MANGIA BENE

Traditional Recipes of Italy

Mangia Bene

Traditional Recipes of Italy

Pasqualina Rio Gregory

Photographs by Joseph P. Costa

HALE
MARY
PRESS

Dedication

This book was written for my grandchildren—Jonathan, Leo, Jesse, Patricia, Katya, Rebecca, Robin, Victoria, and Anarie—with hope that they will continue to enjoy and carry on the family traditions.

First Edition 2003
03 04 05 06   5 4 3 2 1

Library of Congress Cataloging-in-Publication Data
Gregory, Pasqualina Rio, 1932–
   Mangia bene : traditional recipes of Italy / Pasqualina Rio Gregory ; photographs by
Joseph P. Costa.
      p. cm.
   ISBN 0-9643477-9-2 (alk. paper)
      1. Cookery, Italian. I. Title.
   TX723.G76523 2002
   641.5945—dc21   2002017250

For information concerning this book write to:
Hale Mary Press, 423 East Ellis Street, East Syracuse, New York 13057-2413, U.S.A.,
e-mail *sumdp@earthlink.net*

Hale Mary Press was founded to commemorate all women who lost their ethnic, given names at Ellis Island and who were renamed "Mary" in legal immigration papers.

Design: Elizabeth Wixson
Photographs: Joseph Costa

Manufactured in China

CONTENTS

FOREWORD
A Doctor's Advice

The recipes in this exceptional cookbook present foods that not only
are exquisite in flavor and aroma, but also exemplify the highly regarded
Mediterranean pyramid of a healthful diet. Those who believe the adage,
"If food tastes good, it can't be good for you," are in for a very pleasant
awakening.

The extraordinary appeal of Italian foods hardly needs to be mentioned.
If one walks into a kitchen and smells the aroma of garlic being sautéed in
olive oil, or savors a salad of fresh vegetables laced with extra virgin olive oil
and balsamic vinegar, he or she will readily agree that this food is both pleasant
to the nose and satisfying to the taste. Is not the oil really the *nectari* of Greek
mythology?

The attributes of Italian food have been ascertained and proclaimed by
numerous investigators. It is their findings that have led to the compilation
of the Mediterranean pyramid of the most nutritious diet, renowned for
decreasing the incidence of arteriosclerosis, cardiac arrest, and various forms
of cancer.

The Mediterranean pyramid is a modification of the USDA pyramid which
categorized foods in levels of healthfulness from a broad base of the most
desirable, which should be consumed daily, to a narrow apex of the least
healthful, to be eaten only rarely. The two pyramids are alike in their broad
bases of grains and breads, and in the second levels comprising fruits and vegetables. The Mediterranean version, however, places protein-rich legumes and
nuts in the fruits and vegetables level instead of the higher level of meat and
poultry. It differs also by according olive oil, the primary fat, a separate level
immediately above fruits and vegetables. Unlike the USDA pyramid in still
another way, the Mediterranean version limits the dairy products of the next
level to cheese and yogurt.

From this level upward, the pyramids are similar. Red meats are at the top
of both with recommendations to consume them only a few times a month.
Fish, poultry, eggs, and sweets are on another level just below red meats with
instruction to limit them to a few times per week.

The quantity of fat consumed by Italians is not much less than that consumed by Americans and the peoples of northern Europe, but the great
difference is in the quality of fat. While the fat consumed by Italians, especially
the Italians of southern Italy, consists almost entirely of olive oil, which is a
monounsaturated fat, Americans and northern Europeans consume most of

their fats in the form of fatty meats, butter, margarine, and vegetable shortening. Margarine and vegetable shortening, which many mistakingly perceive as less harmful than butter, consist mostly of unsaturated fat hydrogenated to be firm at room temperature. The process of hydrogenation creates trans-fatty acids which, when consumed, are similar to the saturated fats that raise cholesterol levels.

A survey published in the *London Times* in April 1994, showing life expectancy rankings among the nations of the world, had Italy ranked fifth behind Japan, Iceland, Switzerland, and Sweden. The United States was ranked fifteenth and Britain seventeenth.

Many studies have been undertaken and are ongoing in Italy on diet and health. The first study to link a low incidence of heart disease to the Mediterranean diet was the Seven Countries Study conducted by the Americans Ancel and Margaret Keyes in 1974. A second by this researching couple, published in 1986, revealed that the monounsaturated fat consumption is important because it has protective characteristics related to cancer death rates as well as to those from cardiovascular disease.

Italian doctors have been reaching similar conclusions in studies of thousands of individuals in nine different medical centers. They have reported that the extensive use of olive oil in the diet of the middle and southern regions of the country is contributing to lower blood cholesterol, lower blood pressure, and lower blood sugar. They have found that northern Italians, who have a diet more similar to that of the United States and northern Europe, have a higher rate of cholesterol, higher blood pressure, and higher blood sugar.

In recent years, Italian food has become very popular in countries outside Italy, including the United States. Unfortunately, most of the Italian restaurants in the United States do not use the same high-quality food as that found in Italy. High-quality, pure, natural, organically-grown foods are not so readily available as they are in Italy. The cost of imported foods from Italy is higher than that of the domestic products but well worth the difference.

The Mediterranean pyramid and the research behind it confirm the value not only of this book, but also of the author's first book, the popular *Bean Banquets from Boston to Bombay*, which presented a variety of protein-rich legumes as healthful substitutes for meat. Since its appearance more than a decade ago, the book has been through many printings, and now is translated into Japanese. Friends to whom I have given the book rave about the hearty, healthy, and tasty recipes.

Like *Bean Banquets*, Pasqualina's new book will not sit on the shelf as just another cookbook. It will be cherished and used repeatedly. All the healthful foods of the Mediterranean pyramid are reflected, and the recipes have been tested and refined through the years in her laboratories, that is, the kitchens of her home in the United States and her residences in Italy. With her family and friends, I have been the lucky recipient of some of these experiments in her American home. The kitchen is not equipped much differently from yours or mine. The setting, however, if far different from mine and, I am sure, provides her inspiration. She and her husband, Robert, live in Pompey in upstate New York in a pastoral setting of rolling hills, a pond, a creek, and a beautiful forest. The setting conjures up images of the hills of Tuscany.

As a general surgeon I have spent more than thirty years treating illnesses that might have been prevented. The medical profession treats heart disease mostly with coronary artery bypass surgery and treats cancer usually by excision. The operations are sometimes not successful. It is refreshing to consider the possibility that some of these operations can be prevented by the Mediterranean diet. I consider it a rare opportunity to recommend this dietary style and this delightful book.

Enjoy the book and its recipes! I am sure you will agree that the tastes are *squisito*, and you can rest assured that the food will be good for you.

Fred W. Rio, M.D., F.A.C.S.

ACKNOWLEDGMENTS

My husband, Robert, who is Italian only through marriage to me but truly Italian at heart, has been extremely helpful and always supportive. I can say the same about our daughter, Theresa, and her husband, Robin Matchett, and our son, Robert, and his wife, Eva. Also my brother and sisters and their families—Fred and Charlene Rio, Nancy and Mort Sogaard, and Rosemary and Ken Dewhirst—and our niece, Allison St. Dennis. Others in North America include Albert Anella, Sylvana Emprin, Leonardo Fonte, Norman Kutcher, and John Usher. In Switzerland I am indebted to Cristina Dembinski, and in England to Hansa Pandya.

Many in Italy also helped with this project. Our wonderful close friends and relatives contributed recipes and shared with us many memorable meals and happy times. Others were also helpful. I discussed food with friends, chefs, housewives, restaurant owners and anyone who had the patience to talk with me. They always had valuable suggestions and usually insisted that I taste their special dishes. Unfortunately, I cannot list everyone.

I want to thank especially Lina and Alessandro Coglianese and Yolanda, and also Antonetta Grieco of Oliveto Citra; Raffaelina and Tonia Lambiase, Anna Maria Cirillo, Raffaella Apicella, and Angelina Cirillo of Salerno; Antonio Scorza of Palomonte; Donatella and Gino Nicolais of Napoli; and Vicki and Guido Indelli, and the Contessa Federica Picolomini and Marissa of Firenze.

The owners and staff of the following restaurants were particularly generous with samples and suggestions: I Due Cannoni of Oliveto Citra; Il Cenocolo of Salerno; I Conti of Reggio Calabria, U Giancu of San Massimo; Rapallo; La Campannina of Torino; and Vecchia Bari of Bari.

For assistance in editing I am grateful to Lina Coglianese for the Italian titles and my sister Nancy for family recipes. Special thanks also to Mary Demetrick, editor of Hale Mary Press, who started the publication process, and her senior designer, Elizabeth Wixson, who designed the book and prepared the final copy. Mary Selden Evans, executive editor of Syracuse University Press, supervised the eventual publication.

INTRODUCTION

As explained in the foreword by my brother, Fred, Italy is renowned for the tasteful and healthful qualities of its food. These qualities are attained by the use of a variety of natural foods with an emphasis on carbohydrates, fish, meats, cheeses, fresh vegetables, and fruits, all balanced for maximum nutritional value and prepared as far as possible with the finest and most wholesome olive oil.

For me, one of the most essential ingredients in Italian cooking is olive oil. Italians insist on having the highest quality of olive oil because they believe that it is not only the most flavorful, but also the most healthful. "Extra virgin," as most readers of this book will already know, is the classification given to Italy's finest olive oil which comes from the first pressing of the olives and is cold-pressed rather than heat-treated.

Aware that olive oil undergoes an undesirable chemical transformation at high temperature, Italians, when cooking, carefully watch the changing color of the slices of garlic while heating their olive oil. When the garlic begins to brown, they know that the oil is just right for the addition of vegetables or meat.

During the fall of 1988 my husband and I had a rare opportunity to sample the extra virgin oil of Tuscany just after it was pressed. At an old villa surrounded by vineyards and olive groves, high in the Chianti area outside Florence, we were offered a flask of rich, peppery olive oil fresh from the press, together with country bread toasted over an open fire, cloves of garlic, and salt. We were shown how to rub each piece of toast with a garlic clove, dribble olive oil over the top, and sprinkle with salt. Thus we prepared the simple, rustic, and so delicious Tuscan *bruschetta*, and again following instructions, we washed it down with the villa's own Chianti *vino novello*, the new wine. Unfortunately, this delightful experience is almost impossible to duplicate in most countries outside Italy because olives and grapes are rarely grown in the same vicinity. The olive oil loses its peppery, pungent flavor within two weeks after the pressing, and the new wine cannot retain its unique qualities much longer.

Beginning with Greek and Roman times, the peoples of Italy have attached great importance to fine olive oil. They believed that it was a remedy for many ailments, and they applied it as a moisturizer for the skin and hair. Women believed that the liberal use of the oil on their skin would prevent premature wrinkles. They also prized it as the most suitable substance for the delicate skin of their babies.

Throughout Italy the people consume different forms of cereals on a daily basis. While *pasta* is cherished in the southern regions, *risotto* (rice) and *polenta* (cornmeal mush) are favored more in the north. The Italians also have some form of wheat bread at almost every meal. They derive about 60 percent of their daily caloric intake from these various cereals which provide them also with vitamin E, the essential B vitamins, some protein, and important dietary fiber. In other countries the daily caloric intake from cereals is usually much less. In the United States the average is only 19 percent.

Italians prefer to eat their main foods separately. *Pasta*, *risotto*, or *polenta* is taken as the *primo piatto* (first course). Whatever the form, it is not consumed in such large quantity as in the United States, nor is it drowned in sauce. The *pasta* is always cooked *al dente* (to the tooth), meaning firm. Mushy *pasta* is not tolerated. Meat, poultry, or fish is a *secondo piatto* (second course). These dishes are consumed in modest portions and, in some families, are not a daily fare.

Legumes, including dried beans and lentils, are enjoyed throughout Italy and especially in Tuscany. The Florentines are sometimes referred to, with a humorous tone, as *mangia fagioli*, the bean eaters. They prefer the *cannellini* beans but enjoy also the *borlotti* beans, chick peas, and lentils. All the legumes are known to reduce cholesterol and contribute calcium and other minerals as well as vitamins such as thiamin and niacin. Another desirable feature is that they are low in sodium but high in protein. For the vegetarians of the world legumes are the principal source of protein.

Fresh vegetables and fruits are other important foods in the daily diet of the Italians. They are usually brightly colored and have vibrant flavors. Both raw and cooked, the root, leafy, and other vegetables are consumed on a daily basis. In Florence one can buy spinach, swiss chard, and other greens already cleaned, boiled, and formed into balls needing only warming and the addition of flavorings to be ready for the table. It is so easy to prepare greens and many other foods when most of the work is done for you. Vegetables show up often with the *antipasto*, the first and second courses, and also constitute the salad. Choice freshly-picked fruits with superb flavor are always served at the end of a meal.

Meat, though taken sparingly in Italy, is as healthful as meat can be because it is very lean and organically produced. Italians prefer veal to fully developed beef, and in Milan and other northern cities they have it as almost a daily fare. The Italian pork, another popular food, is exceptionally lean and flavorful. Lamb and kid, eaten mostly in the southern regions, have the same qualities. Chicken, turkey, and rabbit, which are consumed throughout Italy, exhibit the taste and lack of fat derived from an out-of-doors, free-range growth. The eggs have yokes of a deep orange. Italians will not accept animal foods that have artificial hormones or other additives. Moreover, they value all parts of their animals. The heads of their smaller animals and the organ meats are highly prized, and tripe is a favorite in Florence and northern cities.

The Italians' beef cattle reflect the concern for healthful food. In the Val di Chiana, Province of Arezzo in Tuscany, the cattle are the largest, tallest, and probably the finest beef-producing animals in the world. This white *Chianina* breed grows quickly to a massive size without artificial hormones. In a year a bull can weigh as much as one thousand pounds and in two years two thousand pounds. The meat has virtually no fat and is renowned for its flavor. *Chianina* beef, or more precisely *vitellone* (young beef), is used for the famous *bistecca alla fiorentina*. Florentine butchers cut it into one-inch thick or even thicker steaks, the same cut as a porterhouse steak. The meat is then simply grilled over coals of a hot fire and served rare. This is the only dish that I know in Italy which includes such a large portion of meat. In fact, it is often shared by two persons.

In southern Italy, where until recent years poverty was endemic, the people never acquired the meat habit to the extent of the northerners. Today the southerners enjoy all the meats but do not indulge on a daily basis. They attach more importance to fish, cheeses, and vegetables.

Fish of many varieties, including shellfish, has always been important in the diet of Italians throughout Italy and especially along the coast. There are many rivers inhabited by fresh-water fish, and, in comparison with most other countries, Italy has an exceptionally long coastline. In many areas fish are a part of almost every course. Along the spectacular Amalfi coast which tourists frequent, the restaurants serve seafood for the *antipasto,* include it in the *pasta* for the first course, and make it the main item of the second course. Fish is thus another ingredient in the healthful Italian diet.

Flavorful and healthful cheeses are also enjoyed throughout Italy. The cheese consumed more than any other in the south is the fresh, moist, *mozzarella di bufala* made there from buffalo milk, but southern Italians consume a host of other cheeses, especially *ricotta* and *provola*. In the north the best known is the *Parmigiano Reggiano, fontina,* and *gorgonzola,* but there are many other superb cheeses.

Garlic, onions, and herbs, which have their own nutritional properties, are used generously to enhance the flavor of meats and vegetables. The popular herbs include parsley, basil, rosemary, sage, bay leaves, mint, marjoram, thyme, oregano, capers, and fennel.

One of the principal means to flavor foods is the application of what I have heard referred to as the "holy trinity" of olive oil, garlic, and *peperoncini*. The *peperoncini* are the tiny, dried, red hot peppers. These three ingredients, used in combination, require little preparation but provide a healthful and delicious flavoring for *pasta,* vegetables, and many other foods. Italians feel that the triple combination keeps them from showing age. Another combination of flavorings, used mostly in the middle regions of Italy, is the *battuto,* finely chopped onion, celery, and carrot sautéed in olive oil. Herbs, and sometimes tomatoes, are added for making a sauce for many different foods.

The main meal of the day, *il pranzo,* is very important. It takes place in early afternoon. On weekdays throughout Italy, shops, government offices, and schools close at this time so that the family can assemble, eat at leisure, and relax in conversation until work and study are resumed. On Sundays and other holidays relatives and friends often gather to eat their main meal together.

This full-course meal, which is prepared at home, includes several courses and begins with an *antipasto.* This starter-course may consist of *prosciutto, salami,* preserved fish, olives, marinated artichoke hearts, and other preserved vegetables, or a number of other foods as described in the recipes of this book. At the beginning of this course, wine and bread, and often mineral water, are put on the table and remain there through the meal.

Il primo piatto, the first course to follow the *antipasto,* consists of *pasta, risotto, polenta,* or soup. Only one serving of moderate size is offered, but it is this dish that provides most of the carbohydrate. Bread is never eaten with *pasta* or *risotto* and seldom with soup which in Italy may be as substantial in its food value as the cereal dishes. The soup is usually thick with vegetables and frequently contains pieces of left-over bread, *pasta,* or rice.

Il secondo piatto (second course), which provides most of the protein in the meal, may take the form of meat, poultry, fish, or, if vegetarian, a combination of vegetables, some prepared with cheese. The vegetarian dish would most likely include some legume that would be rich in protein. One or two vegetables are usually served with the *secondo piatto* as a side dish called *il contorno.* In addition, there may be a salad, although the salad is more often a separate course that follows the *secondo.* The salad is often accompanied by cheese and sometimes dried sausage and *salami* if they were not served with the *antipasto.* Fresh fruit is usually the last food to be eaten, and it is sometimes followed by the traditional *espresso* coffee.

With all courses most Italians drink moderate quantities of wine. On special occasions the meal may be followed with one of the Italian liquors, such as *grappa, strega,* or *limone liquori,* which is served with or after the *espresso.* Unlike in the United States, the desserts, which are equally appreciated in Italy, are usually taken apart from the main meal.

The Italian meal can be very complex on special occasions. In Salerno, we shared one of these occasions with our hospitable neighbors, the extended family, twelve in all, of Felice and Raffaelina Lambiase. For the *antipasto* they offered *prosciutto, salami,* three types of olives, various marinated vegetables, eggplant preserved in olive oil, homemade sun-dried tomatoes, *mozzarella di bufala* in tiny balls the size of cherry tomatoes, fried peppers and eggplant, and roasted pepper salad. For the *primo piatto* we ate homemade *gnocchi alla Sorrentina*.

The *secondo* began with breaded veal cutlets, fried batter-dipped eggplant, fried small green peppers, roasted red and yellow peppers, grilled eggplant made into a salad with garlic, *oregano, peperoncini,* vinegar, and oil, and roasted peppers in a salad. Then, to our further surprise, came another *secondo* which included sausage and *broccoletti* (greens with little broccoli flowers).

Following these courses, another series opened with roasted chestnuts and white wine. White wine, they said, was always served with roasted chestnuts. After the chestnuts, melon, and other fruits were passed, then, successively, *biscotti* (chocolate spice cookies), *gelato* (ice cream), *caffé* (coffee), and *liquori*. Through all these servings, the table held bread and bread sticks, red and white wines, and mineral water both plain and *con gas*. The Lambiase family, to whom we will always feel indebted, had obviously laid out the red carpet for their American guests.

Cooking Italian is on the whole neither difficult nor time-consuming. Certain dishes require time and patience to prepare, but for those who want to turn out meals quickly and want healthful foods, most of the dishes in this book can be very helpful. The ingredients conform to the traditional recipes with only a few minor changes. Most recipes have been kept as true to the original as possible.

Although I have recommended extra virgin olive oil for its healthful qualities and excellent flavor, I have tried to minimize all fats, even olive oil. In those recipes from the north that specify butter, I have used a minimum of butter and made up the loss with olive oil. When eggs are called for, I have used a minimum of egg yolk and made up the difference with egg white. Some of the desserts include more fat, but I recommend eating them in small quantities. I have not included many recipes for organ meats or those that require pig's blood because these foods do not appeal to most Americans and because I had to limit the number of recipes.

One may say that my cooking, at least within the Italian context, is eclectic in its combination of both northern and southern recipes. I come from a family of excellent cooks, and the compilation of this book was possible mainly because of my family's rich cooking tradition. My mother was my first teacher. Her father, from northern Italy, came from a town near Torino in Piemonte, and her mother learned much of her cooking from her husband's family. My mother's mother was born in Andretta, a small mountain town in Campania, where southern cooking predominated. My mother also learned southern cooking from my father's mother who resided in Oliveto Citra, another small mountain town inland from Salerno in Campania.

My grandmother on my father's side came from another mountain town in Campania, Laviano. Her family ran an inn with stables and prepared meals for the guests of the inn. One of their guests, Ferdinando Rio from Oliveto Citra, riding in on his white stallion, took a room, had a fine meal, and spotted the beautiful inn keeper's daughter, Pasqualina. It was love at first sight or perhaps after the first meal. They married, rode off to Oliveto Citra and raised a family of five, the youngest being my father, Giuseppe Rio. My grandmother, Pasqualina, for whom I was named, knew how to prepare a wider variety of excellent dishes than was known in her small locality. She learned at her parents' inn. She passed on her cooking talents to her daughters and daughter-in-law, Theresa, my mother.

What I learned from my family was augmented by extensive travel and residence in Italy. In 1955 when newly married, I spent six weeks in Torino and visited many other cities with my husband who as an historian was investigating Italy's relations with East Africa. In subsequent years during each of my husband's research visits to Africa, we always traveled in Italy, both going and coming. During the school year 1988-89 we were teachers in the Syracuse University Center in Florence. While my husband lectured on Italian history, I taught courses on Italian cooking, and I learned much about the antique dishes epitomized in Florence, the historic center of European cuisine. In the fall of 1993, and again in the winter of 1996, we spent three months in Salerno, near my father's home, where I concentrated on southern Italian foods.

This varied experience in Italy, combined with what I have learned from my family and friends has made me fully realize how healthful and delicious the Italian foods are and has inspired me to undertake this work. I want to share what I have learned.

Incidentally, all the recipes in this book, and many more, were judged separately by members of my family and any other relatives or friends who through the years happened to be sitting at our table. Each person was asked to rate a dish on a scale of one to ten, with ten being the most favorable. If the average were six or less, a discussion would be held on whether the recipe could be improved. A few passed the test on second try. In the end only the most favored recipes were included in this book. The book has been a long time in compilation, and you can understand why. I know that after trying these recipes you will agree that in Italy *si mangia molto bene* (one eats very well).

Greve

Gli Antipasti

Appetizers

The *antipasto* stimulates the taste buds in preparation for the courses that follow. Cured meats such as *prosciutto, bresaola,* and a variety of *salami* are frequently used for the *antipasto.* The all-time favorite is *prosciutto* with melon or figs.

Preserved olives, eggplant, mushrooms, artichoke hearts, and other vegetables also are popular. So are fresh, raw vegetables to be dipped into a golden-green, extra-virgin olive oil. The list of *antipasti* goes on, from delightful seafood salads to small toasts (*crostini*) with tasty toppings.

Small amounts are consumed because additional courses follow to complete the meal.

Facing page: Settignano

Perhaps the most popular *antipasto* is *prosciutto e melone*.
When fresh figs are in season they are frequently offered with the *prosciutto*.

PROSCIUTTO E MELONE
Italian Ham and Melon

1 sweet cantaloupe, honeydew melon, or a combination of melons, chilled
6 large, paper-thin slices of *prosciutto*

Cut melon in thin wedges, removing seeds and skin. Place attractively on 6
plates with a slice of *prosciutto* alongside the melon. Serves 6.

Carpaccio, the raw meat *antipasto,* is especially appreciated in Torino and other areas of Piemonte. Use only best quality beef, organically raised. If you cannot find the best quality of beef, you may use *prosciutto* or *bresaola* in this recipe.

It can be served as a first course, as a light lunch, or even as a main course.

CARPACCIO
Raw Beef Antipasto

beef loin, sliced paper-thin
extra virgin olive oil
asparagus spears, optional
a few drops of wine vinegar
salt and freshly ground, black pepper
shavings of *Parmigiano Reggiano* cheese
shavings of fresh *porcini* mushrooms or white truffles, optional
parsley, *arugula,* or watercress for garnish

1. Coat the beef slices on both sides with olive oil and place them around the edge of the plates.

2. Steam only the tenderest part of asparagus spears until tender-crisp, about 12 minutes. Coat with olive oil, a few drops of wine vinegar, salt, and pepper. Let them cool and arrange them on the plates with the beef.

3. Sprinkle with shavings of cheese and *porcini* mushrooms or truffles, if available.

4. Garnish with parsley, *arugula,* or watercress.

One of the best known *antipasti* in Piemonte is *bagna cauda* meaning "hot bath."
This anchovy dip is kept warm in a pottery bowl with a candle warmer under it.
Individual bowls are sometimes used but more often a larger bowl is placed in the center
of the table into which all dip pieces of fresh vegetables and bread to be enjoyed with
red wine, especially the new wine, *vino novello*. It always creates a jovial atmosphere.
Usually more butter is added to the *bagna cauda* than is used in this recipe.
I prefer it without the butter.

BAGNA CAUDA
Hot Anchovy Dip

1 tablespoon butter
1 large clove garlic, finely mashed
1/2 cup extra virgin olive oil
8 fillets of anchovy, finely chopped
vegetable pieces for dipping: cardoons, bell peppers, celery, cauliflower,
broccoli, boiled potatoes, radishes, artichokes, Belgian endive, and *radicchio.*
Italian bread

1. Melt butter and stir in garlic over very low heat. Be careful that
butter and garlic do not color.

2. Add the oil and anchovies and stir until anchovies dissolve. Place
in a warmed pottery bowl set over a warming candle. Serve with a
combination of fresh vegetables and bread to 4 or more.

One of the most delightful ways to enjoy *bagna cauda* is with roasted peppers. The colorful peppers make an attractive and appealing *antipasto*.

PEPERONI CON BAGNA CAUDA
Peppers with Hot Anchovy Dip

4 meaty red and yellow peppers
1 recipe *bagna cauda*

1. Broil the peppers under high heat, turning them often, until they are blistered and blackened on all sides.

2. Remove peppers from the broiler and place them in a paper bag to help loosen the skins. When they begin to cool, peel and remove core, ribs, and seeds. Do not wash peppers because flavor will wash away.

3. Cut the peppers in 1-inch wide strips and place, inside up, on a large, round plate, alternating red and yellow strips going out from the center to the edge in a star pattern.

4. Prepare *bagna cauda* and while hot, spoon evenly over the peppers. Serve with Italian bread to 6.

Roasted peppers are wonderful to have on hand. They not only make an attractive *antipasto*, but also are a tasty addition to a *pasta* salad or in sandwiches, and they can always be a side dish on the table.

PEPERONI ARROSTITI SOTT'OLIO
Roasted Peppers in Olive Oil

6 large red, or 3 red and 3 yellow peppers
2 large cloves of garlic, peeled and sliced
salt and pepper
about 1/3 cup extra virgin olive oil

1. Broil the peppers under high heat until they are blistered and blackened on all sides.

2. Remove peppers from the broiler and place them in a paper bag until cool enough to handle.

3. Peel the peppers, halve them lengthwise, and remove the core, seeds, and ribs. Cut them into strips about 1-inch wide, lengthwise.

4. Layer them in a glass or pottery container, cover each layer with salt and pepper and slices of garlic placed here and there, and coat each layer with olive oil.

5. Place in refrigerator several hours or overnight and use as needed. To serve at the table, remove garlic if desired, and bring to room temperature.

At the *La Capannina* restaurant in Torino, which specializes in the best of the regional foods, my husband and I were served for the *antipasto* the most eye-appealing salad that we had ever seen. In the center of the plate was a mixture of fresh, chopped vegetables tossed with *bagna cauda* sauce, and around the edges of the plate were opened squash flowers. The result was a beautiful sunflower.

INSALATA DI FIORI
Flower Salad

deep yellow *zucchini*, pumpkin, or other squash flowers
assorted salad vegetables: tomatoes, cucumbers, celery, carrots, radishes, fennel, etc., chopped
bagna cauda, cooled (page 24)

1. Open squash flowers and fan out around the edges of individual plates to resemble a sunflower.

2. Toss vegetables with the *bagna cauda* sauce and spoon a good portion of them in the center of each plate.

This attractive dish of roasted peppers with a savory breadcrumb topping is great, hot or cold, as a tempting *antipasto*. It also may be served as a side dish with a main course.

PEPERONI ARROSTITI AL FORNO
Baked Savory Roasted Peppers

2 large or 3 medium red peppers
2 tablespoons extra virgin olive oil
1 clove garlic, mashed
8 Gaeta black olives, pitted and coarsely chopped
1 rounded teaspoon drained capers
1 rounded tablespoon chopped parsley
a pinch of *oregano*
1/4 cup dried, plain breadcrumbs
salt and pepper
lemon wedges

1. Broil the peppers under high heat until they are blistered and blackened on all sides.

2. Remove peppers from the broiler and put them into a paper bag until cool enough to handle.

3. Peel the peppers, halve them lengthwise, and remove the core, seeds, and ribs. Cut them into strips about 1-inch wide, lengthwise.

4. Place them in a single layer, in an attractive baking dish, that can go directly from the oven to the table.

5. Pour 1 tablespoon of the olive oil in a small bowl. Stir in the garlic, olives, capers, and parsley. Add the *oregano,* breadcrumbs, salt, and pepper. Toss mixture with a fork until well mixed.

6. Sprinkle breadcrumb mixture over peppers and dribble the remaining olive oil evenly over the top. Bake in a preheated 400° F. oven for 10 minutes or until golden. Serve to 4 with lemon wedges.

Overlooking Florence and the Arno River

Anna Maria and Francesco Cirillo, our dear friends in Salerno, entertained my husband and me in their home for *il pranzo*, the main midday meal. Anna Maria served this fresh and tasty *antipasto* with crusty Italian bread. All their family were there to share the many courses of a delightful meal. The *arugula* must be young, mild flavored, with small leaves.
A mixture of wild greens may be used instead of the *arugula*.

BRESAOLA CON RUCOLA
Bresaola with Arugula

4 large or 8 small, thin slices of *bresaola*
1 bunch of arugula or mixed wild greens
2 tablespoons extra virgin olive oil
1 tablespoon fresh lemon juice
salt and pepper
shavings of *Parmigiano Reggiano* cheese

1. Place the slices of *bresaola* evenly over 4 salad plates.

2. Mix the rinsed greens with the olive oil, lemon juice, salt and pepper.
Place a few greens over each plate atop the *bresaola*.

3. Distribute some shavings of the *Parmigiano* cheese over the greens. Serve
to 4 with fresh Italian bread.

Variation: GAMBERI CON RUCOLA—*Shrimp with Arugula*

1. Boil a pound of shrimp, in just a little salted water, for about 2 minutes or
until cooked through but not overdone. Peel shrimp and chill.

2. Mix *arugula* or mixed wild greens salad as above. Put some salad on each
of 4 salad plates and distribute shrimp evenly over salad. Serves 4 as an
antipasto or a light lunch.

This vegetable *antipasto* is simplicity itself and requires only the freshest raw vegetables and the best extra virgin, cold-pressed olive oil, preferably from Tuscany.

PINZIMONIO

Extra Virgin Olive Oil Dip for Raw Vegetables

a selection of raw vegetables for dipping into the oil, e.g., celery, carrots, fennel, yellow and red peppers, radishes, baby artichokes, and green onions
extra virgin, cold-pressed, Tuscan olive oil
salt
freshly ground black pepper

1. Cut vegetables into strips for dipping.

2. Pour olive oil into small individual bowls and add a little salt and pepper.

3. Arrange the vegetable strips attractively for diners to dip into the oil and enjoy with crusty Italian bread.

One of my greatest culinary experiences was having the rustic *bruschetta* with newly pressed olive oil in the Chianti hills of Tuscany. The unique peppery flavor of the oil lasts only about two weeks. Crusty, unsalted Tuscan bread was toasted over an open fire, cloves of garlic were offered to rub over the bread, and the superb green olive oil was poured over and absorbed by the bread.

The new wine *Chianti vino novello* is ready at about the same time, so we had the perfect accompaniment to the *bruschetta*.

BRUSCHETTA O FETTUNTA
Toasted Bread with Olive Oil

slices of country-style, crusty wheat bread
cloves of garlic
the finest cold-pressed, Tuscan, extra virgin olive oil
salt
freshly ground black pepper

1. Toast the bread, preferably over an open fire, or under the broiler, on both sides.

2. Offer the diners the garlic cloves to rub over the toast. Then offer olive oil to dribble or spoon over the toast. Also pass the salt and pepper.

3. Enjoy with a glass of red *Chianti* wine.

These toasts with liver spread certainly are the most popular *antipasto* in Florence. They can be served as an *antipasto*, with soup, or in the afternoon only with a glass of red *Chianti* wine.

CROSTINI DI FEGATINI
Small Toasted Bread with Liver Spread

1/4 onion, finely chopped
2 tablespoons extra virgin olive oil
2 bay leaves
4 chicken livers, cut in 3 or 4 pieces
1/4 cup dry *Marsala* wine
about 1/4 cup chicken broth
freshly ground pepper
2 fillets of anchovy, finely chopped
1 tablespoon drained capers, chopped
3/8 to 1/2-inch sliced Italian bread

1. Sauté onion in olive oil with the bay leaves. When onion is soft and golden, add the chicken livers. Fry the livers to brown.

2. Add the Marsala and cook until it has reduced by half. Add the chicken broth, cook until livers are cooked through but not dry, and add the pepper.

3. Chop the cooked liver mixture and mash with a fork. It should be coarsely mashed, not a smooth paste. Stir in anchovies and capers.

4. Cook mixture again adding a little more broth, if necessary, to produce a moist spread rather than a thick paste. Taste and add a pinch of salt if necessary.

5. Toast the bread under the broiler without burning it. Spread with some of the liver mixture. Serves 6.

Crostini, toasted bread with toppings, are very popular in Italy. This recipe for *crostini* from the Naples area is exceptionally tasty. Of course, homemade Italian bread is ideal for them. The next best would be bread bought in an Italian bakery. The bread must have substance and not be mushy.

CROSTINI ALLA NAPOLETANA
Toasted Bread with Toppings of Naples

slices of Italian bread
extra virgin olive oil
mozzarella cheese, sliced
anchovies in olive oil
basil, chopped
fresh tomato, chopped
salt and pepper
grated *pecorino Romano* cheese

1. Put bread slices on a baking sheet and dribble with olive oil.

2. Cover each slice of bread with a slice of *mozzarella*.

3. Cut anchovies in half, lengthwise, and put 2 strips over each *crostino*.

4. Spoon over each some chopped basil and tomato, then sprinkle with salt, pepper, and grated cheese.

5. Put *crostini* in a preheated, 350° F. oven for 10 to 12 minutes until they are heated through and the cheese has melted. Serve while they are hot.

Another *crostini* from the south is simple and tasty. It comes from *Oliveto Citra*, the town in the mountains where my father was born, and is served at the *Due Cannoni* restaurant there.

CROSTINI AL POMODORO
Toasted Bread with Fresh Tomatoes

sliced Italian bread
1 clove of garlic
chopped fresh tomatoes
oregano
salt and pepper
extra virgin olive oil

1. Toast the bread, lightly under the broiler, on both sides.
The toasts may be kept whole or cut in halves.

2. Rub one side of the toasts, lightly, with the garlic clove.

3. Spoon some chopped tomatoes on each toast. Add salt, pepper and very little *oregano*. Dribble with olive oil.

4. Put the toasts back under the broiler, briefly, and when hot, serve immediately.

These *crostini* are tasty and healthful. They should be served with knife and fork as a first course or perhaps with beans for lunch. They are simply *broccoli di rape* or *rapini* greens which have the little *broccoli* flowers on them, boiled, and served on the toasted bread with garlic, lemon, and extra virgin olive oil.

CROSTINI DI RAPINI
Toasted Bread with Rapini Greens

1 bunch *rapini* greens
4 large slices Italian bread
1/2 clove garlic
4 tablespoons extra virgin olive oil
juice of 1/2 lemon
freshly ground black pepper

1. Wash the *rapini* well and cut off tough ends. Blanch them in boiling, salted water until tender but not too soft. They should still maintain a bright green color. Drain and set aside.

2. Toast the bread slices under the broiler. Do not let them become too dark. Place one slice on each of 4 plates and lightly rub the tops of the toast with the half piece of garlic.

3. Distribute the greens evenly over the *crostini*, dribble a tablespoon of olive oil over each, and then squeeze some fresh lemon juice on them. Top with pepper and serve either warm or at room temperature to 4.

The success of this *antipasto* depends on the freshest, moist *mozzarella*, red, vine-ripened tomatoes, the best quality of extra virgin olive oil, and fresh basil.

INSALATA CAPRESE
Tomato and Mozzarella Salad of Capri

4 ripe but firm tomatoes, sliced
1 pound *mozzarella di bufala*, sliced
extra virgin olive oil
salt
freshly ground black pepper
fresh basil leaves

1. Arrange the slices of tomatoes and *mozzarella*, overlapping them in an attractive pattern, among 4 individual plates.

2. Drizzle the olive oil over them and season with salt and pepper.

3. Tear the basil leaves, or leave them whole if they are small, and distribute evenly over the tomatoes and *mozzarella*. Serve to 4.

This colorful *antipasto* has eye appeal as well as taste. It emanates from the family of Alberto Ianelli in the small, southern mountain town of Montemurro near Potenza.

ANTIPASTO DI MONTEMURRO
Antipasto of Montemurro

Italian *salami*, sliced paper thin
imported *provolone* cheese, sliced
pickled beets, sliced
roasted peppers, peeled, with seeds and membranes removed, cut into strips
(or from a jar)
flat fillets of anchovy, packed in olive oil
capers
dried black olives

1. Line a platter with *salami* slices and layer attractively over it the *provolone*, beets, roasted peppers, anchovies, capers, and olives.

2. Serve as a first course or even as a light lunch with crusty Italian bread.

These hot, cheese-filled sandwiches are quick to prepare and always are appreciated whether they are served as an *antipasto*, as a snack, or with soup or salad for lunch. Some Italians like them with a fillet of anchovy tucked inside, and others prefer them plain.

MOZZARELLA IN CARROZZA
Mozzarella in a Carriage

2 eggs
2 tablespoons milk
salt
8 slices firm, homemade-type Italian bread, sliced about 1/2-inch thick
1/2 pound *mozzarella*, sliced about 1/4-inch thick
4 anchovy fillets (optional)
olive oil for frying

1. Beat eggs with milk and salt in a broad-bottomed bowl.

2. Prepare the sandwiches: cut the crusts from the bread and cover 4 of the slices with slices of cheese without overlapping the cheese slices. Do not let the cheese extend beyond the edge of the bread.

3. If using anchovies, rinse and dry them and place one on each sandwich. Cover with the remaining 4 slices of bread.

4. Dip each sandwich on both sides, holding them carefully so that the cheese does not fall out, into the egg mixture. Allow the sandwiches to soak up the egg. Let the sandwiches sit in the egg mixture until all of it is absorbed into the bread.

5. Meanwhile heat oil about 1/4-inch deep in a frying pan. When it is hot, lift the sandwiches with a broad spatula into the oil. Fry until lightly browned on one side. Turn over the sandwiches and fry the other side. Drain on paper towels and serve immediately.

These croquettes from Rome are called "telephone wires" because when they are cut the mozzarella cheese stretches into strings resembling the wires. They can be enjoyed as an *antipasto* or as a snack. They are a treat at parties and can be eaten hot, warm, or at room temperature. Making them is a good way to use up leftover *risotto*.

SUPPLI AL TELEFONO
Telephone Wires

1 tablespoon butter
1 cup *Arborio* rice
20 to 22 ounces light chicken broth
1 egg yolk
1/4 cup grated *Parmigiano* cheese
salt and pepper
10 to 12 1/2-inch cubes of *mozzarella* cheese
1 egg plus 1 tablespoon water
1 cup fine dry bread crumbs
olive oil or canola oil for deep frying

1. Melt the butter, in a saucepan, over low heat. Add the rice and sauté until rice turns opaque.

2. Meanwhile, in another saucepan, bring broth to a simmer. Add broth to the rice, a little at a time, while stirring. Allow the rice to absorb the broth before adding more.

3. The rice should be cooked through and all the liquid absorbed in approximately 20 minutes. Put the rice in a cold mixing bowl to cool.

4. Stir into the rice, the egg yolk, *Parmigiano* cheese, and salt and pepper. (If chicken broth is salty, additional salt may not be necessary.)

5. Take a heaping tablespoon of rice in the palm of one hand. Place a cube of *mozzarella* in the center, press the rice around it and shape into a ball. Continue to make balls with the remaining rice and *mozzarella*.

6. Beat together the egg and water. Roll each ball in the beaten egg and coat with the bread crumbs.

7. Heat the oil until hot but not yet smoking. Fry the balls, 3 or 4 at a time, for about 5 minutes until they are golden brown. Drain well on paper towels. Makes 10 to 12 balls.

Outside Café, Florence

One of the favorite *antipasto* items that I have grown up with is my mother's pickled eggplant. I relished eating it on a slice of her homemade bread. This is a shortcut version of her recipe. This preparation of eggplant along with roasted peppers is a great addition to a *pasta* salad.

MELANZANE CON OLIO E ACETO
Marinated Eggplant

1 or 2 firm, slender, eggplants, 1 to 1 1/4 pounds
extra virgin olive oil for coating eggplant slices
salt
1 teaspoon *oregano*
1 stalk celery, coarsely chopped
2 small hot green peppers, seeded and sliced
3 tablespoons olive oil
3 tablespoons red wine vinegar
2 large cloves garlic, quartered

1. Cut off the stem and the other end of each eggplant. Peel and slice eggplant about 1/4-inch thick and cut slices in halves.

2. Layer eggplant slices on a plate, salting each layer. Cover with another plate and put a weight on top. Let eggplant sit for one hour or until the excess water drains out. Rinse and dry eggplant slices.

3. Line a large baking sheet with aluminum foil and coat foil with a little olive oil. Arrange eggplant slices close together, in one layer, on the baking sheet.

4. Bake in a preheated, 375° F. oven for 15 minutes. Turn eggplant slices over and bake another 10 to 15 minutes until eggplant begins to brown. Eggplant slices may also be broiled.

5. Remove eggplant from the baking sheet and put into a bowl. Add *oregano*, celery, peppers, olive oil, vinegar, garlic, salt, and pepper. Mix well, cover, and store in refrigerator at least 24 hours. Stir occasionally to distribute flavors.

Verona and the Adige River

Pickled mushrooms are always popular on an *antipasto* tray on which you have an assortment of items, or they are delightful on their own.

FUNGHI SOTT'OLIO E ACETO
Marinated Mushrooms

1 pound button mushrooms with about 1/2-inch caps
3 cups white vinegar
3 cups hot water
1/4 cup extra virgin olive oil
1 1/2 teaspoons salt
2 teaspoons peppercorns
2 cloves garlic, peeled and quartered
1 teaspoon mace
white wine vinegar

1. Wash and rinse well a 1-pint screw-top jar.

2. Wash mushrooms being careful to remove all soil. Place mushrooms in saucepan and cover with the vinegar and hot water.

3. Bring to boiling over high heat and cook 5 minutes. Drain mushrooms and place in a bowl.

4. Add to the mushrooms the olive oil, salt, peppercorns, garlic, and mace. Stir mixture and pack in the jar. Cover mushrooms with white wine vinegar, screw cap onto jar, and store in the refrigerator for at least 2 days. Serve cold or at room temperature.

Vernazza

I Primi

First Courses

Le Minestre

Soups

Italian soups are mostly hearty, chock full of vegetables, thickened with rice, *pasta* or bread, and always enriched with good quality olive oil. As substantial as they are, they are served only as a first course and never take the place of the main meal.

Soups are enjoyed in all areas in Italy but are very important in the northern regions. The best known Italian soup is, of course, the *Minestrone* of Milan. Other soups have gained prominence too. In Florence bean soups are especially popular. Other Florentine soups, such as the Bread and Tomato Soup (*Pappa al Pomodoro*) and the Reboiled Vegetable Soup (*Ribollita*), are thickened with the local crusty bread.

In Trieste a rich Cream of Potato (*Zuppa Crema di Patate*) is favored, and in the cities and towns along the Italian coast many types of fish soups are prepared with the wonderful seafood of the Mediterranean.

Rich cream soups are popular in the north. This creamy soup from
Trieste is less rich than most but retains a fine flavor.

ZUPPA CREMA DI PATATE
Cream of Potato Soup

1 leek, the white part, coarsely chopped
1 teaspoon chopped fresh marjoram
1 tablespoon butter
1 pound potatoes, peeled and cubed
2 cups vegetable or chicken broth
1 egg yolk
1 1/2 cups milk
salt
black pepper
Parmigiano Reggiano cheese, grated

1. Sauté the leek and marjoram in butter until softened but not brown.
Stir in the potatoes and then add the broth. Let boil slowly until potatoes
are soft.

2. Mash the potatoes in the broth.

3. Beat the egg yolk and gradually combine it with the milk. Slowly pour
the egg and milk mixture into the soup while stirring. Add salt and when
soup is very hot but not quite boiling, serve to 4. Pass a pepper mill and the
Parmigiano cheese at the table.

The literal meaning of *acquacotta* is "cooked water." It is a popular soup from the Tuscan Maremma area around Grosseto. The fertile countryside with rolling hills is famous for its "cowboys," who round up long-horn cattle and wild horses, and is a hunting ground for wild game.

ACQUACOTTA
Cooked Water

1/2 ounce dried *porcini* mushrooms
1 cup hot water
1 large onion, chopped
2 stalks celery, chopped
1 carrot, chopped
1 large clove garlic, mashed
1/4 cup extra virgin olive oil
1 1/2 cups peeled and chopped, Italian-type, plum tomatoes
1/3 pound spinach or swiss chard, coarsely cut
6 cups hot water
3 eggs
1/4 cup grated *Parmigiano Reggiano*
salt and freshly ground black pepper
8 thin slices of homemade-type Italian bread

1. Briefly rinse and soak mushrooms in 1 cup of hot water for 15 minutes. Remove soaked mushrooms, saving the soaking water, and chop finely.

2. Sauté onion, celery, carrot, and garlic in the oil until soft. Add mushrooms and continue to sauté. When everything has a golden color, add the tomatoes, the spinach, and the mushroom soaking water except for the last 2 tablespoons in case some sand has fallen into it.

3. Add the remaining 6 cups of water. Bring soup to a boil, reduce heat, and simmer 15 minutes.

4. Beat the eggs with the cheese. Add salt and pepper to the eggs and to the soup.

5. Toast the bread and place 1 or 2 in the bottom of each of 4 warmed, shallow soup plates. Rub the toast lightly with a piece of garlic and dribble with a little olive oil.

6. Pour the eggs and cheese slowly into the boiling soup and stir gently until eggs are barely cooked.

7. Ladle soup over the toast. Pass additional *Parmigiano* cheese. Serves 4.

Ponte Vecchio, Florence

This thick, tasty, colorful soup is featured at the well-known Cibreo restaurant, on via dei Macci in Florence, across from Mercato di Sant'Ambrogio, a neighborhood farmers' market. The soup will have a nice color if you use peppers that are deep yellow. You may even use one orange pepper with the yellow if the yellow peppers are pale.

PASSATO DI PEPERONI
Thick Pepper and Potato Soup

2 tablespoons extra virgin olive oil plus more for serving
1 carrot, peeled and chopped
1 stalk celery, chopped
1 onion, chopped
2 cloves garlic, peeled and coarsely chopped
a pinch of crushed, dried, hot red pepper
1 1/2 pounds large deep-yellow peppers, about 3 or 4, cored, seeded, and cut into small pieces
2 medium-large baking potatoes, peeled and cubed
2 cups chicken broth
2 cups water
salt

1. Heat the olive oil in a large saucepan and cook carrot, celery, onion, garlic, dried red pepper and yellow peppers, stirring often, until vegetables are golden but not brown.

2. Add potatoes, and chicken broth. Cook gently until vegetables are soft.

3. Puree soup thoroughly in batches in a food processor or blender and return to the saucepan. Add water and salt and simmer, stirring occasionally, until soup is hot. Serve in warm, rimmed soup bowls topped with a "C"-shaped drizzle of olive oil.

Young fruit vendor, Capri

Ribollita means "reboiled." This famous, thick Florentine vegetable soup is made in abundant quantities. Traditionally, it is prepared a day ahead, reboiled, and eaten the next day. The flavor is enhanced when allowed to sit overnight. The success of this soup depends upon using a good homemade-type bread and an excellent quality olive oil.
Additional oil is dribbled over each serving in a "C"-shape.

RIBOLLITA
Reboiled Vegetable Soup

1 1/2 cups *cannellini* or great northern beans
5 cups cold water
4 tablespoons extra virgin olive oil
1 onion, finely chopped
2 cloves garlic, mashed
1 large stalk celery, finely chopped
1 large carrot, finely chopped
1 thin slice of *pancetta* (Italian bacon), chopped
1 potato, peeled and diced
1/2 pound kale or savoy cabbage, chopped
1 tablespoon fresh thyme or 2 teaspoons dried
2 mature tomatoes, peeled, seeded and chopped
6 cups beef broth
1 bunch swiss chard or beet greens, cut in large pieces
salt
freshly ground black pepper
about 3/4 pound country-style, homemade-type Italian bread, stale
(preferably whole-wheat)

1. Boil beans in 5 cups water for 2 minutes. Allow to rest for 1 hour or longer. Cook beans gently until tender.

2. Heat oil in a large saucepan over medium heat. Add onion, garlic, celery, carrot, and *pancetta*. Sauté until vegetables are golden. Add potato, cabbage, and thyme. Continue to sauté another 2 minutes.

3. Add tomatoes, broth, and liquid from cooked beans. Bring to a boil and add swiss chard. Simmer until vegetables are soft.

4. Mash half of the beans and add to the soup with the whole beans. Season and add a little more water if too thick.

5. Cut bread in 1/2-inch slices and put them in a low oven on racks until very dry and golden, but not toasted.

6. Place a layer of dried bread on the bottom of a large flameproof casserole. Ladle half of the soup over the bread and place another layer of bread on the soup. Ladle remaining soup into the casserole. Set aside, covered.

7. If saving for the next day, it should be refrigerated, then reheated in the oven before serving. Serve the steaming thick soup into shallow, rimmed bowls and top with a "C"-shape of best extra-virgin olive oil and freshly ground black pepper. Enough for 8 or more.

Although this is meant to be a *primo piatto* (first course), it is hearty enough to serve as a vegetarian main course if you double the recipe. In either case it goes very well with *bruschetta,* the toast with olive oil and garlic. Chickpeas take an hour or two and sometimes longer to cook. Home cooked are always better, but you can use the canned chickpeas, without preservatives, in this Tuscan recipe.

CECI IN ZIMINO
Chickpea Stew with Greens

1 cup dried chickpeas or one 14-ounce can, with no preservatives
1 small bunch beet greens or swiss chard
3 tablespoons extra virgin olive oil
1 onion, chopped
1 clove garlic, finely minced
1 stalk celery, coarsely chopped
1/4 teaspoon dried, crushed red pepper
1 cup chopped canned tomatoes

1. If using dried chickpeas, put them in a saucepan with water about 2 inches above the top of the chickpeas. Bring to a rolling boil and let boil about 5 minutes. Cover pan, remove from heat, and let rest for 2 hours.

2. Bring the chickpeas to a boil again and let simmer for 1 hour or longer. Chickpeas vary in the time they take to cook. When soft, they are done. Drain them, and save some of the cooking water.

3. Wash the greens and cut in halves or fourths lengthwise and then in 3-inch lengths. Slice the stems.

4. Heat the olive oil in a large saucepan and sauté the onion, garlic, celery, and pepper until vegetables are golden and soft. Stir in the greens until they are coated with the oil and begin to wilt.

5. Add the tomatoes and let simmer until greens are nearly done. Add chickpeas, 1/2 cup of the cooking water of the chickpeas, and salt. Let all cook together for a few minutes until chickpeas are soft and flavors have blended. Serves 3 or 4.

Villager's window, Tuscany

This is a typical and very popular soup served in most of the *trattorie* of Florence.

PAPPA AL POMODORO
Bread and Tomato Soup

1/2 cup extra-virgin Tuscan olive oil
3 garlic cloves, peeled and mashed
1/8 teaspoon or more of dried, crushed red pepper or 2 or 3 of the tiny,
dried, red hot peppers
1 medium-large leek, chopped
1 large stalk celery, chopped
1 1/2 pounds fresh, deep red, ripe tomatoes, peeled, some of the seeds
removed, and coarsely chopped
6 cups chicken broth
2 rounded tablespoon chopped parsley
15 leaves of fresh basil, chopped
12 ounces day-old, homemade-type Italian bread, cubed (If not dried out,
put into a low oven for a while. Do not toast it, just let it dry.)
salt

1. Heat olive oil and add garlic, red pepper, leek, and celery. When they turn
golden, add tomatoes and broth. Slowly boil until vegetables are soft.

2. Add parsley, basil, bread cubes, and salt. Cook slowly for 15 minutes.
Remove from heat, cover, and let stand about an hour until you are ready to
reheat and serve.

3. Reheat the soup, stirring often. Add a little water if soup becomes too
thick. Check salt. Serve with a "C"-shape of fresh olive oil on top of each
serving. The success of this soup depends on the quality of the oil, tomatoes,
bread and the use of fresh basil. Serves 6.

Our Aunt Margherita, who lived until age 96, came from the mountain town of Oliveto Citra inland from Salerno. She remembered as a girl the wild asparagus, in springtime, which would be the main ingredient in this tasty soup. You may use one less egg yolk if you are concerned about the fat content.

ZUPPA DI ASPARAGI
Asparagus Soup

1 1/2 pounds asparagus
3 tablespoons extra virgin olive oil
1 large clove garlic, peeled and cut in half lengthwise
2 1/2 cups water
salt and pepper
1 egg and 2 additional egg whites or 2 whole eggs
2 tablespoons grated *pecorino Romano* cheese

1. Cut off the tough portion of the asparagus stalks and peel the stalks about 2 inches up from the bottom. Cut them in 1-inch lengths.

2. Heat the olive oil in a soup pan and add the garlic clove and asparagus. Sauté until asparagus and garlic are just beginning to brown. Add water and simmer gently until asparagus is tender. Add salt and pepper.

3. Beat the egg and whites together and add the cheese, salt, and pepper. Slowly pour the egg mixture into the soup. Stir gently until egg is just cooked, about 1/2 minute. Serve immediately to 4. Accompany this soup with fresh, whole-wheat Italian bread.

The *Minestra d'Agosto* is so called because the ingredients—pears, *zucchini*, potatoes, and tomatoes—are in abundance in the month of August. This unusual combination produces a delightful soup.

MINESTRA D'AGOSTO
August Soup

1 onion, chopped
3 tablespoons extra virgin olive oil
4 tomatoes or 1 14-ounce can of Italian-type tomatoes, peeled and chopped
1 potato, peeled
1 pound small *zucchini*
2 large or 3 medium size pears, peeled
salt and pepper
2 tablespoons chopped fresh basil

1. In a soup pan, cook the onion in the olive oil until golden. Add tomatoes to the pan and bring to a slow boil.

2. Quarter the potato lengthwise and cut in 1/4-inch slices. Add the potatoes to the pan.

3. Quarter the *zucchini* lengthwise, cut in 1/4-inch slices, and add them to the soup pan.

4. Quarter the peeled pears, remove the cores, and cut in 1/4-inch slices. Add them to the soup.

5. Add 2 cups hot water and allow soup to cook until potatoes and *zucchini* are done but not breaking apart.

6. When soup is almost done, add salt, pepper, and basil. Serves 4.

This is a special soup for late fall and winter when chestnuts are available. Chestnuts combine wonderfully with the beans for a rich-flavored, satisfying soup.

ZUPPA DI FAGIOLI E CASTAGNE
Bean and Chestnut Soup

3/4 cup dried *cannellini* or great northern beans
12 ounces chestnuts
2 cloves garlic, cut in halves lengthwise
4 tablespoons extra virgin olive oil
a pinch of crushed, dried red pepper
1 rounded tablespoon chopped parsley
salt

1. Sort through beans, rinse and cover with water 2 inches over the beans. Bring to a fast boil and let boil for 2 minutes. Cover pan, remove from heat, and let beans rest for 2 hours.

2. Bring them to a very slow boil and cook about 40 minutes or until beans are softening but not quite cooked through.

3. Boil the chestnuts for 1 hour. Drain and peel off the outer and inner skins of the chestnuts as soon as they are cool enough to handle. Some will be whole and some will break into pieces. Boil peeled chestnuts in water to cover for about 15 minutes or until chestnuts are tender but not mushy.

4. In a large saucepan, sauté the garlic pieces in the olive oil until they are golden. Add the crushed red pepper and when the pepper darkens a little, after a few seconds, add the beans with their water.

5. Pour the chestnuts and their water into the beans. Add parsley and salt. Let everything cook together until beans and chestnuts are soft. Add water if soup becomes too thick. Serves 4.

I do not know why this soup is called "crazy water." Perhaps because, despite its simplicity, a lot of flavor is created. This recipe includes beaten eggs and *Parmigiano* cheese as optional items.

One of the recipes in this book features fish poached in *Acqua Pazza*. It describes a delightful way to prepare fish. The eggs and cheese would not be included to cook fish.

ACQUA PAZZA
Crazy Water

8 cups water
1 tablespoon extra virgin olive oil
1 medium-small onion, finely chopped
1 stalk celery, chopped
1 carrot, chopped or cut in rings
salt and pepper
3 small Italian-type plum tomatoes, peeled, some seeds removed, and coarsely chopped (Use fresh tomatoes if in season.)
1 rounded tablespoon of parsley, chopped
2 eggs, beaten (optional)
1 tablespoon grated *Parmigiano* cheese (optional)

1. Bring water to a boil and add olive oil and onion. Let cook slowly while you prepare the remaining vegetables.

2. Add celery, carrot, salt, and pepper and let the soup continue to simmer until vegetables are tender. Add the tomatoes and parsley.

3. Shortly before serving the soup, slowly add the eggs which have been beaten with the cheese, salt, and pepper. Stir the mixture gently into the soup until it shreds. Serve immediately to 4.

This hearty soup from Campania is chock full of vitamins and is easy to prepare.

ZUPPA DI LENTICCHIE E SCAROLA
Lentil and Escarole Soup

1/2 pound lentils
3 tablespoons extra virgin olive oil
2 cloves of garlic, peeled and halved lengthwise
1 onion, chopped
1/8 teaspoon dried, crushed red pepper
1/2 teaspoon *oregano*
1 head of *escarole* or endive, washed and cut in 2-inch lengths
1 tomato, fresh or canned, peeled, seeded, and chopped
2 cups water
salt

1. Rinse lentils and put to boil in water about 2 inches above the lentils (about 3 1/2 cups). Let boil vigorously for 1 minute. Cover pan and remove from heat. Let the lentils rest for 2 hours or longer.

2. Bring lentils to a gentle boil and cook until tender.

3. In a soup pot, heat olive oil and lightly brown garlic pieces. When they begin to take color, add the onion, pepper, and *oregano*. Cook slowly until onion is soft and lightly browned.

4. Add *escarole*, tomato, and water. Cook about 10 minutes until *escarole* is tender.

5. Add lentils, with their cooking broth, and salt. Let soup cook another few minutes to blend flavors. Serves 4 to 6.

This well-known soup combines many fresh vegetables and herbs in a tasty broth and is topped with the world famous *Parmigiano Reggiano* cheese which, like the soup, is produced in Lombardy.

MINESTRONE ALLA MILANESE
Vegetable Soup of Milan

1 ounce lean *pancetta,* diced
1 onion, chopped
3 tablespoons extra virgin olive oil (The original recipe calls for butter.)
1/2 sprig fresh rosemary, chopped
4 sage leaves, chopped
1 bay leaf
2 stalks celery, coarsely chopped
2 carrots, quartered lengthwise and sliced
2 *zucchini* (about 8-inches long), quartered lengthwise and sliced
1 leek, the white and pale green part only, quartered lengthwise and sliced
1 potato, peeled and diced
1 pound green beans, topped, tailed, and cut in 1/2-inch lengths
1 cup, packed, coarsely chopped savoy cabbage
1/2 cup *Arborio* rice
6 cups meat broth (Homemade is preferable.)
1 1/2 cups peeled and chopped tomatoes, fresh or canned
1/2 cup frozen peas
1 cup cooked beans (*Borlotti, cannellini,* or great northern beans may be used.)
1 large clove garlic, mashed
1/4 cup chopped parsley
1 heaping tablespoon chopped fresh basil
salt and pepper
grated *Parmigiano Reggiano* cheese

1. Sauté *pancetta* and onion in olive oil until onion is golden. Add the rosemary, sage leaves, and bay leaf. Stir and add celery, carrots, *zucchini,* leek, potato, green beans, and savoy cabbage.

2. Sauté the vegetables for 5 minutes and add rice. Stir the rice, and when it is opaque, add the broth and tomatoes. Cook slowly until vegetables are tender.

3. Add peas, beans, garlic, parsley, basil, salt and pepper. Cook for 10 to 15 minutes longer until flavors have blended. Add water as necessary. Adjust seasonings and serve to 6 to 8. Add some grated *Parmigiano* on each serving.

The Duomo at dawn, Milan

This delicate, thick onion soup (*cipolla* means onion) of Umbria traditionally uses pork fat for flavor. I prefer using just 1 ounce of a lean *pancetta,* which is an unsmoked Italian bacon. Begin the preparation of this soup the night before because the thinly sliced onions should soak in cold water for 12 hours.

CIPOLLATA
Onion Soup

2 pounds large onions, sliced thinly
4 tablespoons extra virgin olive oil
1 ounce lean *pancetta,* chopped
6 leaves fresh basil, chopped
salt and pepper
14 ounces Italian-type tomatoes, peeled and crushed
4 cups water
2 eggs
1/4 cup grated *Parmigiano Reggiano* cheese

1. Soak onions in a large bowl of cold water for about 12 hours. Drain.

2. Heat the oil with the *pancetta* in a large, heavy pan and then add onions. Cover the pan, lower the heat, and cook, stirring occasionally, until onions are soft but not colored.

3. Add basil, salt, and pepper. Stir and add tomatoes and water. Stir well, cover pan, and simmer over low heat for about 1 1/2 hours. Test the seasonings.

4. Beat the eggs well and season. Remove the pan from the heat, immediately sprinkle the *cipollata* with the *Parmigiano* cheese, and add the eggs, stirring gently.

5. Serve immediately to 4 with slices of coarse Italian bread, toasted.

This light soup requires a well-flavored broth, which can be chicken, other meat, or vegetable. Use only the outer green leaves of the *escarole*. Save the pale center leaves for salad.

SCAROLA IN BRODO
Escarole in Broth

4 cups well-seasoned broth
1 large head of *escarole*, only the outer green leaves, washed and cut in
2-inch pieces
1 egg
2 tablespoons grated *pecorino Romano* cheese
salt and pepper

1. Bring broth to a boil and add the *escarole*. Let cook until *escarole* is tender.

2. Beat egg with cheese, salt, and pepper. Add the egg slowly to the soup and run a fork gently through the egg to feather it.

3. Serve immediately to 3 or 4.

Variation: SCAROLA IN BRODO CON POLPETTINE—*Escarole in Broth with Tiny Meatballs*

Mix about 1/3 pound of ground beef or veal with some breadcrumbs, grated cheese, egg, parsley, salt, and pepper. Make tiny meatballs and add to the soup before the *escarole*. Cook meatballs and *escarole* together until both are cooked through.

When my mother served this chicken soup at home, she usually made homemade noodles to go with it. Sometimes she would add *tortellini* or *raviolini* instead. However, she also made chicken *pastina* soup by cooking *pastina* and adding it to the soup together with a mixture of beaten egg and grated *Romano* cheese. If the chicken proves to be too much to eat with the soup one can save the breast meat for chicken salad to be prepared at a later date.

ZUPPA DI POLLO
Chicken Soup

1 3-to-5-pound chicken, minus giblets
4 quarts water
2 stalks celery and some leaves, cut in 2-inch lengths
1 large onion, peeled and quartered
salt and pepper
1/2 cup parsley

1. Place the washed chicken in water in a large soup pot and bring to a boil over high heat.

2. Meanwhile add celery, onion, and salt. Skim off the foam from the surface of the water, as it collects, and discard. Lower heat and let soup simmer for 2 hours. Check salt.

3. Remove chicken, skim fat from the surface of the broth, and strain broth into a clean pan. Skin and bone chicken, if desired, and pour a cup of broth over meat to keep it moist. Keep chicken meat warm.

4. Before serving soup, cook egg noodles, preferably homemade, in salted, boiling water until done. Meanwhile add parsley to broth and bring to a boil.

5. Drain the noodles and place in a soup tureen or in individual soup bowls. Pour soup over noodles and serve with the chicken. Makes about 2 1/2 quarts of broth.

Variation: ZUPPA DI POLLO CON PASTINA E UOVA—*Chicken Soup with Pastina and Eggs*

To make chicken *pastina* soup, boil the tiny *pastina* instead of the noodles. In a small bowl beat 2 eggs, 2 tablespoons grated *Romano* cheese, salt, and black pepper. Drain the *pastina* and add it to the boiling broth. Slowly stir in the egg and cheese mixture. Serve immediately.

Settignano

Italians in the coastal cities and towns boast of their wonderful soups comprised of the excellent seafood of the Mediterranean Sea. Although the soups vary from area to area because of the different varieties of shellfish and octopus, they all contain the *scorfano,* similar to rock fish.

From Napoli along the Amalfi coast to Salerno the soup is called simply *zuppa di pesce* or *zuppa di crostacei.* In the Marches and Rome, in Rimini, and in other coastal cities along the Adriatic it is known as *brodetto,* and in Livorno, the seaport of Tuscany, as *cacciucco.* In Liguria, farther north, it has the name *burrida.*

The following recipe, using a variety of American seafood similar to that found in Italy and the shellfish prepared and served in their shells, produces a flavorful and eye-appealing soup.

ZUPPA DI PESCE
Fish Soup

1 dozen small mussels
1 dozen small cherrystone, littleneck, or Maine clams
1/2 pound rock fish or red snapper fillets
1/2 pound swordfish
1/2 pound shrimp
2 small squid, cleaned
1/4 pound bay scallops
1/4 cup extra virgin olive oil
4 cloves garlic, peeled and halved lengthwise
1/8 teaspoon dried, crushed red pepper
1 (14-ounce) can peeled Italian-type plum tomatoes, chopped
5 cups water or fish stock
salt
1/4 cup chopped parsley
whole-wheat Italian bread, toasted (optional)

1. Clean the mussels and clams with a stiff brush under cold water and put into a large bowl of cold, salted water. Cut the fish in 2-inch pieces, removing skin and bone, and set aside. Clean the shrimp by removing the shells and black vein.

2. If squid is not cleaned, remove the sac and the membrane so that the squid is white. Cut off the tentacles and slice the squid body in rings. Set aside the squid and scallops.

3. Heat the olive oil in a large-bottomed pan and lightly brown the garlic on both sides. Add the red pepper and remove pan from heat so that pepper does not burn but will turn a shade darker in the hot oil.

4. Add tomatoes, fish stock or water, and salt. Bring to a boil and simmer 15 minutes. Add the pieces of fish, mussels, and clams. Cover the pan and bring to a boil over moderately high heat.

5. Let boil 3 or 4 minutes or until shells open. Add the *Zuppe di Pesce*, shrimp, squid, scallops, and parsley. Cover pan and cook over medium heat for 5 minutes or until all the seafood is cooked through.

6. Discard any shellfish that have not opened and check seasoning. If desired, rub a piece of garlic lightly over the toast, set pieces of toast on the bottom of large, shallow soup bowls, and dribble with olive oil. Serve seafood and broth over the toast. Soup also may be served without the toast and with Italian bread on the side. Serves 6.

To clean the mussels for this richly flavored soup, run them under cold water and scrub each one with a stiff brush. Remove the beards and drop the cleaned mussels into a bowl of salted cold water with a tablespoon of cornmeal, until you are ready to cook them.
After the mussels are cleaned, the dish is very quickly prepared.

ZUPPA DI COZZE
Mussels Soup

3 1/2 pounds small mussels
1/4 cup extra virgin olive oil
2 large cloves garlic, halved lengthwise
pinch of dried, crushed, hot pepper
2 cups tomatoes, peeled, seeded, and chopped
1 cup dry white wine
salt and pepper
1/4 cup chopped parsley

1. Clean the mussels as described above and drop in cold, salted water.

2. Heat the oil in a large saucepan and sauté the garlic pieces until they begin to color on both sides. Add the crushed pepper and when it darkens slightly, add the wine. When it has reduced by half, add the tomatoes, salt, and pepper. Cook slowly 10 minutes.

3. Raise heat and bring liquid to a boil. Meanwhile scrub mussels once again and put into the saucepan. Cover pan and cook mussels 5 minutes. Sprinkle with parsley, stir mussels, and cook another 1 or 2 minutes until shells have opened.

4. Remove and discard any mussels that have not opened. Spoon into soup bowls, shells and all with some of the broth. Leave a little of the liquid in the pan in case some sand dropped to the bottom.

5. Serve with Italian whole-wheat bread (*pane integrale*), toasted, rubbed with garlic, dribbled with extra virgin olive oil, and seasoned with salt and pepper as *bruschetta*.

6. Have some empty bowls on the table so that discarded shells may be placed into them. Serves 6.

Around the Bay of Naples

This tasty soup that my mother prepared so well could be made with other seafood, but my favorite is the shrimp.

ZUPPA DI GAMBERETTI
Shrimp Soup

3/4 pound fresh shrimp, not too large
2 tablespoons extra virgin olive oil
1/2 onion
2 cups canned chopped tomatoes with puree
6 cups water
1/2 cup *pastina* or other tiny *pasta*
1 clove garlic, mashed
1/4 cup chopped parsley
salt and pepper

1. Remove the shells and the black veins from the shrimp and set shrimp aside.

2. Heat olive oil and sauté onion until it is soft and golden. Do not brown the onion

3. Add the tomatoes and water and bring to a boil. Let cook gently about 15 minutes. Raise heat and, when boiling rapidly, add *pastina*. Stir and let cook about 9 minutes until *pastina* is nearly done.

4. Add the shrimp, garlic, parsley, salt, and pepper. Let cook until shrimp is done, about a minute or 2 depending on their size. Do not overcook shrimp. Serve at once to 4 or 6.

This is yet another way the Italians have found to use up their stale bread and turn it into a tasty dish. The Calabrians make a *frittata* out of bread crumbs, eggs, cheese, and herbs. They slice it and put it into a tasty broth. *Eccola, Mariola*!

A *mariola* is a swindler or cheat. I suppose the title indicates that one is swindled when eating this meatless soup with stale bread.

MARIOLA
Swindler's Soup

2 eggs and 3 egg whites
1 cup bread crumbs, made from homemade-type, day-old Italian bread
1/3 cup grated *pecorino* cheese
1 tablespoon chopped parsley
1/2 tablespoon chopped marjoram
salt
pinch crushed dried red pepper
4 cups broth (Vegetable, chicken, or meat broth may be used.)
2 tablespoons extra virgin olive oil

1. Beat the eggs in a bowl and add bread crumbs, cheese, parsley, marjoram, salt, and pepper. Mix well.

2. Bring broth to a simmer while making the *frittate*.

3. Heat oil in a small skillet and add half the egg mixture. Spread it out with a spatula. Lightly brown it on one side over medium-low heat, turn it over, and cook the other side. Remove *frittata* from pan and make another one with the remaining egg mixture.

4. Cut the *frittate* into thin strips and then into 2-inch lengths. Add the pieces to the simmering broth and let all cook together for several minutes.

5. Pour soup into a tureen and sprinkle with more *pecorino* cheese. 4 servings.

La Pasta

Pasta

Pasta must be considered the signature food of Italy. In the south it is the first course of the main meal every day. Naples is the center of the south for dried *spaghetti* and hundreds of other shapes of the dried *macaroni*. Other cities in the south have special *pasta* too, such as the *orecchiette* (little ears) of Puglia.

Pasta is a frequent addition to the menu in the northern regions too. Bologna is the center where the filled *pasta* and freshly made ribbon noodles such as *tagliatelle* reign. Fresh ribbon noodles are made throughout Italy, however, and in Liguria, where they are called *trenette*, they are prepared with their famous *pesto* sauce.

Today every type of *pasta*, fresh or dried, is enjoyed throughout Italy and in most other countries. One word of warning: fresh commercial *pasta*, available in almost every grocery store, will not have the flavor and texture of that made at home.

Facing page: Venice

In some regions, especially in the north, Italians use only eggs for the moisture in their dough recipes. In other areas they use a combination of eggs and water. Some *pasta* dishes require a dough made with no eggs. My mother usually combined the eggs and water to reduce the richness of the dough, but the result was the most delicious *pasta* that I have had. She also made egg noodles without the water, especially for soup.

PASTA DELLA MAMMA
My Mother's Pasta

5 cups unbleached flour
3 eggs
3/4 cup water

1. Mound the flour on a pastry board and form a well in the center. Make certain that the wall around the well is firm so that cracks will not appear and allow the egg-water mixture to run out through the cracks. It is safer to use a large bowl or pan.

2. Break the eggs into the well and add the water.

3. Gradually work the flour from the walls of the well into the egg mixture. I use one hand to mix. When the flour and the liquid are combined, knead the dough by pushing away with the heels of both hands. Then fold the dough over toward you and push away with the heels of the hands again. Turn the dough as you knead. The dough should be firm. If too moist, add flour. If too dry, add a little water. When the dough is well kneaded, form into a ball and place a bowl over it or cover with plastic wrap. Let it sit for about 20 minutes. It will become softer as it sits. Scrape the board clean.

4. Cut the ball of dough into slices. Flour and run the slices through the rollers of a *pasta* machine at the thickest setting. Then set the rollers at a medium thickness and run the strips through the rollers again, always dusting the strips with flour. Finally, adjust the setting to the desired thickness of the *pasta* and run the strips through again. Lay the strips of dough on a dry cloth and dust them with flour once again.

5. Dough may also be rolled out with a rolling pin. In this case you would roll dough into a circle like a large pie crust. To cut the dough in desired widths, you roll up the *pasta* sheet like a jelly roll and slice.

6. The strips of dough can be used for lasagna or ravioli or cut in 4-inch lengths for *cannelloni*. They may also be run through the cutters on the *pasta* machine for making *spaghetti* or ribbon noodles.

7. If making *cavatelli*, roll the slices of dough into ropes, the thickness of a small finger, and run the ropes through a *cavatelli* machine. If you do not have a machine, you can cut the ropes into half-inch pieces and roll each piece against the pastry board with the fingers or thumb in the same way you would form *gnocchi*. *Cavatelli* may also be made with the eggless *pasta* dough. They are especially good with beans in *Pasta e Fagioli* (*Pasta* and Beans). Makes about 2 pounds of dough, enough to serve 6 to 8.

Variations:

1. PASTA CON L'UOVA E FARINA—*Pasta with Eggs and Flour Only*
Combine 5 cups flour and 6 eggs in the method described above.

2. PASTA SENZA UOVA—*Pasta Without Eggs*
Combine 5 cups flour, approximately 1 1/4 cups water, and 1 tablespoon olive oil to make a medium-firm dough. Follow directions above.

We all considered my mother's *ravioli* the best there were.
I am sure you will agree after trying these.

RAVIOLI DELLA MAMMA
My Mother's Ravioli

2 pounds good quality *ricotta* sold in bulk in Italian grocery stores
(Do not use *ricotta* in the plastic containers displayed in the dairy case or the
very moist type.)
3 eggs
1/2 cup grated *pecorino Romano* cheese
2 tablespoons chopped parsley
salt and pepper
1 recipe of my mother's *pasta* dough (page 78)
1 recipe of meat sauce (See index for *Braciole di Manzo e Spaghetti* or
Lasagne al Forno e Polpettine.)
1 tablespoon extra virgin olive oil
grated *pecorino Romano* cheese

1. Drain *ricotta* overnight, in the refrigerator, to remove any excess moisture.

2. Combine drained *ricotta*, eggs, cheese, parsley, salt, and pepper. Set aside.

3. Roll out *pasta* strips thinly, about 3 inches wide. Place a rounded teaspoon
of *ricotta* mixture along the center of the strip about 1 inch apart.

4. Bring the long edge of the strip over the *ricotta* mounds, joining the two
long edges. Press between each mound of *ricotta* and also along the long
edges.

5. Cut a sliver off the long, jagged edge and cut where pressed, between each
mound. With the tines of a fork, press around the edges for decoration and
to be sure that the *ravioli* are well sealed.

6. Place the completed *ravioli* on a dry cloth and continue to make them until all the *pasta* and *ricotta* mixture are used.

7. Cook the *ravioli* in a large pot of boiling, salted water, with a tablespoon of olive oil, stirring frequently with a wooden spoon.

8. When *ravioli* are tender, drain them, put about 1/3 of them on a large warmed platter, and top with sauce and cheese. Put on another 1/3 with more sauce and cheese, and add the last with additional sauce and cheese. Makes 85 to 100 *ravioli*.

Variation: RAVIOLI DI SPINACI E RICOTTA—*Ravioli of Spinach and Ricotta*

In Tuscany the filling for *ravioli* usually is made by combining about 1 1/2 pounds spinach, cooked, drained well, and finely chopped with 1 pound *ricotta*, drained, 1/4 cup grated *parmigiano,* 2 eggs, salt, pepper, and a pinch of nutmeg.

The *lasagne* that my mother prepared is by far the best that I have had of this dish. This recipe includes her marvelous sauce with meatballs. The sauce may be prepared for use with any type of *pasta* or *polenta*. In Salerno and other southern Italian cities *lasagne al forno* is the specialty at *Carnivale* to begin Lent. Actually, it is not found on the menu often in Italy.

LASAGNE AL FORNO E POLPETTINE DELLA THERESA TENORE RIO

Baked Lasagne and Meatballs by Theresa Tenore Rio

MEATBALLS:

1 1/2 pounds ground chuck (fairly lean)
2 cloves garlic, mashed
3 slices homemade-type Italian bread, soaked in water, squeezed to remove water, and shredded
salt
1/2 teaspoon black pepper
2 rounded tablespoons grated, imported *pecorino Romano* cheese
1/4 cup finely chopped parsley
3 eggs
extra virgin olive oil for frying or baking meatballs

1. Mix all ingredients, except olive oil, thoroughly.

2. To make 24 meatballs, dampen the palms of the hands and roll meatballs lightly to about 1 1/2 inches in diameter and until smooth and round. For *lasagne*, set aside less than 1/4 of the meat mixture and make very small, marble size meatballs.

3. You may fry the meatballs or bake them. To fry, heat olive oil in a large, heavy-bottomed saucepan and place meatballs in the oil. Do not crowd them, but turn them as they brown on all sides. Remove meatballs as they are browned and add more until they all are fried.

4. To bake meatballs, line a cookie sheet with foil coated with a little olive oil. Preheat the oven to 350° F. Place meatballs on the baking sheet and put in the oven for 10 minutes.

If you are baking small meatballs, 10 minutes will be enough time to complete the baking. Set aside the small meatballs for assembling the *lasagne*. For the larger meatballs, loosen them with a spatula and bake another 10 minutes or until brown.

SAUCE FOR LASAGNE:

approximately 18 meatballs
2 large cloves garlic, mashed
1/8 teaspoon dried, crushed red pepper
1/8 teaspoon black pepper
1 (28 ounce) can crushed tomatoes
1 (28 ounce) can tomato puree
1 cup water
1 rounded tablespoon fresh chopped basil
2 rounded tablespoons chopped parsley

1. If meatballs were fried, remove all but 1 tablespoon of fat from saucepan, and add garlic, red and black pepper. Fry briefly until garlic is golden. Do not allow to brown.

2. If meatballs are baked, heat 1 tablespoon of olive oil in a large heavy-bottomed saucepan. Add garlic, red and black pepper and fry briefly until garlic is golden but not brown.

3. Add tomatoes, tomato puree, water, half of the basil and parsley, and salt. Simmer for 30 minutes, add only the larger meatballs and continue to simmer for 1 hour.

4. Add remaining basil and parsley and check seasonings. Add very little more water if sauce becomes too thick. The sauce should not be thin for *lasagne.*

FILLING:

2 pounds *ricotta* cheese sold in bulk, drained overnight to lose as much moisture as possible (Do not use the *ricotta* in those plastic containers displayed in the dairy case.)
4 eggs
1/2 cup grated *pecorino Romano* cheese
salt
1/8 teaspoon black pepper
1/4 cup chopped parsley

Mix all ingredients thoroughly.

LASAGNE ASSEMBLY:

Approximately 1 pound fresh *lasagne* noodles. To make the *lasagne,* use 2 1/2 cups flour, 2 eggs, and 3 1/2 tablespoons water. Follow directions for my mother's *pasta* above or use the food processor to form the dough and the *pasta* rolling machine to roll out the strips of dough as described under *Cannelloni* (page 88), but leaving the strips of dough long.
sauce
ricotta cheese filling
tiny meatballs
8 ounces *mozzarella* cheese, thinly-sliced
grated *pecorino Romano* cheese

1. Into 6 quarts of boiling salted water with a tablespoon of olive oil, add *lasagne* strips, one at a time, and when water returns to the boil cook until *lasagne* are barely tender, about 2 minutes. Stir with a wooden spoon so that the *lasagne* do not break and do not over cook.

2. Pour out most of the hot water and add cold water to the pot to cool the noodles. Drain into a colander and stack noodles on a cutting board. Cut noodles to fit *lasagne* baking pan.

3. In a *lasagne* pan, approximately 9 x 13 x 2 1/2-inches or even a little larger, spoon just a little sauce to barely cover bottom. Place a layer of noodles, side by side to completely cover sauce. Spoon a layer of *ricotta* filling over noodles, put a few tiny meatballs and a few slices of *mozzarella* here and there. Sprinkle with grated *Romano* cheese and spoon a layer of sauce over the cheese. Do not use too much sauce or it will become soupy. Set in place, side by side, another layer of *lasagne*.

4. Continue to make layers until pan is nearly full. Fill to not more than 1/2 inch from the top of the pan, ending with a layer of noodles, sauce, and grated cheese. Use a more generous layer of sauce on top. Do not over fill pan because this puffs during baking and will spill over.

5. Bake in preheated, 350° F. oven for 35 to 40 minutes or until puffed and cooked throughout. Cut into rectangles and serve to 8. The meatballs may be served as a *secondo* after the *lasagne* or may be offered with. Pass additional sauce, thinned just a little and heated, and grated cheese at the table.

Cannelloni are made with rectangles of *pasta* rolled around a filling of ground chicken, *ricotta* cheese, and other ingredients. They are topped with cheeses and sauces and baked. They were very tempting when my mother would take them out from the oven steaming hot.

Several preparations are necessary before the assembly: the filling, the white sauce, the tomato and basil sauce, the *pasta*, and the topping.

CANNELLONI
Filled Pasta Rolls

FILLING:

1/2 pound *ricotta* cheese
2 tablespoons extra virgin olive oil
1 onion, chopped
1 clove garlic, peeled and halved
1 1/2 pounds boned, skinned, and defatted chicken thighs, cubed
(You also may use veal or a combination of the two.)
1/4 cup dry white wine
1/2 cup freshly grated *Parmigiano Reggiano* cheese
1 egg
salt and pepper
dash of nutmeg

1. Drain the *ricotta* overnight in the refrigerator to reduce the moisture.

2. Heat olive oil in a large skillet and sauté onion and garlic until golden. Add chicken and continue to cook, stirring occasionally, until meat is cooked through and tender, but not browned or dry.

3. Add the wine and cook until it evaporates. Set aside and let cool. Grind chicken mixture through the finest blade of a grinder, twice, or run it through a food processor.

4. Combine meat mixture and *ricotta*. Mix thoroughly with the *parmigiano* cheese, egg, salt, pepper and nutmeg. Cover and keep refrigerated. This could be made a day ahead.

BESCIAMELLA SALSA (White Sauce):

6 tablespoons butter
6 tablespoons flour
2 cups milk, scalded
3 cups chicken broth

1. Melt butter in a saucepan and blend in flour. Cook while stirring until mixture is golden and well combined. Add hot milk, all at once, whisking vigorously to prevent lumps from forming.

2. When sauce is smooth, stir in chicken broth and bring to a gentle boil. Cook at a slow boil, stirring occasionally, for about 10 minutes. Add salt, if necessary.

FRESH TOMATO AND BASIL SAUCE:

1 tablespoon extra virgin olive oil
1 rounded tablespoon finely chopped onion
4 or 5 fresh red, ripe tomatoes, peeled, seeded and diced (about 2 cups tomato pulp)
1/3 cup chicken broth
8 leaves fresh basil, chopped
salt

1. Heat the olive oil in a saucepan over medium-low heat
and sauté the onion until soft, but do not brown.

2. When the onion is soft, add tomatoes and chicken broth. Simmer 15 minutes and add basil and salt. If sauce becomes too thick, add a little more broth. Set aside.

PASTA:

2 cups unsifted, unbleached flour
2 eggs
2 tablespoons plus 2 teaspoons water

1. This could be mixed in a food processor, with the plastic blade, by putting flour in the bowl and running the motor while adding eggs and water. Once it is combined, process 20 to 40 seconds or until the dough forms a ball. Knead the dough with the heels of the hands a few times on a floured pastry board. Shape into a ball, cover with an inverted bowl, and let rest 20 minutes. Personally, I like to mix the dough by hand, but the food processor does it very quickly. If the dough does not form a ball, it means that the dough is slightly dry. Add 1/2 teaspoon water and run the motor again. Makes 14 ounces of dough.

2. To make by hand, mound the flour on a large pastry board and make a well in the middle. Put eggs and water in the well. Gradually mix the flour with the eggs and water, using one hand, until well combined. Add more flour or more water, as necessary, to achieve a firm but pliable dough.

3. Knead dough with both hands, on a floured board, until it is elastic. Shape into a ball and cover with an inverted bowl. Let dough rest 20 minutes. Scrape the board clean.

4. Cut dough in 1/2-inch thick slices. Flatten, widen, and flour them. Roll out dough one slice at a time, thinly as you would *lasagne* strips, or ribbon *pasta*, about 4 inches wide, using a *pasta* machine with rollers. Run the strips through 3 or 4 times, beginning with the widest setting on the dial. Turn the dial each time for a thinner setting until the correct thinness is achieved. You may roll out dough with a rolling pin but it is easier and more even with the machine.

5. Flour the strips of dough, stack them, cut off the narrow ends and cut them in 4-inch lengths. Separate the squares and set them on a floured board or cloth. Makes about 20 squares.

6. Drop the *pasta* squares, a few at a time, in a large pan of boiling, lightly salted water with 1 tablespoon olive oil. Bring water back to the boil and cook 2 or 3 minutes or until *pasta* squares are cooked through but are still firm. Drain them and set them out, separated, on a pastry board or work counter.

TOPPING:

1/2 pound of Italian *stracchino* or *crescenza* cheese (A soft *mozzarella* may be substituted, if necessary.)
2 sauces, described above
freshly grated *Parmigiano Reggiano* cheese

ASSEMBLY:

1. Divide filling into 20 parts (about 2 tablespoons each). Form one of the parts of filling into a log and place it along an uneven edge of a *pasta* square. Roll to form a *cannelloni*. Continue to form *cannelloni* with the remaining *pasta* and filling.

2. Pour a layer of *besciamella* sauce on the bottom of 2 approximately 10 x 14-inch baking dishes. Place *cannelloni*, seam side down, in the baking dishes allowing about an inch between them. Top each of the *cannelloni* with about a tablespoon of *stracchino* or *crescenza* cheese.

3. Spoon the *besciamella* sauce to coat each of the *cannelloni*. Then spoon about 1 1/2 tablespoons of tomato sauce evenly over each of the *cannelloni*. Keep warm the remaining *besciamella* sauce and the remaining tomato sauce.

4. Sprinkle *cannelloni* with *Parmigiano* cheese. Place the baking dishes in a preheated, 425° F. oven for 15 to 20 minutes, or until hot and bubbling. To serve, lift out 2 *cannelloni* with a spatula onto a warmed plate. Spoon some additional sauce around the *cannelloni* on the plate. Continue to serve the remaining *cannelloni* in the same manner. Makes 20 *cannelloni*. The *cannelloni* may be made ahead and frozen for up to a month.

Variation: TORTELLINI AL FORNO—*Baked Tortellini*

Boil *tortellini* until tender but not too soft. Combine *besciamella* and tomato sauces and spoon some on the bottom of a baking dish. Put the cooked *tortellini* in the baking dish, put some *stracchino* or *crescenza* cheeses here and there and spoon sauce over all. Sprinkle with grated *Parmigiano* cheese and bake in a preheated 425° F. oven 15 minutes or until hot and bubbling.

Spinach *linguine* is especially attractive and tasty with white clam sauce.
My sister-in-law, Charlene Rio, who prepares this so well, claims that it is quicker
to use frozen spinach, but fresh spinach may be used if well chopped.
The recipe for the white clam sauce follows.

LINGUINE DI SPINACI
Spinach Linguine

1 10-ounce package of frozen chopped spinach or 12 ounces fresh
1 pound (about 3 1/2 cups) unbleached flour
2 eggs
1/2 teaspoon salt
1 tablespoon extra virgin olive oil

1. Cook spinach according to package directions. When cool, squeeze out as
much water as possible. If using fresh spinach, wash it well, drain, and cook it
in only the water clinging to its leaves. Chop the spinach finely and squeeze
out as much water as possible.

2. Combine spinach with all other ingredients and mix and knead either
by machine or by hand. All can be mixed and extruded in a *pasta*-making
machine or mixed in a food processor in a few seconds. If making by hand,
put the flour on a pastry board, make a well, put the wet ingredients in the
well and gradually mix with fingertips of one hand, bringing in the flour, a
little at a time, until well combined. Knead dough and shape into a ball, cover
with a bowl and let sit 20 minutes.

3. Cut the dough in slices, flour and flatten them, and run through the
widest setting of a *pasta* machine. Flour them again and run them through at
a medium setting, and then again at a thin setting. Flour the strips and cut
into *linguine* or other ribbon noodles with the machine. *Pasta* may also be
rolled out with a rolling pin into a large thin disk, floured, rolled, and cut
with a knife into the desired width. Makes enough for 4.

Gnocchi di Patate, which originated in Piemonte, where my grandfather was
born, are popular throughout Italy and in other countries. They are often
called *strangolapreti* (priest stranglers). In Piemonte and other areas of the north
they are served topped with butter infused with sage leaves, or with a *gorgonzola*
cheese sauce made by combining *gorgonzola*, melted with cream and a little butter.
Pesto, the well-known basil and olive oil sauce of the Ligurian coast, is another favorite topping.
These sauces are then sprinkled with grated *Parmigiano Reggiano* cheese. Our family favored a
tomato meat-based sauce for *gnocchi*, topped with grated *pecorino Romano* cheese,
but some prefer a fresh tomato-basil sauce and *Parmigiano Reggiano* cheese.

GNOCCHI DI PATATE
Potato Gnocchi

1 pound Idaho-type baking potatoes
1/2 pound unbleached flour (scant 2 cups)

1. Boil potatoes in water until cooked through. Drain potatoes and peel
them quickly, while still hot. Put them through a ricer or mash them
thoroughly. It is important to work quickly so that the potatoes remain hot.

2. Put 1/3 of the hot potatoes onto a pastry board. Add about 1/3 of the
flour. Mix together quickly with the hands and push to the side of the
board. Take another third of the potatoes, mix with another third of the
flour, and add it to the first potato-flour mixture. Continue to combine the
remaining potato and flour.

3. Bring the whole quantity of potato and flour mixture to the center of the
board and knead thoroughly until mixture is smooth and elastic.

4. Form the dough into a loaf, cover with an inverted bowl or with plastic
wrap, and let sit for 20 minutes. Scrape the board to remove any dough that
has stuck to it. Place a little flour in the upper corner of the board.

5. Cut a slice of dough from the loaf, dip it into flour, shape and roll it into a long log the thickness of a finger. Cut the log into 1/2-inch to 1-inch lengths.

6. Roll each length of dough lightly against a floured board using two fingertips or the side of the thumb or index finger. Push the finger or thumb right across the dough without much pressure so that the dough forms a little roll (*gnoccho*). Some cooks roll the pieces of dough against the prongs of a fork, which forms grooves, or against a grater. Some do not roll them at all.

7. Continue to form logs. Cut them into small pieces, and roll into *gnocchi* until all the dough has been used. Place the *gnocchi* on a tea towel or on a floured board as they are being made, separated, so that they do not stick together.

8. Cook the *gnocchi* in a large pot of boiling, salted water about 5 minutes or until cooked through so that they have lost their raw taste. They should be soft but firm enough to hold together.

9. Drain the *gnocchi* and place in a warmed shallow bowl. Cover with your favorite sauce and top with grated cheese. Serves 4.

This is a Sunday or holiday meal. The sauce may be used to flavor any *pasta* but I prefer *gnocchi* or *ravioli*. The meat is sliced and arranged on a platter to show off the attractive egg center. In Italy, it is served as the main course after the *pasta*.

GNOCCHI CON POLPETTONE ARROTOLATO AL SUGO
Gnocchi with Rolled Meatloaf in Tomato Sauce

3 extra-large eggs
3 large slices of Italian bread (about 4 ounces)
1 1/2 pounds lean ground beef
4 cloves garlic, mashed
1/4 cup grated *pecorino Romano* cheese
4 tablespoons finely chopped parsley
salt and pepper
2 ounces of sliced *prosciutto*
4 ounces of *Fontina* cheese, sliced
flour for coating meatloaf
2 tablespoons extra virgin olive oil
6 cups coarsely ground or crushed tomatoes
1/2 cup water
1 tablespoon chopped basil
1 1/2 pounds *gnocchi*, *ravioli*, or other *pasta*
grated *pecorino Romano* cheese

1. Put the three extra-large eggs in a saucepan, cover with water, and bring to a boil. Lower heat and simmer eggs for 15 minutes. Remove from heat, cool eggs in cold water, peel, and set aside.

2. Soak the bread with cold water. Squeeze as much water out as you can, shred the bread and put into a large bowl. Add to the bowl the ground meat, 2 cloves of the mashed garlic, grated cheese, 2 tablespoons of the parsley, the uncooked eggs, salt and pepper. Mix well. I use my hands to do this.

3. Flatten mixture on a sheet of plastic wrap. Form a rectangle about 8 x 12 inches. Cover meatball mixture with a layer of *prosciutto* slices and a layer of *Fontina* cheese slices.

4. Place the peeled eggs along a short edge of the meat. Begin to roll the meat over the eggs with the help of the plastic wrap. Continue to roll the meat until it is all one neat roll. Seal the edge and pinch together both ends. Sprinkle flour around the roll.

5. Heat 2 tablespoons of oil in a large, non-stick saucepan. Lift the roll into the oil. Carefully turn the roll to let it brown on all sides.

6. Add the tomatoes to the saucepan along with the remaining garlic. Season the sauce with salt and pepper. Bring to a boil, lower heat and simmer for 2 hours, turning meat occasionally. If sauce is too thick, add 1/2 cup of water. Add the remaining parsley and the basil. Check seasonings and allow to cook for another 20 minutes.

7. While sauce simmers, cook *gnocchi* or other *pasta* until done. Drain and put into a large shallow bowl. Sprinkle with grated cheese and spoon some sauce over. Stir gently to coat the *pasta*. Spoon more sauce over top and sprinkle with cheese. Serve to 6 as a first course with the sliced meat as the second.

This is a family favorite requested every Friday evening by my brother, Fred, who refers to them as the "green and whites." His wife, Charlene, prepares this with her homemade spinach *linguine* (page 91) which makes it special.

LINGUINE VERDI ALLE VONGOLE IN BIANCO
Green Linguine with Clams in a White Sauce

36 small clams or 2 5-ounce cans whole baby clams with juice
1/3 cup extra virgin olive oil
6 cloves garlic, sliced lengthwise
6 tiny dried hot peppers or 1/4 teaspoon dried, crushed red pepper
1/4 teaspoon *oregano*
1/2 cup dry white wine
1 cup bottled clam juice
salt
1/4 cup chopped fresh parsley
1 to 1 1/4 pounds fresh spinach *linguine* or *fettuccine*

1. If using fresh clams, remove sand by first scrubbing and setting them in salted water sprinkled with cornmeal for 30 minutes or longer. Shortly before cooking scrub clams again. If using canned clams drain and reserve clams and juice separately.

2. Put a large pot of lightly salted water over heat for boiling *linguine*.

3. Heat oil in saucepan and add garlic slices. When beginning to brown, add peppers and *oregano*. When garlic slices are a medium brown and peppers turns a shade darker, remove pan from heat. Do not burn pepper. Remove half of the garlic slices and half of the whole peppers to pass at the table. Leave remaining garlic and peppers in the pan.

4. If using canned clams, add them and sauté briefly in the oil. Add the wine and cook over high heat until wine is reduced by half. Add the reserved and the bottled clam juice. Bring to a boil, lower heat, and simmer 5 minutes. Add salt and parsley.

5. If using fresh clams, after removing half of the garlic and peppers, add wine, over high heat, to the remaining oil, garlic, pepper, and *oregano*. When it is reduced by half, add bottled clam juice and *linguine* and bring to a boil.

6. Remove fresh clams from the water and add them to the pan. Cover pan and cook about 5 minutes or until clams open. Add salt and parsley.

7. While sauce is being prepared and nearly done, cook but do not overcook. Drain *linguine* and immediately transfer to a warm, shallow bowl.

8. Add almost all the sauce and toss *linguine* until it is completely coated. Place opened clams over *linguine*, removing most of the shells and discarding those that did not open. Spoon remaining sauce evenly over *pasta* and serve at once to 4. Pass reserved garlic and peppers at the table.

Tortelli di Zucca are *ravioli* stuffed with pumpkin, *amaretti* cookies, and *Parmigiano* cheese.
This specialty of Mantua in Lombardia is served strictly as a *primo piatto* (first course).
The *tortelli* are traditionally served with melted butter and sage leaves.
To cut down on the richness of the topping, I like to mix the butter with some
light olive oil and to use both sparingly.

TORTELLI DI ZUCCA
Pumpkin Tortelli

1 piece of pumpkin or other mealy yellow squash, e.g., butternut squash
weighing about 1 pound
1 cup grated *Parmigiano Reggiano* cheese
1/4 cup Italian *amaretti* cookies, finely crumbled
salt and pepper
1 3/4 cups unbleached flour
2 eggs
3 ounces unsalted butter or a mix of half butter, half light olive oil
6 to 8 fresh sage leaves

1. Remove the seeds from the pumpkin or squash and bake or steam until
tender. Peel pumpkin, cut in cubes, and put through the food processor.
Strain the pumpkin if it is wet. It should be floury. Measure 1 cup of
pumpkin puree and put into a bowl. Add half the cheese, crumbled *amaretti*,
salt, and pepper. Mix well.

2. Mound the flour on a pastry board and make a well in the center. Break
eggs into the well. Work the eggs into the flour with the fingertips of one
hand until it is mixed. Then knead with both hands until smooth and elastic.
Place a bowl over the dough and let it sit 20 minutes.

3. Take one slice of dough at a time from the ball of dough, flour and run each slice through the widest setting of the rollers of a *pasta* machine. Then put them through a medium setting and finally through a thin setting. The strips should be about 3 inches wide and rolled very thinly.

4. Place mounds of filling, each about a rounded teaspoonful, along the center of each strip, about 1 inch apart. Bring the long side of the strip across the mounds to join the other long edge. Press firmly between each mound of filling and along the long edges of the strip. Cut a sliver off the jagged edge and cut between each mound of filling.

5. Make an impression around the edge of each of the *tortelli* with the tines of a fork to make sure that the filling is well sealed. Each may also be cut out with a *ravioli* cutter that has a fluted edge.

6. Cook the *tortelli* in a large pot of boiling, salted water until tender. Drain, place on a platter, dribble with the butter mixture and sage leaves. Top with cheese. Makes about 60 *tortelli*.

This is an elegant, healthful, and attractive vegetarian *pasta* dish. It is topped with a tomato sauce or often just with melted butter and cheese.

ROTOLO DI PASTA E SPINACI
Pasta and Spinach Roll

3/4 pound *ricotta* cheese
2 tablespoons extra virgin olive oil
1 onion, chopped
4 cups peeled and chopped Italian-type tomatoes, fresh or canned
2 tablespoons chopped, fresh basil
salt and pepper
3 pounds fresh spinach
1 egg
1 3/4 cup grated *Parmigiano Reggiano* cheese
pinch nutmeg
2 cups flour
2 eggs
1/4 cup tepid water

1. Set the *ricotta* in a bowl, covered with waxed paper, and let it drain out the excess water overnight. Discard the water.

2. Prepare the sauce: heat the olive oil in a saucepan and sauté the onion in it until softened and golden. Add the tomatoes and simmer for 30 minutes. Shortly before sauce is done, add the basil, salt, and pepper. Add a little water if sauce becomes too thick.

3. When washing the spinach, remove the large, fibrous stems. Drain the spinach and cook it in the water clinging to its leaves. Boil the spinach for 5 or 6 minutes. Drain and cool the spinach and squeeze it to remove as much water as possible.

4. Chop the spinach finely, drain, and combine it with the *ricotta*, 1 egg, half of the grated cheese, nutmeg, salt, and pepper. Mix well and set aside.

5. Prepare the *pasta*. Mound the flour on a large board and make a well in the center. Break 2 eggs in it and add the water. Mix the liquid, gradually working in the flour with one hand until you have a soft dough. Knead the dough with both hands until it is smooth and pliable. You may add some flour to the board while you are kneading. Form the dough into a ball, set a bowl over it, or wrap in plastic wrap and let it rest for 20 minutes. It may also be mixed in a food processor with the plastic blade.

6. Scrape the board, flour it, and roll out the dough with a rolling pin into a thin, large rectangle, about 17 x 19 inches.

7. Spread the spinach mixture over the dough about 1 inch from the edge. Roll it up and press the ends to seal in the spinach. Wrap the roll in cheesecloth and tie the two ends.

8. Bring salted water to a boil in a long pan like a fish poacher or deep roasting pan. Set in the spinach roll, making sure that the water completely covers the roll, and let it cook for 45 minutes.

9. Lift the roll from the water and remove the cheesecloth from the roll. Cut some 1-inch slices and place them around a warmed platter. Set the remaining uncut part of the roll in the center of the platter to be cut later. Serve tomato sauce and cheese separately at the table. Serves 4 to 6.

Trenette are the famous Ligurian ribbon noodles, similar to *tagliatelle* but slightly thicker and narrower. They can be made with white flour or with a mixture of white and whole-wheat flours. When whole-wheat flour is added, the noodles are called *trenette avvantaggiate*. Frequently, as in this recipe, potatoes and green beans are added to the *pasta*. Sometimes *cannellini* beans are used instead of the potatoes.

Pesto is the internationally known sauce of Liguria where the best *pesto* is made because of the region's fragrant basil and olive oil. Our son-in-law and excellent cook, Robin Matchett of Canada, adds a little lemon juice or vitamin C to his *pesto* so that it retains its bright green color.

TRENETTE E VEGETALI AL PESTO
Trenette and Vegetables with Pesto Sauce

1 cup fresh basil leaves, lightly packed
2 cloves garlic, peeled and mashed
1/4 cup pine nuts
1 teaspoon salt
freshly ground black pepper
1/2 cup grated *Parmigiano Reggiano* cheese, or half *Parmigiano* and
half *pecorino Romano*
1/2 cup extra virgin olive oil
2 medium-size potatoes, peeled, cut in half lengthwise,
and sliced about 1/4-inch thick
1 pound tender green beans, topped, tailed, and cut in 1-inch lengths
1 pound fresh *trenette* or other ribbon noodles

1. Prepare the *pesto*. In Liguria this usually is done with a mortar and pestle by pounding the basil leaves, garlic, pine nuts, salt, pepper, cheese, and oil until a fine paste is produced. *Pesto* can also be made successfully in a food processor. You may add a little lemon juice or vitamin C while processing it so that it will retain a brighter green color.

2. Bring to a boil, in a large pan, 4 or 5 quarts of salted water. Add the beans and cook them approximately 8 minutes. Add the sliced potatoes and cook them about 6 minutes.

3. Add the noodles to the vegetables, bring to a boil, and cook until done, from 3 to 5 minutes. Noodles should be cooked through but have some resilience to the bite.

4. Drain *pasta* and vegetables and put into a shallow serving bowl. Pour the *pesto* over the mixture and toss well. Pass additional grated cheese at the table. Serves 4.

Variation: TAGLIATELLE AL PESTO—*Tagliatelle and Pesto Sauce*

Prepare *pesto* sauce and serve it over *tagliatelle* with additional *Parmigiano* cheese but without vegetables.

Ravioli Nudi are so named because they are similar to spinach and *ricotta ravioli* without the *pasta*. They make a delightful, light starter course. The traditional topping for them is heated butter infused with fresh sage leaves. Some enjoy instead the colorful, light tomato sauce that accompanies the recipe.

RAVIOLI NUDI
Nude Ravioli

1/2 pound *ricotta* (1 cup, drained)
3/4 pound spinach (1 cup cooked, drained, and chopped)
2 eggs
1/2 cup *Parmigiano Reggiano* cheese, grated (plus extra for topping)
2 tablespoons flour
salt and pepper
1/8 teaspoon nutmeg

1. Let the *ricotta* drain in the refrigerator for several hours or overnight to reduce the water content.

2. Wash, drain, and cook the spinach with only the water remaining on its leaves. Cook until spinach is tender and drain. Cool and squeeze out, with your hands, as much moisture as possible. Chop spinach finely and squeeze again, or put through a food mill.

3. Combine well, in a large bowl, the *ricotta*, spinach, eggs, *Parmigiano* cheese, flour, salt, pepper, and nutmeg. Refrigerate for an hour or for as long as 24 hours.

4. Bring 6 quarts of salted water to a boil. Flour the palms of your hands and form little, oval dumplings. Set the dumplings on a floured board.

5. Cook the dumplings in slowly boiling water until done, about 6 to 8 minutes. They will rise to the surface and puff a little.

6. Remove with a slotted spoon and drain. Place *ravioli nudi* on a warmed platter. Top with grated *Parmigiano* cheese and serve immediately with tomato sauce and additional cheese passed at the table. Makes 4 servings.

TOMATO SAUCE:

3 tablespoons finely chopped onion
2 tablespoons extra virgin olive oil
2 cups peeled, seeded and chopped tomatoes (fresh or canned)
salt and pepper
8 large basil leaves, torn

1. Sauté onion in olive oil until golden and soft. Do not brown. Add tomatoes, salt, and pepper. Cook 20 to 30 minutes.

2. Shortly before serving add basil. If sauce becomes too reduced, add a little water. Check seasonings.

A delightful combination are these tasty beef rolls with *spaghetti*, *ravioli*, *lasagna*, or other *pasta*. They are normally served for Sunday dinner in our home, along with an Italian dry red wine.

SPAGHETTI E BRACIOLE DI MANZO
Spaghetti and Beef Rolls

1 pound flank steak, cut 1/4 inch thick into approximately 4 x 5-inch steaks. Pound steaks with mallet if necessary. This should make 9 or 10 thin steaks. You also may use thin sandwich steaks.
3 cloves garlic, mashed
salt
freshly ground black pepper
1/3 cup plus 2 tablespoons minced fresh parsley
1/4 cup raisins (6 to 8 per roll)
grated *pecorino Romano* cheese
1 tablespoon extra virgin olive oil
6 cups canned crushed tomatoes
1/2 cup water
1 rounded tablespoon chopped fresh basil
dash crushed red pepper
1 pound *spaghetti*, homemade, or Italian imported 100 percent *semolina*

1. Set out flattened flank steaks. Using 1/2 of the mashed garlic, spread a little on each steak. Reserve remaining garlic. Add to the steaks, salt, pepper, 1/3 cup of the parsley, raisins, and a sprinkling of grated cheese.

2. Roll up each steak and tie or skewer to hold together.

3. Heat olive oil in a large, heavy-bottomed saucepan and fry steak rolls until brown on all sides. Remove meat rolls from the pan and reserve.

4. Add 1 tablespoon olive oil to the saucepan and lightly fry the remaining garlic, red pepper, and black pepper until garlic is barely golden. Do not allow to brown.

5. Add tomatoes, water, half of the basil, and salt. Bring to a slow boil. Reduce heat and simmer for 30 minutes. Add meat rolls. Simmer for 1 to 1 1/2 hours or until meat is very tender. Add remaining parsley and basil and a little water if sauce becomes too thick.

6. Lift meat rolls from sauce and remove strings or skewers. Coat lightly with sauce and keep warm. Continue to simmer sauce while *spaghetti* cooks.

7. Cook *spaghetti* in a gallon of rapidly boiling, salted water until *al dente*. Do not overcook. Drain well and put into a large *pasta* bowl.

8. Sprinkle some of the cheese and spoon some of the sauce over *spaghetti*. Toss to coat all of the strands of *spaghetti*. Spoon more sauce to cover top of *spaghetti* and sprinkle with more cheese. Serve immediately with *braciole*, or serve *braciole* later as a second course. Serves 4. Pass remaining sauce and grated cheese at the table.

My mother would prepare this chicken with *pasta* for Sunday dinner or for company because it was special. She would carefully sew the chicken so that the stuffing would not come out and would cook the chicken in the sauce, very attentively. I make this more frequently with an unstuffed chicken or with chicken cut into serving pieces.

The *pasta* would be served as the *primo piatto* and the chicken, nicely carved, and the stuffing, sliced, would be served as the *secondo*. The *pasta* often would be homemade *tagliatelle,* but also *spaghetti, gnocchi, ravioli,* or *fusilli* would be used.

TAGLIATELLE COL SUGO AL POLLO RIPIENO
Tagliatelle with a Stuffed Chicken Sauce

1 whole frying chicken with the liver, gizzard, and heart.
4 tablespoons extra virgin olive oil
4 cloves garlic, peeled, 2 cut in halves, lengthwise, and 2 mashed
salt and pepper
4 eggs
1/2 cup grated *pecorino Romano* cheese
1/4 cup parsley, chopped
1/8 teaspoon dried, crushed, red pepper
1 28-ounce can crushed tomatoes
1 28-ounce can tomato puree
1/2 cup water
10 leaves fresh basil, chopped
1 1/2 pounds fresh *tagliatelle*

1. Wash chicken inside and out with salt and water. Pat dry and sew the neck cavity closed. Clean giblets and chop finely.

2. Heat 2 tablespoons of the olive oil in a skillet. Add 2 halves of the garlic to the oil and brown. While garlic browns add giblets to the skillet and brown them with the garlic, stirring occasionally. Season with salt and pepper.

3. Beat 4 eggs with 1 tablespoon of the *Romano* cheese, salt and pepper. Stir in half of the parsley.

4. Turn heat to moderately high under the skillet. Remove and discard garlic. Add egg mixture to giblets and gently stir. When eggs begin to set but are still wet, remove from heat and put into a bowl.

5. Sprinkle chicken lightly, inside and out, with salt and pepper. Spoon the egg mixture into the cavity of the chicken and sew skin to close the opening.

6. Heat remaining olive oil in a wide, heavy-bottomed, 8-quart pan. Brown the chicken on all sides with the remaining 2 halves of the garlic.

7. When the chicken is nicely browned, remove from pan and set aside. Remove and discard the garlic pieces. Remove excess oil. Leave no more than 1 tablespoon of oil in the pan.

8. Fry in the remaining oil the crushed red pepper and a little black pepper for only a few seconds. Add crushed tomatoes, puree, and water. Add also the mashed garlic, 1 tablespoon of the parsley, half of the basil leaves, and salt.

9. Simmer the sauce for 20 minutes and add the chicken and any juices. Continue to cook the sauce with the chicken, barely boiling, for 1 1/4 to 1 1/2 hours or until chicken is cooked throughout but not falling apart. Add a little water if sauce becomes too thick. Check seasonings and add remaining parsley and basil. Simmer a few minutes longer.

10. Cook the *tagliatelle* in a large pot of lightly salted, boiling water until cooked through but not mushy. Drain and put into a large, shallow *pasta* bowl.

11. Sprinkle with some of the grated cheese and spoon over some of the sauce. Toss well and again spoon sauce evenly over *pasta* and sprinkle with cheese. Serve immediately to 6. Pass additional sauce and cheese at the table.

12. Meanwhile keep the chicken and some sauce hot. When time to serve chicken, carve and place on a warmed platter. Slice the stuffing and arrange it next to the chicken. Spoon some hot sauce over and serve. We always had a large, green salad afterwards and ended the meal with fresh fruit.

This was a favorite *spaghetti* dish that my mother prepared for our family. The chopped carrots in the sauce made a healthful and tasty combination with the ground meat.

SPAGHETTI ALLE CAROTE
Spaghetti with a Carrot and Meat Sauce

1 tablespoon extra virgin olive oil
3/4 pound lean ground sirloin
3/4 pound peeled and finely diced carrots
3 cloves garlic, mashed
5 cups peeled and chopped tomatoes with puree
3 cups water
3 tablespoons chopped parsley
salt and pepper
1 pound *spaghetti*

1. Heat the olive oil and brown the meat in the oil. Add the carrots and garlic and continue to sauté for 2 or 3 minutes.

2. Add the tomatoes, water, parsley, salt, and pepper. Bring to a slow boil, reduce heat, and simmer until carrots are tender.

3. Cook the *spaghetti* in 4 quarts of rapidly boiling, salted water, stirring from time to time, until *al dente*, about 10 minutes.

4. Drain *spaghetti* and put in a large, shallow bowl. Spoon about 3/4 of the sauce over *spaghetti*. Toss well. Spoon remaining sauce evenly over *spaghetti*. Serve immediately to 4.

This light and aromatic dish is prevalent in the *trattorie* of the Trastevere area of Rome.

SPAGHETTI ALLA ROMANA
Roman-Style Spaghetti

1/4 cup extra virgin olive oil
1 small onion, chopped
2 cloves garlic, finely minced
1 carrot, chopped
1 stick celery and some leaves, chopped
2 rounded tablespoons chopped parsley
4 basil leaves, chopped
1 very small, dried hot pepper or a pinch of crushed pepper
3 cups fresh tomatoes, peeled, seeded, and chopped (If tomatoes are out of season, canned Italian tomatoes may be used.)
salt
1 pound *spaghetti*
1/2 cup grated *Parmigiano Reggiano* cheese

1. Heat oil in a saucepan and add onion, garlic, carrot, celery, half of the parsley, half of the basil, and the pepper. Sauté slowly for about 20 minutes or until the vegetables are soft but not browned.

2. Add tomatoes, bring to a boil, reduce heat, and simmer for 30 to 40 minutes. Add salt and remaining parsley and basil. Let cook another 5 minutes.

3. Cook *spaghetti* in 4 quarts of salted, rapidly boiling water until *al dente*, about 10 minutes. Drain *spaghetti* and put into a large, shallow bowl.

4. Sprinkle *spaghetti* with 3 tablespoons of the cheese and spoon over the top about half of the sauce. Mix thoroughly. Serve 4 portions of *spaghetti* in warmed plates. Top each plate with additional sauce and additional cheese.

5. Serve to 4 immediately and pass remaining sauce and cheese at the table.

The appealing meat sauce is made with any whole piece of meat or with meatballs. Beef, lamb, veal, chicken, pork, or any combination of these may be cooked in the sauce. Even fish may be substituted for the meats. The sauce can be used over any *pasta* and is very good with *polenta*.

SPAGHETTI COL SUGO ABRUZZESE
Spaghetti with Sauce of Abruzzi

2 pound piece of meat of your choice
2 tablespoons extra virgin olive oil
2 large cloves garlic, peeled and halved
1 onion, peeled but left whole
1 carrot, peeled but left whole
1 28-ounce can ground tomatoes with puree
salt and pepper
1 tablespoon basil
1 tablespoon parsley
1 pound *spaghetti*
2 heaping tablespoons grated *pecorino Romano* cheese

1. Brown meat in olive oil with garlic. When meat is almost browned, add onion and carrot.

2. When meat is browned on all sides, add tomatoes and a little water so that sauce will not be too thick. Add salt and pepper and simmer for 45 minutes, stirring occasionally.

3. Add basil and parsley and cook until meat is tender. Add a little water, if necessary.

4. If using fish, add a firm fish after the sauce has cooked 45 minutes and cook only until fish is cooked through.

5. Cook *spaghetti* in 4 quarts of lightly salted, boiling water, until *al dente*, no more than 10 minutes. Drain *spaghetti* and put into a large shallow bowl.

6. Sprinkle *spaghetti* with 1/2 of the cheese and spoon about 1/3 of the sauce over the cheese. Mix well and spoon another 1/3 of the sauce evenly over the *spaghetti* and sprinkle with the remaining cheese. Serve the remaining sauce at the table with additional cheese. You may serve to 4 with the *spaghetti* as a first course and the meat as a second.

Venice

This popular dish is frequently offered in the restaurants of Florence. The *penne* is boiled and drained while still quite firm because it will be recooked in the sauce and must be served *al dente*.

PENNE STRASCICATE ALLA FIORENTINA
Penne with a Florentine Meat Sauce

1 onion
1 carrot
1 large stalk celery
3 tablespoons extra virgin olive oil
3/4 pound lean ground beef or veal
1 cup water
2 cups Italian peeled tomatoes
salt and freshly ground black pepper
1 pound *penne*
2 rounded tablespoons chopped parsley
1/2 cup grated *Parmigiano Reggiano* cheese

1. Make a *battuto* (a mixture of finely chopped onion, carrot, and celery) and put it in a large sauté pan with the olive oil. Cook over a medium heat until vegetables are tender and beginning to color.

2. Add the meat and brown lightly. Add water and when it comes to a boil, reduce heat to low and cook approximately 30 minutes.

3. Add tomatoes and cut them with a spoon. Add salt and pepper and continue to simmer another 30 minutes. Add a little water if the sauce becomes too dry.

4. Boil the *penne* not more than 7 minutes. Strain and add to the sauce with the parsley.

5. Sauté while stirring for 3 or 4 minutes to allow the sauce to be absorbed by the *pasta*. *Pasta* should be cooked *al dente*. Transfer *pasta* to a warmed platter. Sprinkle with cheese and serve immediately to 4. More cheese may be passed at the table.

Naples

A tasty hot sauce is the feature of this dish, which my sister, Nancy, prepares so well. This dish frequently is prepared very simply without the mushrooms, *pancetta*, or grated cheese. *Spaghetti* is often used for this recipe. *Arrabbiata* (angry) refers to the red pepper, so the sauce should have bite.

PENNE ALL'ARRABBIATA
Penne with Hot Sauce

1 ounce dried *porcini* mushrooms
2 table spoons extra virgin olive oil
1 ounce lean *pancetta* (Italian bacon), finely chopped
2 cloves garlic, finely chopped
1/4 teaspoon hot, dried, crushed red pepper, or to taste
2 cups Italian-type plum tomatoes, peeled, seeded and coarsely chopped
1 pound *penne*
8 leaves fresh basil, chopped
salt
1/2 cup grated *pecorino Romano* cheese

1. Rinse dried mushrooms and soak them in 1 1/2 cups of warm water for 15 minutes. Remove from the water when soft, reserving the water, and dice them.

2. Heat olive oil in a saucepan and brown lightly *pancetta*, garlic, and pepper. Add mushrooms and continue to fry for 1 minute, stir in tomatoes, and add salt. Bring to a boil, reduce heat, and simmer for 15 minutes.

3. Add 3/4 cup of reserved *porcini* soaking water being careful not to include any sand that may have fallen to the bottom. Simmer for 20 minutes.

4. Cook *penne* in 4 quarts of boiling, lightly salted water until *al dente*. Drain and put into a warmed *pasta* bowl.

5. While *pasta* is cooking, add basil to the sauce, and check seasonings.

6. Sprinkle about 3/4 of the cheese over the *penne* and spoon about 3/4 of the sauce. Mix well. Spoon remaining sauce evenly over *penne* and sprinkle with remaining cheese. Serve immediately to 4.

The sauce for this tasty recipe has a subtle, delightful flavor of fresh mint.
If fresh mint is not available, dried mint can be a substitute.

FUSILLI ALLA BENEVENTANA
Fusilli with a Meat and Herb Sauce

1 onion, finely chopped
2 tablespoons extra virgin olive oil
12 ounces lean ground round or sirloin
2 cloves garlic, mashed
1/2 stalk celery, finely chopped
1/2 cup dry red wine
28-ounce can Italian tomatoes with juice, coarsely chopped
2 rounded tablespoons chopped parsley
1 rounded tablespoon finely chopped fresh mint (about 20 leaves) or 1/2
teaspoon dried
salt
1/4 teaspoon crushed dried, red pepper
1 pound *fusilli*
1/4 cup freshly grated *Parmigiano Reggiano* cheese

1. Sauté onion in olive oil until transparent. Add meat and brown over
moderately high heat. While it is browning, add garlic and celery.

2. When everything is lightly browned, add wine. Bring to a boil and cook
until wine evaporates.

3. Add tomatoes, half of the parsley and mint, salt, and pepper. Cook gently
about 1 hour. Add remaining parsley and mint. If sauce becomes too thick,
add a little water. Continue to simmer until *fusilli* are cooked.

4. Cook the *fusilli* in plenty of lightly salted water, stirring frequently, until
tender. Drain and put into a shallow serving bowl.

5. Sprinkle *fusilli* with most of the cheese and spoon over most of the sauce. Mix well, spoon remaining sauce evenly over *fusilli*, and sprinkle with remaining cheese. Serve immediately to 4.

Cultivating the olive groves, Cinque Terre

Pappardelle are *pasta* noodles about an inch wide and slightly thicker than most of the ribbon noodles. *Lepre* is a hare. For lack of a hare, rabbit is a good substitute. The dish is very popular in Tuscany, especially in the fall during the hunting season.

PAPPARDELLE ALLA LEPRE
Pappardelle with Hare Sauce

1 to 1 1/4 pounds hare or rabbit pieces (If using hare, marinate in red wine for 24 hours before cooking.)
1 ounce dried *porcini* mushrooms
3 tablespoons extra virgin olive oil
1 small onion, chopped
1 stalk celery, chopped
1 carrot, peeled and chopped
1 large clove garlic, chopped
1 rounded teaspoon fresh, chopped rosemary
1 rounded tablespoon chopped parsley
salt and pepper
1 cup dry red wine
2 tablespoons tomato puree
1/2 cup water
1 2/3 cup unbleached flour
2 eggs
2 tablespoons water
1/2 cup freshly grated *Parmigiano Reggiano* cheese

1. If using hare, dry the pieces of meat when removing from the marinade. It is not necessary to use a marinade for the domestic rabbit.

2. Soak the dried *porcini* mushrooms in 1/2 cup of warm water for 15 minutes.

3. Heat the olive oil and sauté the onion, celery, carrot, garlic, rosemary, and parsley in a large saucepan. When they begin to wilt, add the rabbit or hare pieces, pushing the vegetables and herbs to the side. Giblets may be chopped and added if desired.

4. Remove mushrooms from the soaking water, reserving water. Chop mushrooms and add to saucepan. Continue to sauté, turning meat and vegetables occasionally. Add salt and pepper. When everything is nicely browned, pour in the wine and let it boil.

5. When the wine has nearly evaporated add the tomato puree diluted with 1/2 cup of water. Add all but 1 tablespoon of the mushroom soaking water. Discard the remaining tablespoon in case some sand has fallen to the bottom. Cover saucepan and let the meat cook until tender, 1 to 1 1/2 hours. Add water as necessary to keep a sauce consistency.

6. To prepare the *pappardelle*, mound the flour on a pastry board and make a well in the center. Break the eggs into the well and add 2 tablespoons water.

7. Work the liquid and flour together with one hand to form a dough. Knead with both hands until smooth and elastic. Shape into a ball. Cover with an inverted bowl or plastic wrap and let it rest for 20 minutes. Dough may also be made in a food processor with the plastic blade. While motor is running, add wet ingredients to the flour. It is done when it forms a ball. Knead dough a few times, shape into a ball and let it rest, covered.

8. Cut the ball of dough into slices and dip each slice in flour. Put each slice through the rollers of a *pasta* machine, rolling each into a thin strip. They should be slightly thicker than ribbon *pasta*, *lasagne*, or *ravioli*. The dough also may be rolled out with a rolling pin.

9. Cut the *pasta* into 1–inch wide strips. Lay them on a cloth not touching one another, and dust with flour.

10. When the meat is tender, remove the pieces from the sauce, cut the meat off the bone, chop it coarsely, and return it to the sauce. Add water if necessary and check seasonings.

11. Cook the *pappardelle* in a large pot of boiling salted water until cooked through but still *al dente*. Drain and toss with the sauce. Sprinkle with *parmigiano* cheese and serve to 4.

Artichokes probably are Italy's favorite vegetable. They are eaten both raw and cooked. They are prepared in numerous ways, and even a liquor is made from them. They combine beautifully with *farfalle*, the butterfly *pasta*, or with *penne*.

FARFALLE AL SUGO DI CARCIOFI
Farfalle with Artichoke Sauce

6 small artichokes (8 if they are very small) or one 9-ounce box of frozen artichoke hearts
3 tablespoons extra virgin olive oil
1/2 onion, finely chopped
1 rib of celery, finely chopped
1 clove garlic, finely chopped
1 slice of lean *pancetta*, a scant 1 ounce, finely chopped
salt
freshly ground black pepper
1/2 cup dry white wine
1 14-ounce can Italian plum tomatoes, chopped
1 cup water
1 pound *farfalle* or *penne*
2 heaping tablespoons chopped parsley
1/2 cup grated *Parmigiano Reggiano* cheese

1. Prepare the artichokes by pulling off the tough leaves. If you hold them at the top and pull straight down, they will break off at the tender part. Peel the stems.

2. Cut each artichoke in quarters, remove the fuzzy choke, if there is one, cut off the very top and any tough parts remaining on the heart. Slice thinly and put into a large bowl of cold water with a little lemon juice in it.

3. If using frozen artichoke hearts, thaw, remove any tough leaves from them, and slice.

4. Heat the olive oil in a large saucepan and sauté the onion, celery, and garlic until golden and softened. Add the *pancetta* and continue to sauté until just turning color. Drain the artichokes, add them to the saucepan, and cook at a moderately high heat. Add salt and pepper.

5. When the artichokes and onion are very lightly browned, add the wine and cook until most of the wine has evaporated.

6. Add the tomatoes and water and let the sauce cook at a gentle boil until artichokes are cooked and sauce has been reduced but is still fairly thin.

7. Cook the *farfalle* in a large pot of lightly salted, rapidly boiling water until cooked through but still retaining a slight firmness. This takes about 10 minutes. Stir frequently.

8. While *farfalle* are cooking, add parsley to the sauce. Check the salt.

9. When *farfalle* are cooked, drain and put into a large, warmed bowl. Add 2/3 of the cheese and 2/3 of the sauce and toss until *pasta* is thoroughly coated. Add the remaining sauce and cheese and serve immediately to 4.

This is a very old recipe from Amatrice, in the area of Rome, and very popular throughout the region. It is quick to make and really tasty. I always buy the leanest *pancetta* and use only an ounce, which imparts plenty of flavor. *Bucatini,* the long, thin, tubular *pasta,* may be used instead of *spaghetti.*

SPAGHETTI ALL'AMATRICIANA
Spaghetti in the Style of Amatrice

1 ounce lean *pancetta*, finely chopped
1 onion, finely chopped
1 tablespoon extra virgin olive oil
1 small piece of hot dried pepper or 1/4 teaspoon crushed red
hot pepper
2 cups peeled, seeded, and chopped tomatoes
salt
1 pound *spaghetti*
1/3 cup grated *pecorino Romano* cheese

1. Sauté *pancetta* in a saucepan, over moderate heat, until it begins to color. Add onion, olive oil, and red pepper. Continue to sauté, stirring occasionally, until onion is very soft.

2. Add tomatoes. When sauce comes to a boil, lower heat and boil slowly for 20 minutes. Add a little water if sauce becomes too thick.

3. While sauce simmers, bring 4 quarts of water lightly salted, to a boil. Put into the water the *spaghetti*. Stir, put a lid on the pan, and quickly bring water back to boiling. Remove lid. Stir *spaghetti* occasionally and cook until *al dente*.

4. Drain *pasta* and put into a large, shallow bowl. Sprinkle 3/4 of the cheese and spoon 3/4 of the sauce over the *pasta*. Mix well. Spoon remaining sauce evenly over top and sprinkle with remaining cheese. Serve immediately to 4.

Summertime is when you prepare *Spaghetti d'Estate* because the fresh, uncooked tomato sauce requires red, ripe, garden-grown tomatoes and fresh basil. Because of its fresh tomato flavor, this is the favorite sauce of our son, Robert, and his wife, Eva.

SPAGHETTI D'ESTATE
Summer Spaghetti

1 1/4 pound fresh tomatoes, peeled, seeded, and chopped
5 tablespoons extra virgin olive oil
1 large clove garlic, mashed
4 rounded tablespoons chopped fresh basil
salt
freshly ground black pepper
12 ounces *spaghetti*

1. Put prepared tomatoes in a bowl. Add olive oil, garlic, basil, salt, and pepper. Mix well and let sit for an hour or longer.

2. Cook *spaghetti* in lightly salted, boiling water until *al dente*, about 7 minutes.

3. Drain *spaghetti* and put back into cooking pot or into a large skillet. Put over heat and add the tomato mixture. Toss for a couple of minutes, until *spaghetti* is well coated with the sauce. Check seasonings. It is important to serve the *spaghetti al dente*.

4. Serve immediately as a first course to 4.

Eggplant or *zucchini*, *pasta*, and cheese combine superbly in this casserole which can be made ahead and baked just before serving. The dish freezes well too.

MELANZANA E PASTA AL FORNO
Baked Eggplant and Pasta

1 eggplant, 1 1/4 to 1 1/2 pounds
2 medium-sized eggs
salt and pepper
3/4 cup dried bread crumbs
2 rounded tablespoons plus 1/3 cup grated *Parmigiano Reggiano* cheese
extra virgin olive oil for frying eggplant slices (Use about 2 tablespoons per batch.)
1/4 cup extra virgin olive oil
2 cloves garlic, cut in halves
pinch crushed, dried red pepper
1 28-ounce can crushed tomatoes
1 cup water
1/4 cup chopped parsley
8 leaves fresh basil, chopped or 1 teaspoon dried
12 ounces *tagliatelle* or other noodles
8 ounces *mozzarella* cheese, sliced

1. Cut eggplant in 1/2 inch slices.

2. Beat the eggs in a bowl with 1 tablespoon water and add salt and pepper.

3. Combine bread crumbs, 2 rounded tablespoons of grated *Parmigiano* cheese, salt, and pepper. Dip eggplant slices into eggs and then into bread crumbs and set aside.

4. Heat 2 tablespoons of olive oil in a large skillet. Fry one layer of coated eggplant slices until lightly browned on both sides. Remove from skillet and reserve. Wipe out skillet with paper towels if bread crumbs remaining in skillet become too brown. Add another 2 tablespoons olive oil and fry another batch of slices until all eggplant is fried.

5. Make a sauce: heat 1/4 cup olive oil and brown garlic pieces. Add crushed pepper and swirl around in pan. Add tomatoes, water, and salt. Simmer 15 minutes and add parsley and basil.

6. Cook *tagliatelle* in 3 quarts lightly salted water until done but not too soft. Drain and put into a 2 1/2-quart, 3-inch-deep casserole dish with cover. Spoon about 1/4 of the sauce over the *tagliatelle* and mix well. Remove half of the sauced *tagliatelle* and reserve.

7. Place a layer of fried eggplant slices over the *tagliatelle* in the casserole dish and cover with half of the *mozzarella* slices. Spoon another 1/4 of the sauce evenly over *mozzarella* and sprinkle with *Parmigiano* cheese. Make another layer of reserved *tagliatelle*, eggplant, *mozzarella,* another 1/4 of the sauce, and a sprinkling of *Parmigiano*.

8. Cover casserole and bake in preheated, 350° F. oven for 20 minutes. Remove cover and bake 10 minutes longer. Heat remaining sauce and pass at the table with additional *Parmigiano* cheese. Serves 4 to 6.

Note: if preparing ahead to freeze, place covered casserole in freezer before baking. When ready to use casserole, thaw and bake.

Variation: ZUCCHINI E PASTA AL FORNO—*Baked Zucchini and Pasta*

You may substitute *zucchini* for eggplant in the above recipe.

Whether you are in Venice, Florence, Naples, or most other cities in Italy, you can find this famous dish. Chickpeas are sometimes used instead of beans, and each area makes it slightly different. This is my family's recipe from the region of Campania.

PASTA E FAGIOLI
Pasta and Beans

1/2 pound dried *cannellini* beans (Great northern beans may be substituted.)
1/4 cup extra virgin olive oil
3 cloves garlic, peeled and halved lengthwise
1/8 teaspoon crushed red pepper
1 3/4 cups peeled and chopped tomatoes, fresh or canned
salt
1 rounded tablespoon finely chopped parsley
12 ounces fresh *pasta* 1/2 x 2 inches (*laganelle*) similar to *tagliatelle* cut in 2-inch lengths (*Lasagne* sheets may be cut to size.) or use any small-size, dried or fresh *pasta* made without eggs. *Cavatelli*, made without eggs, is an excellent choice.

1. Sort through the beans to remove damaged ones and any bits of stone or dirt. Rinse and put into a saucepan. Add 4 cups of water and bring to a full boil. Boil for 1 or 2 minutes, cover pan, remove from heat, and let rest for 2 hours.

2. Bring beans to the boil again, reduce heat, and simmer until beans are tender, but not mushy.

3. In a large saucepan, heat olive oil and sauté garlic until lightly browned. Add red pepper, swirl around in the pan, and add tomatoes and salt. Simmer for 20 minutes.

4. Drain the beans and add to the sauce with the parsley. Continue to simmer sauce until beans are soft.

5. Cook *pasta* in plenty of lightly salted water until almost done. Drain *pasta* and add to the sauce and beans. Cook until *pasta* is tender but not overdone. Add a little hot water if mixture becomes too dry. Check seasonings and serve to 4.

This is the most typical of the *pasta* dishes of Bari in Puglia. The *broccoli* they refer to is not the *broccoli* that we use in the United States. Instead it is *rapini*, sometimes called *broccoli di rape*, the greens which have little *broccoli* flowers that sprout from them.
Orecchiette (little ears) are the most popular *pasta* in Bari.

The *rapini* and *orecchiette* are cooked together in a large pot of lightly salted water. Then, before serving, the *pasta* and greens are drained and quickly cooked again in a large skillet in the flavored olive oil.

ORECCHIETTE CON BROCCOLI DI RAPE
Orecchiette with Rapini Greens

3/4 pound *orecchiette pasta*
1 bunch of *rapini*, cleaned, the tough stems removed, and cut in 2-inch lengths
1/3 cup extra virgin olive oil
5 cloves garlic, peeled and halved lengthwise
1/4 teaspoon dried, crushed red pepper
1/4 teaspoon black pepper
salt

1. Put the *orecchiette* in a large pot of boiling, salted water, stirring occasionally. When the water returns to a full boil, let the *orecchiette* cook for approximately 10 minutes and add the *rapini*, a little at a time, so that the water does not stop boiling. *Orecchiette* can take 20 to 25 minutes to cook.

2. Cook the two together until the *orecchiette* and *rapini* are done. Meanwhile, in a large skillet, heat the olive oil and lightly brown the garlic. Add the red and black pepper and remove from the heat when the red pepper turns a shade darker. Do not let it burn.

3. Drain the *pasta* and *rapini*, reserving 1 cup of cooking water. Return the skillet to a moderately high heat. Pour the *pasta* and *rapini* into the skillet. Add salt and toss them around in the oil until thoroughly coated. If mixture is too dry, add a little of the reserved water. It should be neither soupy nor dry. Serve immediately to 4.

Steps, Assisi

This traditional recipe from Reggio-Calabria, combining sun-dried tomatoes, olives, and olive oil, is very much in keeping with today's style of healthful, tasty, easy cooking.

SPAGHETTI ALLA CALABRESE
Spaghetti with Sun-Dried Tomatoes and Olives

2 ounces sun-dried Italian tomatoes
1/3 cup extra virgin olive oil
5 cloves garlic, peeled and halved lengthwise
1/8 teaspoon crushed, dried red pepper
1/8 teaspoon black pepper
1/4 teaspoon *oregano*
12 Italian black or green olives, pitted and quartered
1 pound fresh or dried *spaghetti*

1. Put dried tomatoes in a bowl and pour very hot water over them to cover. Let them soak for 15 minutes to soften. Drain them, remove seeds, and chop tomatoes. Set aside.

2. Heat the olive oil and brown the garlic cloves. Add red and black pepper and *oregano* to the pan. Remove from the heat and swirl around so that the seasonings do not burn.

3. Return pan to the heat and add the chopped tomatoes. Let sauce simmer for 10 minutes and then add the olives. Add 1 cup of water and let the sauce boil slowly for 15 minutes.

4. If sauce becomes too dry, add a little water. Check the salt. If the tomatoes are salty, it will not be necessary to add salt to the sauce.

5. Cook *spaghetti* in plenty of rapidly boiling, lightly salted water until cooked through but still *al dente*. Fresh *pasta* cooks more quickly than the dried.

6. Drain *spaghetti* and put into a warmed bowl. Pour 3/4 of the sauce over the *spaghetti* and toss well. Spoon the remaining sauce evenly over the *spaghetti* and serve immediately to 4.

Vinci

From Catania in Sicily comes this rendition of an eggplant and *pasta* sensation named in honor of Vincenzo Bellini's beautiful opera "Norma." I would not be surprised if Bellini himself created this dish. Apparently, he was an imaginative cook as well as composer.

PASTA ALLA "NORMA"
Pasta with Eggplant

1 1/2 pounds eggplant (about 2 thin, elongated of medium size)
salt
3 tablespoons extra virgin olive oil
1/2 onion, chopped
4 cloves garlic, peeled and halved
1/8 teaspoon dried, hot, crushed red pepper
28 ounce can Italian whole tomatoes, chopped
20 leaves fresh basil, chopped
1 pound *spaghetti*
1/3 cup *pecorino Romano*, or salted, aged *ricotta* cheese, grated

1. Slice the eggplants, salt, and layer on a plate. Place another plate over the slices and top with a weight. Let the eggplants sit for an hour so that they will lose their bitter liquid.

2. Dry eggplant slices on paper towels, brush both sides with olive oil, place slices on a broiler pan, and broil until soft and lightly browned on both sides. Set aside and keep warm.

3. Heat olive oil in saucepan and add onion and garlic pieces. sauté until onion and garlic are lightly browned. Add red pepper. Add tomatoes and simmer 20 minutes. Add salt and basil.

4. Boil *pasta* in 4 quarts of lightly salted water until *al dente*. Drain and put into a large, shallow, warmed bowl. Spoon about 3/4 of the sauce and 3/4 of the reserved eggplant over the *pasta* and sprinkle with half the cheese. Mix well. Spoon the remaining sauce and eggplant evenly over the *pasta*. Sprinkle with the remaining cheese. Serve to 4 immediately.

Zucchini is featured in many Italian dishes. This is one of the tastiest, especially if you use the small, young *zucchini*. It also is easy to prepare.

RIGATONI COI ZUCCHINI E UOVA
Rigatoni with Zucchini and Eggs

1/2 cup extra virgin olive oil
2 onions, chopped
2 cloves garlic, peeled and chopped
a few flakes of dried, hot, crushed red pepper
2 1/2 pounds of small *zucchini*, stems and tails removed
salt and black pepper
1 pound *rigatoni pasta*
4 eggs
6 tablespoons grated *Parmigiano* cheese

1. Heat the olive oil in a large skillet. Add the onion, garlic, and red pepper. sauté until the onion is golden.

2. Cut the *zucchini* in halves, lengthwise, and slice them. Add *zucchini* to the skillet and continue to sauté, stirring frequently. Add salt and black pepper. Cook until vegetables are soft but not browned.

3. Cook the *rigatoni* in 4 quarts of lightly salted, rapidly boiling water until tender.

4. While *zucchini* and *rigatoni* are cooking, beat the eggs in a bowl. Add salt and pepper and 4 tablespoons of the cheese.

5. When the vegetables are done and *rigatoni* are cooked, drain the *rigatoni* and combine them with the vegetables. Keep them over the heat and add the beaten eggs. Keep turning the mixture while the eggs are setting.

6. When the eggs are cooked but not overdone, turn out into a warm platter. Sprinkle with remaining cheese and serve immediately to 4.

Asparagus and *spaghetti* in an olive oil sauce is a simple, but delightful combination and is very quick to prepare.

SPAGHETTI E ASPARAGI
Spaghetti and Asparagus

1 pound fresh asparagus
1/3 cup extra virgin olive oil
1 clove garlic, halved lengthwise
salt
freshly ground black pepper
12 ounces *spaghetti*, broken into 1-inch pieces

1. Cut off the very tough part of the asparagus and peel 2 or 3 inches of the bottoms. Cut asparagus in 1-inch lengths.

2. Heat olive oil and sauté asparagus and garlic until they begin to color. Add salt and a good amount of pepper. Add 1/2 cup water and cook gently until asparagus is tender.

3. In the meantime cook *spaghetti* in lightly salted, boiling water until *al dente*. Add a little of the *spaghetti* cooking water to the asparagus if the sauce is too reduced. Drain *spaghetti* and put into a warmed *pasta* bowl.

4. Pour most of the asparagus and sauce over the *spaghetti*. Mix well and pour the remaining asparagus and sauce over the top. Serve immediately to 4.

On Christmas Eve it is mandatory in my family that we have *Spaghettini Aglio, Olio con Alici* as part of our holiday feast, but one can enjoy this humble, tasty dish any time of the year. I vary it to please the individual tastes. If I omit the anchovies, for those who prefer it without, this recipe becomes *Spaghettini Aglio, Olio e Peperoncini* which is widely popular in Italy and the preference of my daughter-in-law, Eva. I add parsley to my recipe mostly for the aesthetic value, even though my mother did not use parsley in this dish.

SPAGHETTINI AGLIO, OLIO CON ALICI
Spaghettini with Garlic, Oil, and Anchovies

1/3 cup extra virgin olive oil
6 cloves garlic, peeled and cut in halves, lengthwise
2 tiny, whole dried red peppers or 1/4 teaspoon dried, crushed
red pepper
1/4 teaspoon black pepper
1 2-ounce can anchovy fillets packed in olive oil (optional)
1 cup water
1 pound *spaghettini*
1 rounded tablespoon chopped parsley (optional)

1. Heat olive oil and add garlic. When garlic is browned on both sides, add red pepper and black pepper. After a few seconds, add oil from the can of anchovies plus one of the anchovy fillets. Separate remaining fillets, cut in thirds, and reserve.

2. Add water to the sauce, bring to a slow boil, and allow to simmer for 20 to 30 minutes.

3. Cook *spaghettini* in a large pot of boiling, salted water, stirring occasionally, until *al dente*. Do not overcook. Just before *spaghettini* is done, add reserved anchovies and parsley to the sauce.

4. Drain *spaghettini* and put into a shallow bowl. Pour the sauce over the *spaghettini* and toss it well. Serve immediately as a first course to 4.

This antique recipe from the 1700s is featured every day on the menu of the Salerno restaurant, Al Cenacolo. They make their own *pasta* called *pici* which is like a very thick *spaghetti*. Because *pici* are difficult to find, I use fresh, dried *fusilli*. For the success of this dish you must use flavorful potatoes. I find Golden Yukons or new red potatoes good choices, but any potato with good flavor will do.

PICI CON PATATE
Pici with a Potato Sauce

1 small, thin slice *pancetta* (Italian unsmoked bacon),1 rounded teaspoon finely chopped
1 onion, finely chopped
1 pound flavorful potatoes, peeled and cubed
1/2 cup light chicken broth
1/2 cup water
1 pound fresh dried *fusilli*
2 rounded tablespoons coarsely chopped basil
1/2 cup grated *Parmigiano Reggiano* cheese

1. Put the *pancetta* in a saucepan over medium-low heat, stirring frequently. Cook about 3 minutes, not letting it brown, and add the onion.

2. Stir the onion from time to time and do not let it brown. When the onion becomes soft, add the potatoes. Stir them around and add the broth and water. Let this cook slowly until everything is very soft.

3. Cook *fusilli* in 4 quarts of lightly salted, rapidly boiling water until tender. This may take as long as 30 minutes. Test the *fusilli* while it cooks. When it is tender throughout, without having a hard core, it will be done.

4. Mash the potatoes, onion, and *pancetta* in the saucepan. If this potato sauce is too thick, add a little water from the boiling *fusilli*. Add the basil and simmer sauce for a few minutes. Test for salt.

5. Drain *fusilli* and put into a warmed *pasta* bowl. Add the potato sauce and cheese. Mix well and serve to 4.

In the Naples and Salerno areas of Campania, *pasta* is frequently joined with potatoes. This tasty potato sauce has the addition of tomatoes. *Fusilli* is particularly suited for a potato sauce, but other fresh dried *pasta* may be used.

FUSILLI CON PATATE E POMODORO
Fusilli with Potatoes and Tomatoes

3 tablespoons extra virgin olive oil
1 onion, finely chopped (about 1 cup)
1 stalk celery, finely chopped (about 1 cup)
a few flakes of hot, dried, crushed red pepper
2 pounds potatoes, peeled and cubed
1 cup chicken broth
1 cup water
1/2 cup crushed tomatoes
1 pound fresh dried *fusilli*
2 tablespoons chopped parsley
5 tablespoons grated *pecorino Romano* cheese

1. Heat olive oil in a saucepan and sauté the onion, celery, and red pepper until onion and celery are soft and golden.

2. Add the potatoes to the pan, stir them around, and add the broth and water. Bring to a boil, then lower heat and simmer until all the vegetables are tender. Add the tomatoes and cook another 20 minutes.

3. Meanwhile, cook the *fusilli* in 4 quarts of lightly salted, rapidly boiling water. Stir occasionally.

4. Add salt and pepper to the vegetables and mash them with a wooden spoon. They do not need to be completely mashed. A few small pieces of potato in the sauce are desirable. Stir in the parsley. If sauce is too thick, add a little water.

5. When *fusilli* are cooked (they should be tender throughout, not *al dente*) drain them and put into a *pasta* bowl. Add 4 tablespoons of the grated cheese and the sauce. Mix well and sprinkle the remaining cheese over the top. Serves 4.

Venetian Canal

This versatile olive paste is used not only to flavor *pasta*, but to spread on bread as an *antipasto* or to serve with meat and fish. In Liguria usually both green and black olives are blended and some cream is added. In Umbria the paste is served sometimes with a bit of black truffle.

SPAGHETTINI ALLA PASTA DI OLIVE
Spaghettini with Olive Paste

4 ounces black *Gaeta* olives
4 fillets of anchovy
1/2 cup extra virgin olive oil
2 cloves garlic, mashed
1 pound *spaghettini*
1 small black truffle, coarsely grated (optional)

1. Pit the olives. This is not difficult to do if you give a hit to the olive first with a mallet or, as I do, with the bottom of a heavy pottery cup. Place the pitted olives in the bowl of a food processor or in a blender.

2. Add the anchovies to the olives along with half of the olive oil. Process until ground.

3. In a small saucepan, sauté the garlic in the remaining olive oil until golden. Do not brown the garlic. Add the olive mixture to the garlic and oil and keep warm but do not cook.

4. Cook *spaghettini* in a large pan of salted, boiling water until *al dente*. Drain and put into a large, shallow bowl. Toss *spaghettini* with the olive paste, also the truffle if using it.

This colorful, tasty dish is named for the "ladies of the night," probably because it is spicy. Some say it is so named because it is easy to make.

SPAGHETTI ALLA PUTTANESCA
Spaghetti for the "Ladies of the Night"

3 tablespoons extra virgin olive oil
2 cloves garlic, halved
1/4 teaspoon dried, crushed red pepper
28 ounce can crushed tomatoes
1/4 pound black *Gaeta* olives
6 fillets of anchovies packed in olive oil, cut into pieces
2 tablespoons drained capers
1 rounded tablespoon chopped parsley
salt
1 pound dried *spaghetti* or *spaghettini*

1. Heat in a saucepan the oil and garlic pieces. When the garlic is lightly browned, add the pepper.

2. When the pepper darkens a shade (do not burn it), add the tomatoes. Put about 1/2 cup water in the tomato can, swirl it around to remove the last tomato bits and add to the sauce. Let cook about 15 minutes.

3. Pit the olives. To do this easily, smash them lightly with a mallet or, as I do, with the bottom of a cup. The pits can then be easily removed. Cut olives in fourths and add to sauce. Add also anchovies, capers, and parsley. Cook 2 minutes and add salt.

4. Cook the *spaghetti* in 4 quarts of boiling, lightly salted water until *al dente*. Drain *spaghetti* and put into large, shallow, warmed bowl.

5. Add 3/4 of the sauce. Mix well. Spoon remaining sauce evenly over *spaghetti*. Serve immediately to 4.

This colorful dish of Naples looks fantastic in a large Italian *pasta* bowl with the opened clams or mussels placed on top of the freshly cooked *spaghetti*.

SPAGHETTI ALLE VONGOLE
Spaghetti with Clams and Fresh Tomatoes

36 fresh, small quahog clams from Maine, littleneck, or small
cherrystone clams or mussels or both
1 tablespoon cornmeal
1/2 cup extra virgin olive oil
4 large cloves garlic, cut in halves lengthwise
1/8 to 1/4 teaspoon of dried, crushed, red hot pepper
6 small Italian tomatoes, about 1/2 the size of an Italian plum tomato,
unpeeled, or 4 red, ripe, fresh plum tomatoes, peeled, seeded, and cut
in pieces
1 heaping tablespoon chopped fresh basil
salt
2 heaping tablespoons chopped fresh parsley
1 pound *spaghetti* or *spaghettini*

1. Scrub clams. Set them in a large bowl of cold water. Salt the water and sprinkle with cornmeal. Allow to sit for at least 30 minutes or until ready to use them. Scrub once again and leave them in cold water.

2. Heat olive oil in a large saucepan over medium heat. Add garlic pieces and lightly brown on both sides. Add red pepper and when it turns a shade darker, remove pan from heat so that pepper will not burn.

3. Add tomatoes. Stir them around in the pan and squash them as they cook and break in pieces with a wooden spoon. Add basil and salt.

4. Meanwhile cook *spaghetti* in boiling, salted water until *al dente*. The *spaghetti* must not be overcooked in this dish!

5. Just after putting *spaghetti* into the boiling water, remove clams or mussels from water and add them to the olive oil sauce. Cover pan and cook over moderately high heat about 5 minutes or until the shells open. Check seasonings.

6. When *spaghetti* is done, drain and put it into a shallow *pasta* bowl. Pour most of the sauce onto *spaghetti* and toss to coat the strands well. Spoon opened clams over *spaghetti*. You may remove some of the clams from the opened shells and discard empty shells and discard shells that did not open. Leave some clams in the shells on top of the *spaghetti*. Spoon remaining sauce over all. Sprinkle with parsley. Serve promptly to 4.

Lina Coglianese of Oliveto Citra, my father's home town in the mountains of Campania, offers this colorful, tasty, healthful dish. She advises buying the smallest mussels that you can find. *Tubetti* are tubular *pasta* cut very short.

PASTA E FAGIOLI CON COZZE
Tubetti and Beans with Mussels

1 cup dried *cannellini* or great northern beans
3 pounds of small mussels
4 tablespoons extra virgin olive oil
4 cloves garlic, peeled and halved lengthwise
1/4 teaspoon dried, red crushed pepper
1 cup Italian-type plum tomatoes, peeled, seeded, and coarsely chopped
2 rounded tablespoons chopped parsley
salt
1/2 pound tubetti or other *pasta* cut short

1. Rinse beans in a saucepan. Drain and add water to 2 inches above the beans. Bring to a fast boil and cook beans for 1 or 2 minutes. Cover pan, remove from heat, and let beans soak in the cooking water for 2 hours or longer. Bring beans to a slow boil, cook until they are tender, and drain.

2. Scrub mussels well with a brush under cold running water, and pull off their beards. Put the mussels into a bowl of cold salted water. You may also add a little cornmeal to the bowl to help clean them further.

3. Heat 2 tablespoons of the olive oil in a large saucepan and lightly brown 2 cloves of the garlic. Add half of the crushed red pepper and let it darken a shade before removing pan from heat. Do not allow pepper to burn. Stir in the tomatoes.

4. Add half the parsley to the tomatoes, then salt and simmer the sauce for about 15 minutes.

5. Cook the *pasta* in a pot of fast boiling, lightly salted water for 5 minutes or until half cooked. Drain and add to the sauce along with the drained beans. Cook beans and *pasta* slowly in the sauce while cooking the mussels.

6. Heat the remaining 2 tablespoons of olive oil in a large, deep skillet. Brown the remaining 2 cloves of garlic and add the remaining crushed red pepper to the oil.

7. Add 1/2 cup water, turn heat to high, and when water is boiling, lift mussels from the bowl of water into the skillet. Cover skillet and let mussels cook for 4 or 5 minutes or until they have opened. Discard those that do not open.

8. Remove most of the mussels from the shells and stir into the pan of *pasta* and beans. Reserve a few mussels in their shells for garnish and keep warm.

9. Pour most of the water from the cooked mussels into the pot of *pasta* and beans. Do not drain the last bit of water where some sand may have settled.

10. Correct seasonings, and when *pasta* and beans are done, pour into an attractive serving bowl. Place reserved mussels on top and sprinkle remaining parsley over all. Serves 4 to 6.

One of the newer recipes of seafood *pasta*, this appealing dish was wrapped in parchment paper, dramatically opened, and presented by Tonia Lambiase, a beautiful twenty-year-old girl of Salerno.

SPAGHETTI CON FRUTTI DI MARE AL CARTOCCIO
Spaghetti with Seafood Wrapped in Paper

1 pound smallest clams you can find
1/2 pound shrimp
2 small *calamari*, cleaned
1/2 cup extra virgin olive oil
4 cloves garlic, cut in halves lengthwise
some flakes of dried, hot, crushed red pepper
1/4 cup white wine
1/2 cup red, ripe, fresh, peeled, seeded, and chopped tomatoes
salt and pepper
1 pound *spaghetti*
1/3 cup finely chopped, fresh, flat-leafed parsley

1. Scrub the clams with a brush and put into a bowl of cold water. Peel and devein the shrimp. Cut the calamari into rings and cut the tentacles into smaller pieces.

2. Put enough water in a covered skillet to cover the bottom, about 1/3 cup, and bring to a boil. Scrub the clams again and put them into the boiling water, over high heat. Cover the skillet and let the clams cook for 4 or 5 minutes or until they open.

3. Remove clams from their shells, saving the juices, and set aside. Cut them into smaller pieces if they are large. Strain the juices from the skillet and from the clams through several thicknesses of cheesecloth and reserve.

4. Heat the olive oil in a saucepan and add the garlic pieces. When they begin to brown add the red pepper. When the garlic is golden brown, add the *calamari* and shrimp over high heat. Fry and stir for a few seconds and add the wine.

5. Cook with the wine for about 1 minute and when wine has nearly evaporated add the reserved clam juice, clams, and tomatoes. Season with salt and pepper, bring to a boil, and remove from the heat. Preheat the oven to 350° F.

6. Cook the *spaghetti* in a large pot with 4 quarts of lightly salted, rapidly boiling water, stirring frequently, for about 5 minutes or until very *al dente*.

7. While the *spaghetti* is cooking, put a large sheet of oven parchment paper, in which to enclose the *spaghetti*, into a baking dish.

8. When the *spaghetti* is cooked, strain it and put it back into the cooking pot. Add the sauce with the seafood and toss the *spaghetti* and seafood over high heat until well combined, about 1 minute. Check seasonings.

9. Put the *spaghetti* into the parchment paper, sprinkle with parsley, and seal the packet, crimping together the edges. Place the baking dish in the hot oven and bake for 5 minutes. Cut open the paper at the table, and serve immediately to 4.

Pasta combined with vegetables is favored in many parts of Italy, especially in the south. In Sicily cauliflower is often referred to as *vruoccoli*, and *bucatini*, a long, thin, tubular *pasta*, is very popular.

BUCATINI CON VRUOCCOLI ARRIMINATA
Bucatini with Cauliflower

1 small head of cauliflower cut into flowerettes
4 quarts boiling water, salted
3 tablespoons extra virgin olive oil
2 large cloves garlic, halved lengthwise
1 onion, chopped
pinch of crushed, red pepper
2 cups tomatoes, peeled and chopped
1 rounded tablespoon of chopped parsley
1/4 cup *pignoli* (pine nuts)
1/4 cup raisins softening in 2 tablespoons hot water
1/2 teaspoon saffron soaking in 1/4 cup hot water
4 anchovy fillets, cut in small pieces
salt
1 pound *bucatini* or other tubular *pasta*

1. Drop cauliflower pieces into the boiling water. Cover pan and quickly bring back to the boil. Lower heat and cook about 5 minutes. Remove cauliflower and reserve water for cooking the *pasta*.

2. Heat olive oil in a large skillet and sauté garlic pieces and onion until onion is soft. Add red pepper and cauliflower and sauté for 2 minutes. Add tomatoes and simmer until cauliflower is nearly done.

3. Add parsley, *pignoli*, raisins, and saffron with their soaking water, and anchovies. Stir and add salt. Simmer sauce while *pasta* cooks.

5. Bring to a boil the water in which the cauliflower was boiled. Add the *bucatini*. Cook *bucatini al dente*, about 8 minutes. Drain *bucatini* well and add to skillet.

6. Sauté for 2 or 3 minutes while tossing mixture until well combined. Check seasonings and serve at once to 4.

The fountains of Tivoli

My sister, Rosemary, makes *pasta* salads when she has on hand roasted red peppers and preserved eggplants which she prepares frequently. She tosses the cooked *pasta* with olive oil, vinegar, garlic, *oregano*, salt, and pepper. Then she adds pieces of roasted red peppers and preserved eggplant (look for recipes in index). Her husband, Ken, likes to eat this dish when he plays in table tennis tournaments because he requires a high carbohydrate meal for the high energy sport.

The following *pasta* salad is elaborate, but one can simplify it or add to it, depending on the desired taste. Be creative.

INSALATA DI PASTA
Pasta Salad

1/2 pound 3-color *rotelle pasta* or other short-cut *pasta*
1/4 cup extra virgin olive oil
2 tablespoons red wine vinegar
1/2 clove garlic, mashed
salt
freshly ground black pepper
2 tablespoons chopped parsley
1/2 cup packed, preserved eggplant
1/2 cup roasted peppers, cut in bite-size pieces
6 pickled mushrooms, thickly sliced
15 *Gaeta* olives, pitted and halved
1 tablespoon drained capers
3 1/2 ounce can tuna packed in olive oil

1. Cook *pasta al dente* in boiling, salted water. Drain well and put into a salad bowl. Add olive oil, vinegar, garlic, salt, and pepper. Toss well and chill.

2. Add remaining ingredients and toss again. Serves 4.

Variation: INSALATA DI PASTA CON POMODORI E
MOZZARELLA—*Pasta Salad with Tomatoes and Cheese*

Add to the cooked *pasta*, cubed fresh tomatoes, cubed *mozzarella*, extra virgin olive oil, wine vinegar, fresh basil, salt, and pepper. You may use *farfalle* or
penne instead of *rotelle*, if desired.

Sciue sciue is Napoletana slang for a popular *spaghetti* dish that is quickly prepared. It is made with fresh, tiny Italian tomatoes, similar to cherry tomatoes, ripe and red. It can be easily turned into *Spaghetti Arrabbiata* by adding two or more hot peppers.

SPAGHETTI SCIUE SCIUE
Quick Quick Spaghetti

1 onion, finely chopped
5 tablespoons extra virgin olive oil
1 or more small, dried, hot red peppers
1 pound tiny, whole Italian tomatoes (similar to cherry tomatoes), unpeeled
salt
12 basil leaves, coarsely chopped
1 pound *spaghetti*

1. Sauté onion in olive oil over low heat with the red pepper until onion is soft and golden. Do not brown onion.

2. Raise heat to medium-low, add the tomatoes, put a lid on the pan, and cook 10 minutes, stirring from time to time with a wooden spoon. The tomatoes will break open as they cook.

3. If sauce is too moist, remove cover and cook another 10 minutes.
If sauce is too dry, add a little more water and cook slowly. Add salt.
One minute before completing the sauce, stir in basil.

4. Meanwhile boil *spaghetti* in 4 quarts of lightly salted, rapidly boiling water until cooked *al dente*. Do not overcook *spaghetti*, especially in this preparation.

5. Drain *spaghetti* and put into a warmed bowl. Toss with most of the sauce and spoon the remaining sauce over the top. Serve immediately to 4.

Green shutters, Siena

Il Riso e La Polenta
Rice and Cornmeal

Italy produces more rice than any other country in Europe, and rice, along
with *polenta*, is a staple food of the north. Rice and maize are grown
mainly in the fertile basin of the River Po.

When preparing *risotto* (a rice recipe), it is important to buy imported Italian rice. There are
many varieties, and some are preferred over others. *Arborio* and *Vialone Nano* are the best
known, and *Arborio* is the most available. Italian rice is short-grained. While absorbing a great
deal of liquid to obtain the desired creamy consistency of *risotto*, it retains a firmness.
Use only Italian rice for *risotto*.

Facing page: The Campanile, Pisa

Scampi are close cousins to shrimp but are not found outside the Italian seas. Shrimp work very well in this tasty recipe.

RISOTTO CON ZUCCA E SCAMPI
Rice with Pumpkin and Shrimp

3 tablespoons extra virgin olive oil
1 small onion, chopped
1 large leek, trimmed, washed well, and coarsely chopped
1 1/2 pounds pumpkin or other yellow winter squash, peeled, and cut in small dice
1 1/2 cups *Arborio* rice
4 cups chicken broth, simmering
1/2 pound large shrimp, peeled, deveined, and sliced in half lengthwise
1/2 cup grated *Parmigiano Reggiano* cheese

1. Heat oil in large saucepan and add onion.

2. Add rice and stir until rice turns opaque. Add 1 cup of the chicken broth and continue to stir. When broth is absorbed, add more, 1/2 cup at a time, allowing each addition to be absorbed before adding more.

3. About 5 minutes before rice is done, at the time of the last addition of the broth, add the shrimp.

4. Continue to cook and stir until rice is of a creamy consistency but still retains a slight resistance to the bite. It takes 20 to 30 minutes to cook the rice.

5. When rice is done, add cheese, salt and pepper. Mix well, and spoon into warmed serving dish. Serve to 4 immediately.

If you can find them, use very small, tender artichokes for this dish as they do in Florence. The larger artichokes work well too if you are careful to pull off the tough leaves.

RISOTTO CON I CARCIOFI
Rice with Artichokes

4 large or 8 small artichokes, or 9 ounces frozen artichoke hearts
1/4 cup extra virgin olive oil
1 clove garlic, finely chopped
1 1/2 cups *Arborio* rice
5 cups simmering chicken or vegetable broth
salt and pepper
1/2 cup grated *Parmigiano Reggiano* cheese

1. Remove the tough leaves of the artichokes by pulling them straight down and leaving behind the base of the leaf. Peel the stems. Quarter the artichokes and cut out the internal prickly and fuzzy parts keeping the remainder intact. When cleaned, soak in cold water with some lemon juice.

2. Dry them and slice thinly. In a large saucepan quickly sauté them with the garlic in the olive oil.

3. Add 1/4 cup water and cook until artichokes are tender and the water has evaporated. Stir in the rice and cook until rice is opaque.

4. Add about 1/2 cup broth, letting it become absorbed before adding another 1/2 cup. Continue to add broth, a little at a time, until all is absorbed into the rice. Add more if rice is too dry.

5. Cook and stir until the *risotto* is creamy but the rice retains a firm core. Season with salt and pepper and stir in most of the cheese.

6. Pour into a bowl and sprinkle remaining cheese evenly over the top. Serves 4 to 6.

Risotto alla Milanese traditionally accompanies *Ossobuco*. It may be served, however, on its own as a *primo piatto* (first course). It is flavored with saffron and usually includes beef marrow.

RISOTTO ALLA MILANESE
Rice of Milan

1 tablespoon extra virgin olive oil
2 tablespoons butter
1 tablespoon beef marrow
1 onion, finely chopped
1 1/2 cups *Arborio* rice
1/4 cup dry white wine
4 1/2 cups beef, chicken, or vegetable broth, simmering
salt and pepper
1/2 teaspoon saffron threads, crumbled
1/2 cup freshly grated *Parmigiano Reggiano* cheese

1. Melt olive oil, 1 tablespoon of butter, and beef marrow in a heavy-bottomed, large saucepan. Add onion and sauté over moderate heat until onion is golden and softened.

2. Add the rice and stir until it becomes opaque, about 2 minutes. Pour in wine and cook, stirring until it is reduced by half.

3. Add about 1/2 cup of the simmering broth, while stirring, until it is absorbed. Continue to add 1/2 cup at a time until all but the last 1/2 cup has been incorporated.

4. Steep the saffron in the last 1/2 cup of broth and stir it into the rice thoroughly. The *risotto* is done when the rice is still resistant and there is enough liquid to make it creamy and not dry. Add a little more liquid, if necessary.

5. Check the seasoning and gently stir to incorporate the remaining tablespoon of butter and the *Parmigiano* cheese. Pour *risotto* into a shallow serving bowl and serve immediately to 4. Additional grated cheese may be passed at the table.

Fiesole

Rice is a staple food of the Veneto and also of Lombardy where it is combined with flavorful vegetables and fish. This *risotto* is prepared when fresh asparagus is in season, but other vegetables may be substituted.

RISOTTO CON GLI ASPARAGI
Rice with Asparagus

1 1/4 pounds asparagus
3 tablespoons extra virgin olive oil
1 small onion, chopped
1 1/2 cups *Arborio* rice
1 cup dry white wine
3 cups light chicken broth, simmering
1 cup milk, scalded
salt and freshly ground black pepper
1/2 cup grated *Parmigiano Reggiano* cheese

1. Cut off and discard the fibrous ends of the asparagus stalks and peel, from the bottom, about 1/3 of the remaining stalk. Cut the asparagus in 1-inch lengths and set aside.

2. Heat the oil and add the onion. Sauté until onion is transparent and softened. Add asparagus pieces and sauté with the onion until asparagus is half done. You may remove a few of the asparagus tips, at this time, for garnish.

3. Add rice and stir with a wooden spoon until rice becomes translucent, then add the wine and stir.

4. When the wine has nearly evaporated, add 1/2 cup of the broth. Stir the rice while adding the broth 1/2 cup at a time. Wait until the first portion of broth has been absorbed before adding the next.

5. The rice is done when it is tender but is still firm to the bite, *al dente*.

6. Just before serving pour in the milk and stir gently until the milk has been absorbed. Season and add most of the cheese. Pour *risotto* into a serving bowl, sprinkle evenly with the remaining cheese, and garnish with the reserved asparagus tips. Serves 4 to 6.

Cinque Terre

This creamy, tasty *risotto* is named for spring because of its assortment of vegetables, but it can be enjoyed all through the year.

RISOTTO ALLA PRIMAVERA
Rice with Vegetables

5 cups meat or vegetable stock (Bouillon cubes may be used.)
5 tablespoons extra virgin olive oil
1 onion, chopped
1 carrot, chopped
1 stalk celery, chopped
1 medium *zucchini* squash, chopped
2 cups *Arborio* rice
1/2 cup white wine
1 cup frozen peas
1 rounded tablespoon chopped parsley
1 cup milk
1 tablespoon butter
1 cup grated *Parmigiano Reggiano* cheese

1. Bring the stock to a simmer and keep it barely simmering while preparing *risotto*.

2. In a 4-quart, heavy-bottomed pan, heat oil. Cook onion, carrot, and celery until golden. Add *zucchini* and continue to cook, stirring frequently, until vegetables are nearly done.

3. Add the rice and cook until the grains are opaque. Pour in wine and boil until it has almost evaporated.

4. Add 2 cups of the simmering stock to the rice and cook, uncovered, stirring frequently, until most of the liquid has been absorbed.

5. Add remaining stock while stirring, 1/2 cup at a time, until the liquid has been absorbed. Add the peas and parsley with the last 1/2 cup of stock. Cook, while gently stirring, until the rice is creamy but retains a firm core. Cooking time is 20 to 25 minutes.

6. Heat the milk and stir it in with 2/3 of the cheese, salt, if desired, and pepper. Sprinkle remaining cheese over top of *risotto*. Serves 6 to 8.

Tuscan landscape

Lina Coglianese, a teacher in the middle school of Oliveto Citra, Provincia di Salerno, prepares for her husband, Alessandro, and their two children, Pino and Rosaria, a variety of tasty and healthful meals. Her *Risotto coi Funghi* is special because it incorporates a delicious homemade broth.

RISOTTO COI FUNGHI
Rice with Mushrooms

5 cups meat or vegetable broth, homemade or canned
3 tablespoons extra virgin olive oil
1 onion, chopped
12 ounces fresh mushrooms, sliced
1 1/2 cups *Arborio* rice
1/2 cup white wine, optional
salt and pepper
1 tablespoon butter, optional
1/2 cup *Parmigiano*, grated

1. Prepare homemade broth: boil until soft, 2 pounds of veal shank or lean beef round with bone in 2 quarts of lightly salted water with 1 onion, peeled and quartered, 1 carrot, peeled and quartered, 1 stalk celery with leaves, and 2 tomatoes, chopped. Or use canned broth, heated and kept at a simmer.

2. In a large saucepan, heat olive oil and fry onion until golden. Do not brown it.

3. Raise heat under pan and add mushrooms. Stir while frying until mushrooms are lightly browned. Add rice and cook with mushrooms and onion for 5 minutes, while stirring. Turn down heat if necessary.

4. Add wine and stir. When wine evaporates, add 1/2 cup of broth. Stir until broth evaporates and continue to add broth, 1/2 cup at a time, stirring, until all is absorbed into the rice. Rice should have a creamy consistency but should retain a firm core. If rice is too dry, add more broth. Add salt and pepper.

5. Remove rice from heat. Stir in butter and most of the *Parmigiano* cheese. Pour *risotto* into a serving bowl, sprinkle remaining cheese over top, and serve immediately to 4 to 6.

This is a flavorful *risotto* utilizing fish and tomato sauce. Italians serve this as a first course, but I sometimes serve it as a main course with a salad to follow.

RISOTTO AL SUGO DI PESCE E POMODORO
Rice with Fish and Tomato Sauce

5 cups water
1 carrot, chopped
1 stalk celery, chopped
2 onions, chopped
2 tablespoons chopped parsley
salt and pepper
1 pound cod, halibut, swordfish, or other firm-fleshed fish fillets, boned
2 cloves garlic, mashed
1/8 to 1/4 teaspoon crushed, dried red pepper
6 tablespoons extra virgin olive oil
1 14-ounce can peeled and chopped tomatoes
1 1/2 cups *Arborio* rice
1 cup white wine

1. Pour into a saucepan 5 cups water, bring to a boil and add carrot, celery, 1 of the onions, parsley, salt, and pepper. Boil for 15 to 20 minutes until vegetables are tender. Check to see that there are no remaining bones in the fish. Add fish to the broth and cook 10 minutes.

2. In another small saucepan, prepare a tomato sauce. Sauté 1 clove of the mashed garlic and the red pepper in 2 tablespoons of the olive oil until they begin to color. Add the tomatoes and salt, and cook for 15 minutes.

3. Remove fish from broth, cut into small pieces, add to the tomato sauce, remove from heat, and reserve.

4. Measure vegetable-fish broth and add water, to make 5 cups. Keep the broth at a simmer.

5. In a large saucepan, sauté remaining onion and garlic in the remaining 4 tablespoons of olive oil until onion is soft and golden. Stir in rice and cook until rice is opaque.

6. Add wine, while stirring, and let evaporate. Add fish broth 1/2 cup at a time, letting each be absorbed before adding another.

7. When all the broth has been absorbed into the rice, stir in the fish and tomato sauce. Cook until rice is done but not mushy. Check seasonings and serve at once. Serves 4 to 6.

Roman courtyard

This classic, antique recipe was served at the banquets given by the doges in all the territories dominated by the Serenissima (Republic of Venice) when celebrating St. Mark on April 25. The earliest, most tender peas of the season were used.

Risi e Bisi has a consistency of a thick soup instead of a *risotto*. When young peas are not available, frozen tiny peas may be used. The dish may easily be made vegetarian by omitting the *pancetta* and using vegetable broth.

RISI E BISI
Rice and Peas

2 tablespoons extra virgin olive oil
1/2 onion, chopped
1 ounce lean *pancetta*, chopped (optional)
1 2/3 cups *Arborio* rice
4 cups meat broth or more if necessary
2 pounds tender, young, fresh peas in the pod, shelled, or 10 ounces shelled or frozen peas
salt and pepper
2 tablespoons chopped parsley
1/2 cup freshly grated *Parmigiano Reggiano* cheese
1 tablespoon butter

1. Heat olive oil in a large saucepan. Add onion and *pancetta* and cook until onion is soft and transparent but not brown.

2. Stir in rice and add 3 cups of the broth and the shelled peas. If using frozen peas, add them later as they take only 2 or 3 minutes to cook. Cook at a slow boil, stirring occasionally, for about 15 minutes until rice and peas are nearly done. Rice should be firm to the bite. The remaining broth may be added when needed to keep rice moist.

3. If using frozen peas, add them now. Season with salt and pepper and add parsley. Add additional broth as necessary and cook a few minutes longer until rice and peas are tender but not mushy. Mixture should be somewhat liquid.

4. Stir in the *Parmigiano* cheese and butter and serve at once to 6.

Rome

Italy owes a debt to America for its corn which in northern Italy rivals rice as a staple food. *Polenta* is a cornmeal mush consumed in a variety of ways.

Slices of *polenta* can be broiled or fried and topped with *gorgonzola* cheese, *fontina* cheese, grated *parmigiano*, or with wild mushrooms sautéed with garlic and extra virgin olive oil. These could be served as an *antipasto*. My favorite *polenta* dish, served by my mother, was prepared with large spoonfuls of *polenta* put on a serving dish, topped with a meat-based tomato sauce, and sprinkled with *pecorino Romano* cheese. My favorite cornmeal is *farina gialla* imported from Italy, but American cornmeal can also be used. There is a good precooked, boxed, Italian *polenta* which can be ready in five minutes.

POLENTA
Cornmeal Mush

3 1/2 cups water
1 teaspoon salt
1 cup cornmeal

1. In a large saucepan, bring the water and salt to a boil. Over medium heat, take a fistful of cornmeal at a time and sprinkle it into the water through your fingers gradually, like falling rain, while stirring vigorously to prevent lumps from forming.

2. Continue to add cornmeal until all is used. Turn heat to low so that the *polenta* will cook at a slow boil. Continue to stir for 30 minutes to prevent *polenta* from sticking to the bottom of the pan.

3. *Polenta* is done when it is very thick and loses its raw taste.

4. Lift large spoonfuls of *polenta* onto a shallow serving bowl. Cover with meat–based tomato sauce and sprinkle with grated *pecorino Romano* cheese.

5. Also, you may pour *polenta* into a loaf pan and chill. Remove from pan, slice, and broil or fry in olive oil until lightly browned. Add toppings of your choice.

Verona

Dried *porcini* mushrooms from Italy are not so difficult to find, but they are expensive. You use less than one ounce in this recipe, so the price is manageable. Try to find the fine Italian cornmeal *farina gialla* for preparing the *polenta*, but the precooked, ready in 5 minutes *polenta* from Italy can be used successfully.

POLENTA PASTICCIATA COI FUNGHI
Cornmeal Mush with Mushroom Sauce

3/4 ounce dried *porcini* mushrooms
3 tablespoons extra virgin olive oil
1 medium-small onion, finely chopped
1 medium stalk celery, finely chopped
1/2 carrot, finely chopped
1/2 pound lean ground beef
1/4 cup dry white wine
1 14-ounce can chopped or crushed, Italian-type plum tomatoes
salt and pepper
1 tablespoon chopped fresh parsley
1/2 tablespoon chopped fresh basil
7 cups water with 1 1/2 teaspoons salt
2 cups cornmeal
grated *pecorino Romano* cheese

1. Soak mushrooms in 3/4 cup hot water, to soften, for 20 minutes.

2. Heat oil in a saucepan over medium-low heat and sauté the onion, celery, and carrot, stirring occasionally, until vegetables are soft and golden.

3. Break the meat apart as you drop it into the saucepan and cook with the onion mixture until it is lightly browned. Stir, add the wine, and cook until the wine evaporates.

4. Add the tomatoes, salt, and pepper. Cover the saucepan and cook over low heat for 30 minutes.

5. While the sauce simmers, remove the mushrooms from the water, reserving the soaking-water, and cut in small pieces. Add to the sauce with the parsley and basil.

6. Simmer the sauce another 30 minutes, adding a little of the mushroom soaking-water as the sauce thickens. Do not use the last 1/4 cup of the soaking-water because some grit may have dropped from the mushrooms to the bottom of the bowl.

7. To make the *polenta*, bring the 7 cups of salted water to the boil. Reduce the heat to medium and add a handful of cornmeal through your fingers, like falling rain, while stirring vigorously to prevent lumps of cornmeal from forming.

8. Continue to add cornmeal until all is used. Turn heat to low so that *polenta* cooks at a slow boil, and continue to stir for 30 minutes to prevent it from sticking to the bottom of the pan. *Polenta* is done when very thick and has no raw taste.

9. Drop large spoonfuls of *polenta* on the bottom of a warmed, shallow bowl. Spoon some sauce over each mount of *polenta* and sprinkle with grated cheese. Spoon the remaining *polenta* in a second layer and coat with sauce and cheese. Serve 4 to 5. Pass additional sauce and cheese at the table.

This recipe has been in the family for generations. It is spicy, delicious, and healthful.

POLENTA AL FAGIOLI
Cornmeal with Beans

1/2 pound *cannellini* beans
3 tablespoons plus 1/4 cup extra virgin olive oil
5 cloves garlic, peeled and quartered, lengthwise
1/4 teaspoon crushed red pepper
2 cups tomato puree
4 cups water
3 teaspoons salt
2 rounded tablespoons chopped parsley
1 rounded tablespoon chopped basil
1 cup cornmeal
2 or 3 dried red peppers (hot or sweet as desired)

1. Pick through the beans to remove any bits of dirt or stones and rinse. Put beans in a saucepan and add water about 2 inches above the top of the beans.

2. Boil the beans for 1 minute, cover pan, and let rest for 2 or more hours. Simmer the beans until they are tender but not mushy. Drain and reserve.

3. Heat 3 tablespoons of the olive oil in a large saucepan. Brown 2 cloves of the garlic in the oil and add the crushed red pepper. Remove the pan from the heat when the pepper darkens. Do not let burn.

4. Add the tomato puree, water, salt, parsley, and basil. Bring sauce to a boil and simmer 5 minutes. Add the beans to the sauce and bring to a boil again.

5. Very gradually, sprinkle the cornmeal into the sauce and beans while stirring virgorously and constantly, so that the cornmeal will not be lumpy.

6. Continue to cook and stir after the cornmeal has been added until the mixture is thick and the cornmeal does not have a raw taste. Cover the pan and leave it on the lowest possible heat for 20 to 30 minutes, stirring occasionally.

7. In a small saucepan heat the remaining 1/4 cup olive oil and add remaining 3 cloves of garlic, sliced. Fry garlic slices until lightly browned. Break dried peppers into several pieces and remove seeds. Add the pepper pieces to the hot oil an swirl them until they darken a little and become crispy. Do not burn them.

8. Put the *polenta* into a serving bowl and pour the hot oil with garlic and pepper over it. Serve *polenta* with a little of the oil and a couple of pieces of pepper and garlic on each serving. Serves 4 to 6.

Afternoon in San Gimignano, Tuscany

I Secondi

Second Courses

La Carne

Meat

When doing the daily shopping in Italy, it is interesting to go into one of the local butcher shops (*macelleria*). The meat is cut daily, and it is surprising to see such lean meat. The meat looks fresh and is not prepackaged in plastic. There always is some meat which has been rolled and tied with string and is filled with a specialty of the butcher's making. Each roll has a sprig of rosemary, a bay leaf, or some other herb attached. The butcher is always happy to cut whatever pieces of meat you desire. There are spicy fresh sausages in the case and usually some hanging over a bar drying. There are now a few Italian supermarkets which use the typical plastic packing that we do.

The young beef or (*vitellone*) is not aged or marbled. It is not so young as our veal or so mature as our beef, but it is of excellent quality. The veal (*vitello*) is very young and pale pink. Pork (*maiale*) has the best flavor of any that I have had, and the cuts of pork are lean. This pork is the basis for the many types of ham and *salami* that are so flavorful in Italy.

Lamb and kid mostly are eaten in the southern regions and lamb is a favorite meat in Rome. The Romans enjoy their lamb roasted or braised in a sauce with rosemary. The head is highly prized when roasted perfectly with rosemary, garlic, and olive oil.

The excellent *Barolo* wine of the region of Piemonte is used to marinate and to braise the beef which results in a rich and flavorful sauce. Some may think the *Barolo* wine is too fine to be used in cooking. In this case another dry red wine may be substituted.

BRASATO AL BAROLO
Braised Beef with Wine

3-pound piece of lean beef for brazing: rump, eye of round, or sirloin tip
1 bottle of *Barolo* wine, or other dry red wine
1 carrot, peeled and cut in chunks
1 stalk celery, cut in 2-inch pieces
1 clove garlic, peeled and halved
4 or 5 sage leaves
1 small sprig of rosemary
1 bay leaf
3 sprigs parsley
1/4 teaspoon ground nutmeg
salt and pepper
flour for dredging the meat
2 tablespoons extra virgin olive oil
1 onion, chopped
1 tablespoon chopped, lean *pancetta*

1. Place the meat in a large bowl and pour about 2/3 of the bottle of wine over the meat. Add the carrot, celery, garlic, sage leaves, rosemary, bay leaf, parsley, nutmeg, salt, and pepper. Cover the bowl and leave in the refrigerator for approximately 24 hours, turning meat from time to time.

2. Remove meat, reserving marinade, and dry with paper towels. Dust the meat with seasoned flour.

3. Heat olive oil in a heavy-bottomed pan and brown the meat on all sides. While meat is browning, add onion and the *pancetta* and brown the onion and *pancetta* with the meat.

4. When browning is done, add marinade with all its ingredients and pour in the remaining wine from the bottle. Bring to a boil, stirring up the browning from the bottom of the pan, then lower heat, cover pan, and allow to boil slowly for about 2 hours or longer until meat is very tender. Turn meat and stir juices occasionally.

5. When meat is tender, remove from pan. Strain juices into a saucepan and keep hot. Slice meat and place on a platter. Spoon gravy over meat slices and put the remaining gravy in a gravy boat to pass at the table. Serve immediately to 6. *Cipolline d'Ivrea in Agrodolce* (sweet and sour whole baby onions) go well with this dish as do grilled or sautéed slices of *polenta*.

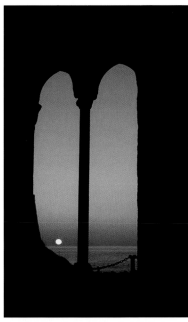

Sunset over Ligurian Sea from inside the Duomo, Vernazza

A boiled meat dinner is for large families or for guests. It is not a meal for only two persons. This is a popular dish prepared in many parts of Italy, sometimes under different names and in a variety of ways.

Bollito Misto is from Piemonte. The broth is often served as a *primo piatto* (first course), or saved for preparing *risotto,* and the variety of meats and vegetables follow with a green sauce. You can use any selection of meats and sausages or even only one.

The southern version, *Maritata,* is so named because the southerners believe that meats and greens make a perfect marriage. The boiled meats are cut in small pieces and are combined with the greens in the broth as a thick soup. The meat is not served with the green sauce.

BOLLITO MISTO
Mixed Boiled Meats

1 large onion, studded with 2 cloves
a handful of celery leaves
8 black peppercorns
1 bay leaf
1 small sprig of rosemary
6 sprigs of parsley
1 cup peeled, seeded, and chopped tomatoes
6 cups water
salt
2 pounds lean beef roast, rump or shoulder, tied
2 pounds veal roast, rump or shoulder, tied
1 3 1/2-pound chicken, cleaned and trussed
4 carrots, peeled
3 stalks celery, cut in 2-inch lengths
4 large potatoes, peeled
4 *zucchini* about 8 inches long

1. In a very large kettle put onion, celery leaves, peppercorns, bay leaf, rosemary, parsley, and tomatoes. Add water and salt.

2. Bring to a boil and add beef. Add more boiling water to cover beef, if necessary. Skim the surface occasionally, reduce heat, and let simmer 45 minutes.

3. Raise the heat, add the veal roast, and let come to a boil again while skimming. Lower heat and continue to cook for 15 minutes. Check salt.

4. Raise the heat again and add the chicken. Add enough water to cover chicken. Bring to a boil while skimming, reduce heat, cover, and simmer for 1 hour or until all the meats are tender.

5. Remove meats from pan, reserve, and add the vegetables to the pan. When vegetables are tender, check the salt and put the meats back into the broth until ready to serve.

6. While *bollito misto* is cooking, prepare the green sauce.

7. Slice the beef, veal, and chicken, and arrange them on a platter. Cut the vegetables in thick slices and put into a serving bowl. Spoon some of the broth over the meats and vegetables. Serve hot with the green sauce. Serves 8.

BAGNET VERD—*Green Sauce:*

1 cup finely chopped parsley
1/4 cup drained and finely chopped capers
1/4 cup finely chopped green onion
6 anchovy fillets, finely chopped
1 tablespoon red wine vinegar
2/3 cup extra virgin olive oil

Combine all the ingredients in a small bowl and whisk until well-blended. Serve with the boiled meats.

Variation: MARITATA—*Boiled Meats and Greens*

lamb shoulder or a combination of beef, chicken, and Italian sausage
2 pounds of mixed greens, e.g., chicory, escarole, swiss chard, and *rapini,* cut in 3-inch pieces

1. Put lamb or the combination meats in water to cover with 2 whole, peeled garlic cloves, 8 peppercorns, 6 sprigs of parsley, and 1 cup of peeled, seeded, and chopped tomatoes. If using a combination of meats, cook as for *Bollito Misto,* adding the chicken and sausage later.

2. Remove the meats from the broth and cut in bite-size pieces. Strain and defat the broth.

3. Blanch the greens quickly in boiling water, drain, and add to the broth. Add the meat and let everything cook together to blend flavors. This is a thick soup and should be served with Italian bread.

Bistecca alla Fiorentina, a very old recipe, is the most popular meat dish in Florence.
It is very simply grilled over an open fire as we do in the United States for our barbecues.
The meat in Florence is not mature, aged beef, nor is it veal. It is somewhere in between.
The beef comes from the massive *Chianina* steers grown in Arezzo, province of Tuscany.
The steak is the same cut as our porterhouse steak, but is bigger and is at least an inch thick.
It may weigh from a pound to one and a half pounds. It has virtually no fat and is a slightly
chewier than our softest steaks, but has excellent flavor. One steak is plenty for two or more.
Try to find organically raised beef.

BISTECCA ALLA FIORENTINA
Florentine Steaks

Porterhouse steaks cut 1 to 1 1/2 inches thick and all visible fat removed
salt
freshly ground pepper
lemon wedges

1. Cook the steaks on a grill over a very hot fire but without flames.
Cook on one side for 4 or 5 minutes without poking them with a fork.

2. Turn the steaks, salt and pepper the cooked side, and cook the other side
about 4 or 5 minutes. The steaks must be cooked rare on the inside and
brown on the outside.

3. Salt and pepper the other side of the steaks and serve immediately with
lemon wedges.

This special occasion roast may be prepared a day ahead, sliced, held in its sauce, and heated before serving. Beef or veal may be used. In Italy, a roast is more often done on the range top than in the oven.

ARROSTO DI CARNE
Roast Beef

3-pound lean roast beef or veal, rib, sirloin tip, or rump, boned, rolled, and tied
salt and pepper
flour for dredging meat
3 tablespoons extra virgin olive oil
2 cloves garlic, peeled and cut in halves lengthwise
1 onion, peeled and chopped
1 carrot, peeled and chopped
1 stalk celery, chopped
a few sprigs of parsley
1 cup dry white wine

1. Wipe the roast with paper towels and sprinkle it with salt and pepper. Season the flour and coat the roast on all sides, shaking off any excess.

2. Heat the oil over medium heat in a heavy-bottomed pan. Brown the meat on all sides. While meat is browning, add garlic pieces.

3. When meat is about half browned, add the onion, carrot, celery and parsley. Let the vegetables and meat brown together.

4. When all are nicely browned, add wine and turn up heat to bring to a boil quickly, turning the meat, for all sides to be in the wine sauce. When wine boils, reduce heat to medium-low, cover pan, leaving lid ajar, and simmer for about 2 hours or until meat is tender. Turn meat from time to time and add a little water as the liquid in the pan evaporates.

5. When meat is done, transfer roast to a carving board and complete the sauce. Add a little water to the pan over medium heat and bring to a boil. When sauce is reduced a little, strain it, mashing the vegetables through the strainer. Test the sauce for seasonings and keep warm.

6. Carve the roast in 1/4-inch thick slices, against the grain, and arrange them on a warmed platter. Spoon the hot sauce over the meat slices and serve to 8. You may hold the meat in its sauce, in the refrigerator, until the next day if you wish.

Tuscan landscape, Settignano

Italians enjoy rolled meats with tasty fillings. Usually, butchers will sell meats already filled, rolled, and tied. In Italy you can find whole rabbits or chickens already boned, kept in one piece, stuffed, and tied, all ready for cooking. The following meat roll can be prepared with any large, thin slice of beef, veal, or turkey breast.

ARROSTO MORTO ARROTOLATO
Filled Meat Roll

1 1/2 or 2 pounds thin slice of beef, veal, or turkey breast
1 clove garlic, mashed
salt and pepper
1/2 teaspoon fennel seeds
6 whole leaves fresh sage
1/2 cup chopped parsley
3 ounces thinly sliced *prosciutto*
3 tablespoons extra virgin olive oil
1 clove garlic, peeled and halved lengthwise
1/2 cup red wine
1 cup broth

1. Lightly pound the meat until evenly thick. Spread the meat with the mashed garlic and sprinkle with salt, pepper, and fennel seeds. Distribute evenly the sage leaves and parsley and cover with sliced *prosciutto.*

2. Roll the meat tightly, beginning with one of the long edges, and tie with kitchen cotton string.

3. In a pan large enough to accommodate the roll, heat the olive oil over medium-high heat. Add the 2 halves of garlic and the meat roll and brown on all sides. Add wine, and when almost evaporated, add broth.

4. Cover and cook gently, about 1 to 2 hours or until meat is tender, turning meat occasionally. Remove meat roll from pan, remove string, and let meat sit for a few minutes before slicing.

5. Place sliced meat on a warmed platter and serve with its juices to 6.

Santa Maria Novella (Detail), Florence

This popular dish of Naples is well-known throughout Italy. It consists of steak quickly cooked in a sauce with the flavors of *pizza*. This dish could also be done with pork steaks, but the meat should be cooked a bit longer. Fish fillets are sometimes done in this manner.

BISTECCHINE ALLA PIZZAIOLA
Beef Steaks with Tomato Sauce

2 tablespoons or more extra virgin olive oil
3 cloves garlic, cut in halves lengthwise
a pinch of crushed red pepper
1 1/2 cups chopped tomatoes
1 tablespoon chopped basil
1 tablespoon chopped parsley
1 teaspoon *oregano*
salt
4 thinly sliced tender steaks (about 1 1/4 pounds total)

1. Heat the olive oil in a large skillet and lightly brown the garlic. Add the red pepper, swirl around in the pan and add the tomatoes, basil, parsley, *oregano,* and salt.

2. Let the sauce cook for 5 minutes. While the sauce cooks, rub both sides of the steaks with olive oil. When the sauce is well-flavored, set the slices of steak, side by side, into the sauce.

3. Let the steaks cook over medium heat, turning occasionally so that they do not stick to the skillet, until nearly cooked through, but not overdone, about 10 minutes.

4. Lift the steaks onto 4 warm plates spooning some sauce over each. Serve with good Italian bread.

The few times that my father cooked, he did a great job of it. He always cooked outdoors over coals and stated that since Roman times, cooking over a fire has been the most prevalent way to cook meat in Italy. He used some sprigs of *oregano* to dip into his sauce to brush over the meat. His method can be followed for beef or lamb steaks, or meat on skewers.

BISTECCHE AL GIUSEPPE RIO
Steaks Grilled Outdoors

1/3 cup wine vinegar
2 tablespoons extra virgin olive oil
1/2 clove garlic, mashed
salt and pepper
several sprigs of dried *oregano*
6 lean, porterhouse or any tenderloin steaks of medium size

1. Have the charcoal fire hot with the coals turning gray and not flaming.

2. Combine vinegar, olive oil, garlic, salt, and pepper. Do not marinate the steaks, but brush them with the vinegar mixture by dipping the *oregano* sprigs into the vinegar and dabbing the steaks. If you do not have sprigs of dried *oregano,* put some dried *oregano* in the sauce and use a brush to apply to the steaks. Set the steaks on the grill over hot coals.

3. Brush the steaks occasionally with the *oregano* sprigs dipped in the vinegar mixture, and turn them when half done. The steaks should be brown, but do not let them blacken.

4. Brush the other side and cook until steaks are at the desired doneness. My father usually made them medium-rare. Give a last brushing on both sides, over the fire, and serve at once to 6.

Artichokes are very important in Florentine cooking. The artichokes are small, tender, and flavorful. Rarely does one have to remove a choke from them. If only larger, older artichokes are available, pull off all the tough leaves and cut out the chokes, the prickly and fuzzy parts from the center above the hearts. Frozen artichoke hearts are a valuable substitute.

INVOLTINI AI CARCIOFI
Rolled Beef Steaks with Artichoke Hearts

2 large or 4 small artichokes or a 9-ounce box of frozen artichoke hearts
3 tablespoons extra virgin olive oil
2 cloves garlic, peeled and halved lengthwise
salt and pepper
4 thin, lean, tenderloin steaks (1/4 to 3/8-inch thick), approx. 4 x 6 inches
1/4 cup dry white wine
1/4 cup water

1. If using fresh artichokes, pull the tough leaves straight down to remove them. Cut off the tops and most of the stem, cut in quarters and remove the prickly and hairy parts from the center, if there are any, located above the heart. Peel the remaining stem. Put the fresh artichoke hearts in a bowl of cold water with a little lemon juice in it. If using frozen, thaw and remove any tough leaves that may remain.

2. Heat 2 tablespoons of the olive oil in a skillet and lightly brown one of the garlic cloves. Meanwhile cut the artichoke hearts in wedges and add them to the garlic.

3. Sauté the artichoke hearts until lightly browned. Add salt and pepper. Add a tablespoon of water, put a lid on the skillet and cook slowly until artichoke hearts are tender. Remove from skillet and reserve.

4. Flatten the steaks and sprinkle with salt and pepper. Place 1 or 2 wedges of artichoke hearts on the end of the steaks, roll them up, and hold the rolls together with wooden or metal picks.

5. Add the remaining tablespoon of olive oil to a skillet and the remaining clove of garlic. Heat the oil and brown the meat rolls on all sides for about 20 minutes.

6. Add the wine and when it has nearly evaporated add the water, salt, and pepper. Let the steaks cook slowly until cooked through, about 10 minutes longer. There should be a little sauce in the bottom of the skillet. If the skillet is dry, add a little more water. If there are any remaining artichoke wedges, they may be added to the pan and cooked with the meat rolls or they may be used for another purpose.

7. Remove the picks from the meat rolls and place them on a warmed platter. Spoon the sauce over them and serve immediately to 4.

My mother's meatloaf is the tastiest that I have had. She varied the meat for it. Sometimes she would use all ground beef, and other times she would use half beef and the other half a mixture of lamb and pork. Often she would bake the meatloaf with potatoes and carrots, and frequently she would top it with peas in a tomato sauce. Any variation was excellent.

POLPETTONE DELLA NONNA
Grandma's Meatloaf

1 1/2 pounds lean ground round or sirloin, or a mixture of half beef and
half lamb and pork
5 ounces Italian bread, homemade, if possible
3 cloves garlic, peeled and mashed
2 eggs
salt and black pepper
2 rounded tablespoons grated *pecorino Romano* cheese
1/4 cup chopped parsley
1/4 cup raisins
extra virgin olive oil

1. Place meat in a large bowl. Cut bread in slices, remove some of the crust, and soak in water. When well-soaked, squeeze out the water with hands, chop the squeezed bread, and add it to the meat.

2. Add garlic, eggs, salt and pepper, cheese, parsley, and raisins. Mix well with hands. If using only very lean beef, add a tablespoon of olive oil. Meatloaf should not be dry.

3. Form into a loaf shape and place in an oiled baking pan. Score the top of the meatloaf and rub with olive oil. Preheat oven to 375° F.

4. If baking with potatoes and carrots, peel and cut potatoes in wedges, and peel and cut carrots in halves lengthwise and in halves again crosswise.

5. Add potatoes and carrots coated with olive oil to the baking pan with the meatloaf. Salt and pepper vegetables. Bake 15 minutes, lower oven heat to 350° F., and bake about 1 hour or until vegetables are done.

6. When preparing the meatloaf with peas and tomato sauce, prepare tomato sauce according to the following instructions, and add about 10 ounces frozen peas.

7. Remove potatoes and carrots from the baking pan and keep hot. Pour tomato sauce with peas over meatloaf and put back in the oven for 20 minutes or until bubbling. Serves 6.

IL SUGO DI POMODORO CON PISELLI—*Tomato Sauce with Peas*

Sauté 2 cloves garlic in 2 tablespoons extra virgin olive oil until garlic begins to color. Add 1 cup tomato puree and 3/4 cup water, salt, and pepper. Simmer 15 minutes. Add 10 ounces frozen peas, 1 tablespoon chopped parsley, and 1 tablespoon chopped basil. Simmer 5 minutes. Check seasonings and pour over meatloaf.

This antique and elegant Florentine dish was served at the baptism of Cosimo I de Medici in 1519. It remains popular today.

POLPETTONE ALLA FIORENTINA
Florentine Meatloaf

1/2 ounce dried *porcini* mushrooms
1 cup warm water
1 onion, finely chopped
1 carrot, finely chopped
1 stalk of celery, finely chopped
1 small bunch of parsley, finely chopped
1 tablespoon butter
3 tablespoons extra virgin olive oil
1 1/2 pounds lean, ground sirloin or veal
2 ounces *prosciutto,* finely chopped
2 ounce slice of homemade-type Italian bread, made into crumbs
1/2 cup grated *Parmigiano Reggiano* cheese
2 eggs
salt and pepper
dash of nutmeg
flour for coating meatloaf
1/2 cup dry white wine
lemon wedges

1. Soak mushrooms in the warm water.

2. In a pan large enough to hold a meatloaf, sauté over a low heat onion, carrot, celery, and parsley in butter and olive oil.

3. In a large bowl mix ground meat, chopped *prosciutto,* bread crumbs, cheese, eggs, salt, pepper, and nutmeg. Mix well.

4. Shape meat mixture into one or two loaves. Roll loaf in flour. Place in pan with vegetables, raise heat to medium, and brown slowly on all sides.

5. Add wine and boil until reduced by half, turning loaf once. Meanwhile, remove mushrooms from water, reserving soaking-water, and chop mushrooms finely. Add mushrooms to the pan. Strain mushroom soaking-water, leaving the last tablespoon behind which might have sand, and add to pan.

6. Turn heat to low and simmer covered for 30 minutes, turning and basting occasionally. Leave pan partially uncovered and cook another 30 minutes. Remove from pan and let sit a few minutes before slicing. Thin sauce with a little water if too thick.

7. Cut into 1/2-inch slices, arrange on a platter, and spoon the sauce on liberally. Squeeze the juice from half a lemon and sprinkle over the top. Pass additional lemon wedges at the table. Serves 6.

In Italy meatballs are served as a second course usually following the *pasta* course. These meatballs from Sicily have an *amaretto* cookie crumbled in which gives an interesting flavor.

POLPETTINE ALLA SICILIANA
Sicilian Meatballs

1 pound lean ground round or sirloin
1 egg
2 tablespoons bread crumbs plus 1/4 cup for coating meatballs
2 tablespoons *pignoli* (pine nuts)
2 tablespoons raisins, softened in a little warm water
salt and pepper
1 *amaretto* cookie, finely crumbled
2 tablespoons extra virgin olive oil for frying

1. Put into a bowl the meat, egg, 2 tablespoons of the breadcrumbs, *pignoli,* raisins (drained), salt, pepper, and *amaretto* cookie. Mix well but do not compact the mixture.

2. Form into balls, lightly, about the size of golf balls, and roll in the remaining bread crumbs to coat.

3. Heat olive oil in a frying pan and fry the meatballs on all sides until nicely browned. Serve hot to 4.

My mother always prepared her roasts by this particular method but used rosemary only with the lamb. Potatoes cooked with the meat are especially tasty.

AGNELLO ARROSTO CON PATATE
Lamb Roast with Potatoes

1 shank end leg of lamb
1/3 cup chopped parsley
1 large clove garlic, peeled and mashed
salt and pepper
extra virgin olive oil
2 or 3 sprigs of fresh rosemary
6 large potatoes, peeled and quartered lengthwise

1. Using a sharp, pointed knife, cut several slits, about 1 inch long and 1 inch deep into the meat, on all sides.

2. Combine parsley with garlic, salt, and pepper. Put about 1/2 teaspoon of this mixture into each of the slits. Place meat into a roasting pan and coat with olive oil. Add the sprigs of rosemary to the pan.

3. Place into a preheated, 350° F. oven. Cook for 30 minutes and remove pan from oven. Place potatoes all around the roast, turning them so that they are all coated with oil in the pan. Add more oil if necessary.

4. Cook for an additional 1 1/2 hours or until lamb is cooked throughout but not overdone and dry. Turn roast and potatoes occasionally during cooking period so that all sides are brown.

5. Remove roast, potatoes, and rosemary from pan. Discard nearly all the oil and the rosemary. Pour a little water into the pan, scraping up the brown. Boil it and season. Carve the meat onto a heated platter and spoon the sauce over the meat.

6. Serve the meat and the potatoes immediately to 6.

Despite the fact that Tuscany was a wool and sheep center centuries ago, lamb today is not eaten much in Tuscany except in the spring for the Easter holiday. This old Tuscan recipe is suitable for pork, rabbit, chicken, or duck as well as lamb.

AGNELLO CON OLIVE NERE
Lamb with Black Olives

3 tablespoons extra virgin olive oil
2 pounds of lean, boneless lamb, cubed
3 cloves of garlic, mashed
1 sprig of fresh rosemary
3/4 cup dry red wine
2 Italian-type ripe plum tomatoes, peeled, seeded, and chopped
15 black Gaeta olives, pitted (You can easily pit them by hitting them with a mallet.)
salt and pepper

1. Heat the olive oil in a large skillet. When the oil is very hot, add the meat and brown it on all sides.

2. While the meat is browning, add the garlic and rosemary.

3. When meat is browned, add the wine and reduce it by half. Stir in the tomatoes and bring to a slow boil. Reduce heat, cover, and let cook about 45 minutes until the meat is tender and the sauce has thickened.

4. Add olives, salt, and pepper and cook another 10 minutes. Add a little water if sauce becomes too thick. Serves 6.

In Rome this succulent dish is usually prepared with *abbacchio,* baby lamb that has never eaten grass. However, American lamb, which is slightly more mature, works well in this recipe.

ABBACCHIO ALLA ROMANA
Roman-Style Lamb

1 1/2 pounds lean lamb meat
4 tablespoons flour
salt and pepper
3 tablespoons extra virgin olive oil
3 cloves garlic, peeled and halved lengthwise
1/8 teaspoon dried, crushed red pepper
1 teaspoon chopped, fresh rosemary leaves
2 fillets of anchovy, chopped
2 tablespoons wine vinegar

1. Cube the lamb meat and lightly dust with seasoned flour. Set aside.

2. Heat olive oil in a wide, heavy-bottomed saucepan over moderately high heat and add 2 of the garlic cloves. When they begin to color, add meat cubes and brown on all sides.

3. Mash the remaining clove of garlic and add it to the meat with the red pepper, rosemary, and anchovy. Stir and add the vinegar.

4. Let everything cook over medium heat until meat is tender. Add a little water when liquid evaporates so that a sauce remains. Serves 4 to 6.

In summer one finds this elegant, cold specialty of Lombardia and Piemonte offered frequently in northern Italy. It can be served as a first course or as a main dish. Its tempting appearance, with its various garnishes, is far different from that of customary veal dishes, and it looks attractive on a buffet table.

Some cooks prepare another version by blending tuna, capers, and anchovies into a homemade or commercial mayonnaise to make the sauce. The following, however, is the traditional preparation. The versatile tuna sauce can be used over other poached, cold meats such as turkey and chicken breasts.

VITELLO TONNATO
Cold Veal with Tuna Sauce

3 1/2 to 4 pounds top round boneless veal, in one piece and tied
1 large onion, coarsely chopped
2 large cloves garlic, peeled and halved
2 stalks celery, cut into chunks
4 leaves fresh sage (optional)
2 bay leaves
about 3 ounces capers packed in vinegar, drained
1 2-ounce can of anchovy fillets packed in olive oil
3 cups dry white wine
1/4 cup white wine vinegar
salt
black pepper
2 cans (6-1/2-ounce) Italian tuna packed in olive oil
1 tablespoon fresh lemon juice
2/3 cup extra virgin olive oil
1/4 cup strained stock

1. Place veal in a pot just large enough to hold it comfortably. Add onion, garlic, celery, sage, and bay leaves, 2 tablespoons of the capers, and all but 3 of the anchovy fillets with the oil from the can. Pour over the meat, wine, vinegar, and enough water to just cover the meat. Salt and pepper lightly.

2. Bring to a boil, reduce heat, and skim the foam as it collects. Simmer gently for about 30 minutes per pound or until tender. Remove pan from heat and let veal cool in the stock for 1 hour. Remove meat, cover with plastic wrap, and chill.

3. Boil up stock and reduce to about half. Strain, reserving both the stock and the solids separately. Remove bay leaves from solids and chill. Also chill stock.

4. To prepare sauce: into blender jar put tuna with its oil, 1 tablespoon of the drained capers, the remaining 3 anchovy fillets, chilled solids from the stock, lemon juice, olive oil, and stock. Blend until smooth and thick. For a lighter-colored sauce, homemade or a commercial mayonnaise may be stirred in.

5. To assemble: remove the strings from the cold meat and cut against the grain in thin slices. Spread the bottom of a serving platter with some of the sauce and arrange slices of veal over this in a single layer, edge to edge. Cover the layer with more tuna sauce and scatter a few drained capers over the sauce. Continue to layer veal slices and sauce and a few capers, saving enough sauce to cover well the top layer. Do not put capers over top layer until ready to decorate and serve.

6. Cover with plastic wrap and refrigerate for 24 hours before serving. It will keep very well in the refrigerator for up to 2 weeks. Before serving decorate it with lemon slices and *cetriolini* (small Italian sour pickles) around the edge of the platter and scatter a few whole capers over the top. Serves 12.

This tasty veal dish from Trentino reflects the Hungarian influence with its use of paprika.

SPEZZATINO DI VITELLO (GULYAS)
Veal Stew with Paprika

2 tablespoons extra virgin olive oil
1 tablespoon butter
1 pound stewing veal, cut in bite-size pieces
1 small onion
5 sage leaves, chopped
1 tablespoon paprika
salt
1/3 cup dry white wine
1/2 cup ripe plum tomatoes, fresh or canned, peeled and chopped
2 tablespoons light cream or milk

1. Heat the olive oil and butter in a saucepan and add the veal. When veal begins to brown, add the onion and brown meat and onion together, stirring often.

2. Add sage, paprika, and salt and continue to brown while stirring. Add wine and stir up any browned bits on the bottom of the pan.

3. When wine is nearly evaporated, add tomatoes. Bring to a slow boil, turn heat to low, and simmer until meat is tender. Just before serving add cream, but do not let it boil. Adjust salt and serve to 4.

Saltimbocca is so good that, as the name indicates, it wants to "jump in the mouth."
For its success you must have fresh sage leaves.

SALTIMBOCCA
Veal, Prosciutto, and Sage Leaves

12 small, thinly sliced veal escalopes
12 thinly sliced Italian *prosciutto,* the same size or smaller than the veal slices
24 fresh sage leaves
3 tablespoons extra virgin olive oil
1 tablespoon butter
1/2 cup white wine
salt and freshly ground black pepper

1. If too thick or unevenly cut, flatten the escalopes with a meat mallet.
Lay a slice of *prosciutto* on each of the escalopes and top each one with 2
sage leaves fastened with wooden picks.

2. Heat the olive oil and butter in a large skillet. When hot, add the veal
slices, sage side up. Cook 1 1/2 to 2 minutes and turn the veal over, sage side
down. Cook another 30 seconds and remove to a heated platter and keep
them warm.

3. Continue to fry the *Saltimbocca* until all the veal is cooked.

4. Deglaze pan with wine and quickly reduce the sauce by about half. Add
salt and pepper to sauce and spoon over *Saltimbocca.* Serve immediately to 6.

Ossobuco alla Milanese is one of the most popular dishes in Lombardia. It requires veal shanks cut in 1 1/2-inch lengths of the round bone with the marrow and the meat surrounding the bone. The dish is usually served with *Risotto alla Milanese*. This is one of the few times that a *risotto* is served with the second course. Frequently a *gremolata* (topping), consisting of parsley, lemon, and garlic, is sprinkled over the dish about 5 minutes before serving.

OSSOBUCO ALLA MILANESE
Braised Veal Shanks

2 1/2 pounds veal shanks, about 4 meaty slices 1 1/2 inches thick
3 tablespoons seasoned flour
3 tablespoons extra virgin olive oil
1 tablespoon butter
1 onion, finely chopped
1 stalk celery, finely chopped
1 carrot, peeled and finely chopped
1 clove garlic, mashed
1/2 cup dry white wine
1 1/2 cups canned Italian tomatoes, finely chopped, with their juice
salt and pepper
1/4 cup chopped parsley
1/2 clove garlic, mashed
grated rind and juice from 1/2 lemon

1. Dredge the veal shanks in the flour. Shake off the excess. Heat the oil and butter in a wide, heavy-bottomed pan over medium heat. Brown the veal shanks on both sides and remove from the pan.

2. Add to the pan the onion, celery, carrot, and clove of mashed garlic. Sauté vegetables for about 8 or 9 minutes until they are golden and softened.

3. Return the meat to the pan and add the wine. Let the meat and vegetables cook together until the wine evaporates, and then add the tomatoes and salt and pepper.

4. Cover the pan and simmer for about 45 minutes. Turn over carefully each piece of *ossobuco,* test seasonings, cover pan, and cook another 40 minutes until meat is fork tender.

5. Prepare the *gremolata:* mix together the chopped parsley, mashed garlic, and grated lemon rind. About 5 minutes before serving sprinkle meat with the mixture and squeeze the lemon juice over each piece. Cover pan and cook for 5 minutes.

6. Carefully lift the pieces of *ossobuco* from the pan onto a warmed platter. Spoon some of the sauce around each *ossobuco* and serve the remainder separately at the table. Serves 4.

This well-flavored, classic, Florentine dish is served traditionally over toasted bread. Fresh garlic can be rubbed over the toast, if desired. Peas are sometimes added and cooked with the meat or they or other vegetables are cooked separately and served with the *stufatino*.

STUFATINO DI VITELLO
Veal Stew

1 1/2 pounds lean veal, cut into cubes
flour for dredging meat, seasoned
3 tablespoons extra virgin olive oil
2 cloves garlic, peeled and halved
pinch of dried, hot, crushed red pepper
1/2 teaspoon rosemary
1/2 cup *Chianti* wine
1 14-ounce can Italian tomatoes, chopped, or 1 3/4 cups, fresh, ripe, tomatoes, peeled, seeded, and chopped
salt and freshly ground black pepper

1. Dust the meat cubes with seasoned flour. Set aside.

2. Heat the oil over a moderately high heat and lightly brown the garlic pieces. Add the red pepper and rosemary and then the meat. Sauté until meat is browned on all sides.

3. Add the wine and cook until wine has almost evaporated. Add the tomatoes and cook slowly until meat is tender. Season with salt and pepper.

4. Toast homemade-type Italian bread and place on dinner plates. Spoon *stufatino* over bread and serve immediately to 4.

We enjoyed this tasty meat dish in Oliveto Citra, Province of Salerno, where my father was born. The recipe was shared by Yolanda, the excellent cook so dear to the Coglianese family.

COTOLETTE ALL'OLIVETO CITRA
Veal Cutlets in the Style of Oliveto Citra

1/2 cup flour
salt and pepper
1 egg
2 tablespoons grated *Parmigiano* cheese
3/4 cup fine, dry, unseasoned breadcrumbs
6 veal cutlets or chops, fat removed, flattened
4 tablespoons extra virgin olive oil
6 lemon wedges

1. Put flour in a shallow bowl and season with salt and pepper.

2. In another shallow bowl, beat the egg with salt, pepper, and 1 tablespoon of the grated cheese.

3. Combine the breadcrumbs, salt, pepper, and 1 tablespoon of the grated cheese in a shallow bowl.

4. Dip each cutlet or chop into the flour. Coat both sides and shake off excess. Next, dip each one first into the egg mixture, coating it on both sides, and then into the breadcrumbs, pressing them in to be sure that the crumbs adhere to the meat. Coat remaining meat with the flour, egg, and crumbs.

5. Heat the oil in a frying pan over medium heat. When oil is hot, fry the meat until nicely browned on both sides. The meat should be just cooked through, even slightly pink, but not over cooked or it will be dry.

6. Serve hot with lemon wedges to 6.

Arista is one of the most popular meat dishes in Florence. The story that I heard as to how it got its name is that in 1439 at a banquet in his honor, a Byzantine patriarch who had come to Florence to attend an ecumenical council savored the delicious roasted pork and then showed his great delight by exclaiming with a Greek superlative term, *Aristos!*

ARISTA ALLA FIORENTINA
Florentine Pork Roast

3 to 3 1/2 pounds of center-cut pork loin roast with the bone
2 cloves garlic
2 sprigs fresh rosemary
salt
coarsely ground black pepper
extra virgin olive oil
1/2 cup white wine

1. Have the butcher saw through the bone between the ribs, keeping the meat intact, to make slicing of the roasted pork easier.

2. Finely chop the garlic and rosemary together with salt and pepper. With a sharp pointed knife, make several cuts in the meat near the bone, and stuff with most of the prepared rosemary and garlic.

3. Lightly score the outside of the meat and rub the remaining rosemary and garlic mixture with more salt and pepper.

4. Place in a roasting pan with the bones on the bottom as a rack for the meat. Cover roast with olive oil and add white wine to the bottom of the pan. Place in a preheated, 350° F. oven. Cook for 2 hours, basting occasionally with the juices.

5. If you wish, you can add peeled potatoes cut in quarters lengthwise when roast is half done. Traditionally, *Arista* is served with *cannellini* beans cooked with fresh sage and extra virgin olive oil and with greens blanched and sautéed in extra virgin olive oil and garlic.

6. When roast is done, it should be nicely browned and have a crispy skin. Remove it to a warmed platter and let it sit for 10 or 15 minutes before slicing. If you have added potatoes, remove them to a warmed serving dish and season them.

7. Skim the fat from the roasting-pan juices, add more wine and some water, and scrape up all the brown bits. Boil slowly for 5 minutes. Season, if necessary, and serve with the *Arista* and with the beans and greens if they are on the menu. Serve to 6.

La Scala, Milan

Spiedini are interesting to put together because you may add any ingredients to the skewer that you prefer. These are floured and dipped in beaten egg, but this procedure is not necessary. What is important is that the meats put on the *spiedini* are cooked through.

SPIEDINI
Skewered Meats and Vegetables

extra virgin olive oil
1/2 pound lean Italian sausage, cut in 8 pieces
1 boned and skinned chicken breast, cut in 1-inch squares
2 cloves garlic, peeled and cut in halves lengthwise
2 small Italian eggplant, peeled and cut in 1/2-inch slices
salt and pepper
Seasoned flour for dredging *spiedini*
2 eggs, beaten with 1 tablespoon water and seasoned
1-inch squares of *mozzarella* cheese, 1/2-inch thick
1-inch squares of Italian bread
8 cherry tomatoes

1. Heat 1 tablespoon of olive oil in a large skillet and fry sausage pieces until cooked through. Remove sausage and set aside.

2. Add 2 tablespoons olive oil to the skillet and add chicken pieces and garlic. When browned, add eggplant slices and sauté until everything is cooked through. Add salt and pepper, remove from skillet, set aside, and cool.

3. Wipe out skillet with paper towel and add 3 tablespoons of olive oil. Form *spiedini* onto eight 6-inch bamboo skewers. Thread the ingredients alternately on each of the skewers. For example, on one skewer, put a square of bread, then a piece of sausage, then a square of *mozzarella*, one of chicken, one of eggplant, if there is enough room, another chicken, and finally a cherry tomato. Add more cheese and bread if space allows. You may also use 8-inch skewers.

4. Heat the oil in the skillet. Lightly coat each skewer with the flour and then dip each into the egg. Fry the *spiedini* on all sides and serve hot, 2 each to 4 persons.

My aunt Margherita prepared this dish often as it was my uncle's favorite. It is piquant, tasty, and easy to prepare. The recipe for the cherry peppers is included in this book, but if you do not have the homemade peppers you can use Progresso brand or another brand that does not add sugar. Add a clove of garlic and some *oregano* to the jar and let it sit for a couple of weeks.

MAIALE ALLE PATATE CON PEPERONI SOTT'ACETO
Pork and Potatoes with Peppers Preserved in Vinegar

3 tablespoon extra virgin olive oil
2 clove garlic, peeled and halved
1 teaspoon fennel seeds
1 pound lean pork steak or boneless baby back ribs, cut in bite-size pieces
5 hot cherry peppers, preserved in vinegar, seeded and cut in pieces
1 1/4 pounds potatoes, about 4, peeled and sliced about 1/4-inch thick

1. Heat 1 tablespoon olive oil in a skillet and add 2 halves of the garlic pieces and the fennel seeds. When they begin to color, add the pork and brown over medium-high heat.

2. When the pork browns, add the peppers and a tablespoon of the vinegar from the jar of peppers. Lower heat, add a little water, cover skillet, and cook slowly until pork is cooked through and the juices have nearly evaporated. The dish should be moist but not soupy.

3. While meat cooks, heat remaining 2 tablespoons of olive oil in another skillet. Add the remaining clove of garlic, and when it begins to brown, add the potatoes. Fry the potatoes, stirring frequently, until they are done.

4. Combine the potatoes and the meat and cook together for 5 minutes. Serve to 4.

For this world famous dish to be at its best, it is obligatory to use the finest, freshest, and most tender calf's liver sliced thinly. It must be cooked briefly so that it does not become dry. The liver and onion combination of Venezia is the most enjoyable that I have had.

FEGATO ALLA VENEZIANA
Liver and Onions

1 large onion, thinly sliced
3 tablespoons extra virgin olive oil
1/3 cup dry white wine
1 pound calf's liver, thinly sliced
seasoned flour for dredging liver
salt
freshly ground black pepper
1 tablespoon chopped parsley

1. In a large skillet, sauté the onion in 2 tablespoons of the oil until golden. Add the wine and cook until the onions are soft and the wine has nearly evaporated. Remove the onions and juices from the skillet and keep warm. Wipe skillet with a paper towel.

2. Dust the liver slices with the flour. Add the remaining tablespoon of olive oil to the skillet. Turn the heat to medium-high. When oil is hot, add liver pieces and sauté quickly until just cooked through. Stir in onions and add salt, pepper, and parsley. Put onto a warmed platter and serve immediately to 4.

Il Pollame ed il Coniglio
Poultry and Rabbit

Chicken and rabbit are popular meats in Italy. Butchers are very happy to bone, stuff, and roll chickens or rabbits to make them ready for a delicious preparation.

Chicken and rabbit provide really versatile dishes. They are cooked in many ways, whether roasted, stewed, fried, braised, boiled, or grilled. Often they are combined with green peppers, as in Chicken or Rabbit *Cacciatore*. Chicken can be prepared with a very delicate or a really spicy sauce.

In the fall during the hunting season, wild pheasants, guinea-fowl, and other fowl are also available, especially in Tuscany and Umbria. In a country *trattoria* you can often see birds of every size slowly turning on a spit over a large wood fire.

Facing page: Poppi, Tuscany

This is the preparation my mother used when she wanted to roast a chicken with some potatoes, put one on the spit for the rotisserie, or even bake chicken cut in serving pieces. Free-range chickens have more flavor.

POLLO ARROSTO CON LE PATATE
Roast Chicken with Potatoes

1 chicken, about 3 1/2 pounds
2 tablespoons extra virgin olive oil
1/2 tablespoon salt
1 large clove garlic
black pepper
oregano
4 baking potatoes, peeled and cut lengthwise in wedges

1. Preheat the oven to 400° F. Cut off all visible fat and wash chicken inside and out. Dry it and rub 1 tablespoon of the olive oil over all of it, inside and out.

2. Put the salt in a pile on a board. Push the garlic through a press, or chop it into tiny pieces, and put it on the salt pile. Mash the garlic with the salt, using the end of a knife blade, until they are blended. Rub this mixture inside and outside the chicken.

3. Sprinkle the chicken lightly with pepper and *oregano*. Set the chicken, breast side up, in a roasting pan large enough to accommodate it with the potatoes. Do not cover pan.

4. Place the roasting pan, with the chicken, in the oven and roast for 15 minutes. Remove pan from oven, add the potatoes to the pan, dribble olive oil over them, and turn them in the oil and any juices that have accumulated.

5. Season potatoes with salt and pepper and put the pan back into the oven. Lower heat to 350° F. and continue to cook for an additional hour. Turn the potatoes once during the roasting.

6. Remove chicken to a carving board and place potatoes in a warmed serving dish. Skim the fat from the juices remaining in the pan. Put a little hot water in the pan and scrape up the brown bits. Bring the sauce to a boil, check seasonings, and spoon over carved chicken which has been arranged on a heated platter. Serves 4 to 6.

Tiled roofs, Vinci

Our daughter, Theresa, shares her favorite Italian recipe. She finds it not only a delicious and attractive dish but one she can prepare quickly in her busy schedule. *Petti di Pollo* are chicken breasts, and *piccata* means something that the diner has set his or her heart on.

PETTI DI POLLO PICCATA
Chicken Piccata

2 chicken breast halves, skinned, boned, and defatted
seasoned flour for coating chicken
3 tablespoons extra virgin olive oil
1 large clove garlic, cut in half lengthwise
2 green onions, sliced
1 tablespoon medium dry *Marsala* wine
1 lemon
2 tablespoons water
salt and pepper

1. Cut the chicken breasts in half, horizontally, so that you have 4 thin slices. Pound them a little if they are much more than 1/4 of an inch thick.

2. Dip the chicken breast slices in the flour, coating them on both sides, and shaking off excess flour. Set aside.

3. Heat olive oil in a skillet and sauté garlic and green onions until lightly browned. Remove from the skillet with a slotted spoon and reserve.

4. Place the chicken breasts in the hot oil and cook until nicely browned on both sides. Remove from the skillet and add *Marsala* wine to loosen the brownings.

5. Cut the lemon in half and squeeze the juice from one of the halves into the skillet. Cut the other half in 4 wedges.

6. Add water, salt, and pepper to skillet along with garlic and green onions. When sauce is bubbling, put chicken breasts and juices back into skillet and cook until chicken is heated throughout and sauce has reduced.

7. If sauce has evaporated, add water, one tablespoon at a time. There should be just a little sauce in the pan. Turn chicken over so that there is some sauce on each side. Place chicken on a heated serving dish and spoon just a teaspoon of sauce over each slice. Squeeze additional lemon juice over chicken.

8. Serve chicken with lemon wedges immediately. Serves 2 to 4.

In the mountains of northern Italy the well-known *Fontina* cheese is produced. It goes very well over the chicken breasts in this recipe from the Valle d'Aosta.

PETTI DI POLLO VALLE D'AOSTA
Chicken Breasts with Fontina Cheese and Mushrooms

6 chicken breast halves, boned, skinned, and defatted
seasoned flour for dredging
2 tablespoons extra virgin olive oil
1 tablespoon butter
8 ounces brown mushrooms, sliced
salt and freshly ground pepper
1/2 cup *Marsala* wine
6 ounces *Fontina* cheese, coarsely grated

1. Pound chicken breasts to flatten. Dip in flour and shake off excess.

2. Heat oil and butter in a frying pan and brown chicken breasts, over moderately high heat, on both sides. Add more olive oil if necessary. Place browned chicken in a single layer in a baking dish.

3. Sauté sliced mushrooms in the same frying pan in the remaining fat. Add more oil if necessary. Season with salt and pepper and spoon over chicken.

4. Pour the wine into the frying pan and reduce by half. The dish could now be kept on hold until you are ready to complete it.

5. When ready to bake the chicken, spoon the reduced wine evenly over the chicken breasts. Bake in a preheated, 350° F. oven for 15 to 20 minutes or until chicken is cooked through. Remove from oven, cover with cheese, and bake an additional 5 to 7 minutes or until cheese is bubbling. Serve immediately to 6.

Pollo alla Diavola is an antique Tuscan recipe which, as its name indicates, requires a good deal of pepper. The chicken is split open along the breastbone, flattened, held flat in a hinged grill, and grilled over hot coals or broiled.

POLLO ALLA DIAVOLA
Chicken, Hot as the Devil

1 young chicken, about 2 1/4 to 2 1/2 pounds
2 tablespoons olive oil
1 clove garlic, mashed
1 lemon, squeeze juice from half and cut the remainder in 4 wedges
salt
freshly ground black pepper
red cayenne pepper
5 or 6 fresh sage leaves, chopped

1. Cut the chicken open, lengthwise, along the center of the breastbone. Do not cut the backbone, but press the opened chicken as flat as you can. You may pound the chicken with a mallet to help flatten it.

2. Combine olive oil, garlic, and lemon juice. Coat the chicken with the mixture.

3. Salt the chicken, coat it liberally with the black and red peppers, and sprinkle with the sage leaves. Place chicken on a two-sided, hinged grate to hold chicken flat, or improvise.

4. Place the chicken about 6 inches from the hot coals or from the broiler element set at 450° F. Turn over occasionally and dab with the oil-lemon mixture. Cook until golden brown, 45 to 55 minutes, or until cooked through and juices are not pink when tested. Cut into 4 parts and serve immediately with lemon wedges.

One of the most popular meat preparations is putting tasty and interesting ingredients on a thin slice of meat, rolling it, and braising it on top of the stove or roasting it. This large turkey roll roast makes a colorful, flavorful, and impressive presentation.

ROTOLO DI TACCHINO O VITELLO
Turkey or Veal Roll

1/2 boneless turkey breast (about 1 1/2 pounds) or a large, thin slice of veal
2 long carrots, peeled
3 cloves garlic
4 tablespoon extra virgin olive oil
8 ounces fresh spinach, washed and drained
salt and pepper
2 eggs
2 tablespoons chopped parsley
2 tablespoons grated *Parmigiano Reggiano* cheese
1/2 tablespoon fennel seeds
2 ounces *prosciutto,* thinly sliced
2 ounces *Fontina* cheese, sliced
1 sprig rosemary
4 sage leaves
1/2 cup white wine

1. If using turkey, cut the breast (or have your butcher do it), horizontally, but do not cut all the way through so that you can open it like a book. Then cut through the thicker half, horizontally, from center to the outer edge but not all the way through, so that it can again be opened and it will be one large, thin slab. Pound it until evenly thin. If using veal, pound the large slice until evenly thin.

2. Steam whole carrots until tender and set aside.

3. Sauté 1 of the garlic cloves in 1 tablespoon of olive oil in a saucepan. When it begins to color, add the spinach with just the water clinging to its leaves. Cover the pan and cook the spinach about 4 minutes. Add salt and pepper. Strain the spinach and cool.

4. Beat the eggs with parsley and *Parmigiano* cheese. Heat 1 tablespoon of the olive oil in a skillet. Pour in the egg mixture to make a thin omelet. Cook the omelet very lightly and set aside.

5. Mash 1 of the garlic cloves and spread it evenly over the flattened meat. Add salt and pepper. Distribute the fennel seeds and slices of *prosciutto* evenly over the seasonings.

6. Layer the *Fontina* cheese slices over the *prosciutto,* then spread the drained spinach. Place the omelet over the spinach and then set the carrots end-to-end across the length of the meat at the long edge where the rolling will begin.

7. Roll the meat tightly to close, beginning with the edge where the carrots are, and tie with cotton kitchen string.

8. In a pot large enough to accommodate the meat roll, heat 2 tablespoons olive oil over medium-high heat and add the meat roll to brown on all sides. While the meat is browning, add the remaining clove of garlic, rosemary, and sage. Add the wine, cover the pan, and let the meat cook approximately 1 1/2 hours. Add a little water if pan becomes dry.

9. Or, place the meat roll in a baking pan with the garlic, rosemary, and sage, cover the meat with a film of olive oil, and roast in a preheated, 350° F. oven for approximately 2 hours. Add the wine after the first hour. Remove meat from baking dish.

10. Heat the sauce from the bottom of the pan. Add a little water if juices are too concentrated. Strain, and spoon some onto a warmed platter. It should just cover the bottom of the platter. Serve the rest separately. Remove the string from the roll, cut 1/2-inch slices, and place slices attractively over the sauce on the platter. Serves 6.

In the autumn, during the hunting season, game birds abound in Tuscany. This is a typical preparation of roasted pheasant in Florence. Farm-raised pheasants are becoming more available in the United States.

FAGIANO ALLA FIORENTINA
Roasted Pheasant

1 2-1/2 to 3-pound dressed pheasant
3 ounces lean *pancetta* (Italian bacon)
2 ounces *prosciutto*
16 fresh sage leaves
3 tablespoons extra virgin olive oil
salt and pepper

1. Cut off any visible fat from the pheasant.

2. Chop the *pancetta*. Reserve three slices of the *prosciutto,* chop the remaining slices, and add them to the *pancetta*.

3. Reserve 8 sage leaves. Chop the remaining sage leaves and add them to the chopped *pancetta* and *prosciutto*.

4. Spoon the chopped ingredients into the cavity of the pheasant. Sew up the opening or fasten with a skewer.

5. Rub 1 tablespoon of the olive oil over the outside of the pheasant. Sprinkle lightly with salt and pepper.

6. Place the reserved sage leaves over the outside of the bird and cover with the reserved slices of *prosciutto*. Tie them in place with string. Tie one piece of string around the wings and breast and another around the legs.

7. Spoon 1 tablespoon of olive oil over the bottom of the roasting pan and place the pheasant in the pan on its back. Spread another tablespoon of olive oil over the pheasant and place it, uncovered, in a preheated, 350° F. oven.

8. Roast for 1 1/4 hours. Turn the bird every 15 or 20 minutes and baste with the juices in the pan.

9. Carve the pheasant as you would a chicken and place on a heated platter. Spoon the stuffing from inside the bird onto the platter so that diners have some to accompany the pheasant meat. Skim the fat from the juices in the pan. Add a little water to scrape up the brown bits, bring to a boil, and spoon the sauce over the carved pheasant. Serves 4 to 6.

Many of the Italian ducks are very large, and the breast is nearly the size of a turkey breast. The meat, however, is tender and succulent and is sold without skin and fat. I cook less than one quarter of a duck breast weighing about 1 1/2 pounds to serve to 4. If you would like to cook duck breast with the skin, I would advise you to sear the skin (without burning it) by placing the breast, skin down on a hot skillet, lightly coated with oil, until the fat melts away from the skin (about 3 to 5 minutes). Then proceed to follow the recipe and remove any remaining fat from the pan in which the duck was baked.

PETTO D'ANATRA AL POMPELMO E PORTO
Breast of Duck with Grapefruit and Port

1 1/2 pounds of breast of duck, boneless and skinless, 2- to 3-inches thick
1 clove garlic, mashed
salt and pepper
extra virgin olive oil
a sprig of fresh sage leaves
1 grapefruit, preferably pink
1 orange
1 rounded tablespoon raisins, plumped in 1 tablespoon port wine
1/4 cup port wine

1. Preheat oven to 400° F. Prepare the duck by spreading the garlic on all sides and sprinkling with salt and pepper. Coat with olive oil and place into baking pan with a fresh sprig of sage on top of the duck breast.

2. Bake 15 minutes, reduce heat to 350° F., and bake another 30 minutes. If breast is thinner, it will take less time.

3. Meanwhile peel the skin (only the yellow) from 3/4 of the grapefruit and from half of the orange. Blanch the peelings in boiling water for about 1/2 minute. Remove and cut in thin strips like needles. Squeeze 1/2 cup of juice from the grapefruit, strain, and reserve.

4. When duck is done, remove from baking pan to a warmed platter and let sit until the sauce is made.

5. Remove fat from the baking pan, add reserved grapefruit juice, raisins, and port wine. Set on a burner on the range or stir up the brown bits and pour into a small saucepan. Bring to a boil and reduce about 1/4. Season and stir in needles.

6. Slice duck breast and arrange attractively on the platter. Spoon the sauce and the needles evenly over the slices. Serve to 4 immediately.

Piazza Repubblica, Rome

Rabbit is a flavorful, lean, and healthful meat. I wish it were more easily attainable in the United States. This is a delightful rabbit stew from Liguria.

CONIGLIO IN UMIDO
Rabbit Stew

1 young rabbit about 2 1/2 pounds
3/4 cup dry white wine
3 bay leaves
1 teaspoon fresh rosemary
1 teaspoon chopped, fresh sage leaves
1 teaspoon thyme
4 tablespoons extra virgin olive oil
1 clove garlic, finely chopped
1 onion, chopped
1 carrot, chopped
2 tomatoes, peeled and chopped or 1 cup canned tomatoes
20 Gaeta black olives, pitted and halved (These are easily pitted by hitting each one with a mallet or bottom of a cup.)
1/2 cup pine nuts
salt and pepper

1. Cut rabbit in serving pieces, put into a bowl and cover with marinade made with the wine, the bay leaves, half of the rosemary, half of the sage leaves, and half of the thyme. Stir and leave for 3 or more hours.

2. Heat the olive oil. Remove rabbit pieces from marinade, reserving marinade, dry, and brown. While rabbit is browning, add the remaining rosemary, sage, thyme, garlic, onion, and carrot.

3. When everything is nicely browned, add the wine marinade and cook until most of the moisture evaporates.

4. Add tomatoes, olives, and pine nuts and season with salt and pepper. Add a little water, cover pan, and simmer for an hour or until the rabbit is tender. Add water as necessary to have some sauce at the end of cooking. Serves 6.

View from Fiesole

My mother prepared this dish superbly. She would use either a whole chicken
cut into pieces or boneless chicken thighs. She always used fresh tomatoes
and basil but said that it was acceptable to use a good quality of
Italian plum tomatoes, canned, when fresh tomatoes were not in season.

POLLO AL POMODORO E BASILICO
Chicken with Tomatoes and Basil

1 3-pound fryer, cut into pieces and the skin removed, or 2 pounds of
boneless, skinless, defatted chicken thighs
2 large cloves garlic, peeled and quartered lengthwise
2 tablespoons extra virgin olive oil
6 tomatoes, peeled, seeded, and chopped
salt and pepper
1/4 cup chopped fresh basil

1. Fry chicken and garlic in olive oil over moderately high heat until golden
on all sides and add salt and pepper. Discard excess fat, spoon tomatoes over
chicken, season, and top with basil.

2. Cover pan and cook slowly for about 40 minutes or until chicken is
tender. Stir after 20 minutes.

3. Remove lid from pan, stir, and cook another 10 minutes or until chicken
is fork tender. Check seasonings, remove garlic pieces, if desired, and serve
to 6.

My aunt Margherita prepared this tasty old family recipe for years for the enjoyment of the family. She usually accompanied it with her special preparation of mashed potatoes. She claimed that you need to make a home preparation of cherry peppers in vinegar with *oregano* and garlic. The recipe for the peppers is included in this book. I find, however, that I get a good result with Progresso hot cherry peppers or another brand that preserves cherry peppers in vinegar without sugar, if I add a clove of peeled garlic and a teaspoon of *oregano* to the jar and let it sit a couple of weeks, or longer, before using them.

CONIGLIO FRITTO CON PEPERONI SOTT'ACETO
Rabbit Sautéed with Peppers Preserved in Vinegar

about 4 hot cherry peppers, preserved in vinegar, seeded and cut into pieces (about 1/2-cup pepper pieces). Double quantity if preparing mashed potatoes to serve with rabbit.
3 tablespoons extra virgin olive oil
1 young rabbit, about 2 1/2 pounds, cut into serving pieces
2 cloves garlic, peeled and cut in half lengthwise
salt
1/4 cup water

1. Fry cherry peppers in about 1 tablespoon of the olive oil in a large frying pan. When peppers are lightly browned, remove from pan and reserve. Add to the pan about 2 tablespoons of olive oil and heat.

2. Fry rabbit and garlic until nicely browned on all sides. Salt rabbit. Return peppers to the pan, add water, cover pan, and cook slowly until rabbit is tender, about an hour. Add a little more water during cooking, if necessary, so that rabbit does not become dry. There should be some sauce.

3. If desired, prepare mashed potatoes to serve with the rabbit. (See index for the mashed potatoes with peppers preserved in vinegar.) Serves 6.

In Italy there are many versions of this famous hunter's stew. Rabbit or chicken was used in our family recipe. Personally, I enjoy the flavor of rabbit, and it is a lean meat.

CONIGLIO O POLLO ALLA CACCIATORA
Rabbit or Chicken Hunter's Style

1 dressed fryer rabbit or chicken, cut in serving pieces
3 tablespoons extra virgin olive oil
1 onion, coarsely chopped
2 cloves garlic, mashed
3 large, green, red, and yellow peppers
1/4 teaspoon hot, dried red pepper flakes
1 28-ounce can tomatoes, chopped
1 teaspoon dried *oregano*
salt

1. Sauté pieces of rabbit or chicken, in heated olive oil, in a large skillet until well browned. Remove meat from pan.

2. Add onion and garlic and sauté slowly until golden. Add peppers and hot pepper flakes and continue to sauté until vegetables are lightly browned.

3. Stir in tomatoes, *oregano,* and salt. Return meat to the pan. Bring to a boil, reduce heat to low, cover pan, and let simmer for 1 hour or until meat is tender. Check seasonings and serve to 6.

Florence

Il Pesce ed i Crostacei
Fish and Shellfish

Fish and shellfish abound in Italy and are some of the most important foods. There are many types of seafood and shellfish that cannot be found outside of Italy. I have suggested substitutions which work well with the Italian recipes.

The largest fish you see are the swordfish (*pesce spada*) which are caught in the straits of Messina and brought to markets of the coastal cities and towns. When a swordfish was brought into Salerno in the early morning, it would be set out on a stone slab in the open air market. Shoppers would wait their turn to buy a slice which would be cut to the desired size. They would carry it home to be enjoyed at the midday meal. They may have also bought some fresh mushrooms to prepare Swordfish with Mushrooms (*Pesce Spada al Funghi*). If swordfish were not the choice for that day, shoppers might instead choose a fish for baking such as *la spigola* and be delighted to enjoy Baked Sea Bass (*La Spigola al Forno*).

Many wonderful clams, of small and smaller sizes, would have just have been brought in from the sea for those who might be preparing them with spaghetti (*Spaghetti alle Vongole*) for the first course.

Facing page: Venice

The large spider crabs of the Adriatic are called *granseole*. They are considered a great delicacy in the regions around Venice. For this recipe other crab meat may be used, such as meat from the legs of king crab or the delicate, sweet lump crab.

GRANSEOLE ALLA TRIESTINA
Baked Crab

1/2 pound crab meat
1 clove garlic, mashed
2 tablespoons chopped parsley
3 tablespoons fresh bread crumbs
salt and freshly ground black pepper
2 tablespoons extra virgin olive oil
juice of 1/2 lemon (2 1/4 tablespoons)
4 tablespoons fresh bread crumbs
grated *Parmigiano Reggiano* cheese
olive oil

1. Combine the crab meat, garlic, parsley, 3 tablespoons of bread crumbs, salt, pepper, 2 tablespoons olive oil, and lemon juice.

2. Pile into 2 or 4 individual cleaned shells or bake-and-serve dishes. Sprinkle with remaining 4 tablespoons bread crumbs and a little *Parmigiano* cheese. Dribble over the top a little olive oil.

3. Bake in a preheated, 400° F. oven for approximately 20 minutes until nicely browned. These may be served to 2 as a main dish or to 4 as an *antipasto*.

In this recipe the bulb of the fennel plant, with its delicate anise flavor, is sliced and added to the sauce, which complements the fish perfectly.

GROSSO ROMBO AL FINOCCHIO
Halibut with Fennel

1 1/4 pounds halibut or other white fish, cut into 4 steaks or fillets
flour for dredging fish
salt and pepper
5 tablespoons extra virgin olive oil
1 bulb of fennel, thinly sliced
1 onion, sliced
1 large clove of garlic, peeled and halved
1 cup white wine
1 cup peeled and chopped tomatoes (Canned tomatoes may be used.)
juice of 1/2 lemon
2 tablespoons chopped parsley

1. Coat the fish steaks in seasoned flour and shake off excess. In a large skillet, heat the olive oil and fry the halibut quickly to brown both sides. Remove from skillet.

2. Add the remaining 2 tablespoons of olive oil to the frying pan and sauté the fennel, onion, and garlic until they are soft and golden.

3. Return the fish to the frying pan and pour the wine over all. When the wine has nearly evaporated, add the tomatoes. Let everything cook together until about half of the liquid has evaporated. Turn fish once so that it does not become overly brown on the underside.

4. Season the sauce and squeeze the lemon juice over the fish. When the fish and vegetables are thoroughly cooked, serve to 4 with a little bit of sauce on the fish steaks. Sprinkle fish with the parsley. Serve the remaining sauce separately.

When my mother prepared this dish, she liked to use large, whole fish fillets of various types. She seldom cooked in small quantities. This is her recipe, using salmon, but cut down to serve 4.

FILETTO DI SALMONE AL FORNO
Baked Salmon Fillet

1 piece of salmon fillet, about 1 1/4 pounds, or 4 portions of salmon, about
5 ounces each and 1/2 to 3/4-inch thick
1 1/4 cup fresh bread crumbs made from homemade-type bread
1/2 clove garlic, mashed
1 teaspoon *oregano*
salt and pepper
6 tablespoons extra virgin olive oil
1 onion, chopped

1. Place the salmon fillet, skin-side down, on a well oiled baking dish. (For easy cleanup, line an unoiled baking dish with aluminum foil.) Salt the fillet.

2. Combine bread crumbs, garlic, *oregano,* salt, pepper, and 2 tablespoons of the olive oil. Mix well and spoon over the top of the fillet.

3. Sprinkle evenly with the chopped onion and drizzle the remaining oil over the salmon.

4. Bake in a preheated, 400° F. oven 25 to 35 minutes or until fish flakes easily and is cooked through when tested with a fork. Serve hot to 4.

Dr. Luigi (Gino) Nicolais, professor of material sciences at the University of Naples, conducts research, teaches, travels a great deal, and is husband and father, but still manages to come up with wonderful culinary creations. His specialty is fish in the tradition of Naples, and he shares this recipe. His wife, Donatella, another excellent cook advises adding white wine to his recipe.

LA SPIGOLA AL FORNO
Baked Sea Bass

1 whole sea bass, scaled, and gutted
extra virgin olive oil
salt and pepper
1/4 clove garlic, mashed
1 heaping tablespoon parsley, chopped
lemon slices
1/2 cup dry white wine

1. Wash and dry sea bass making sure that the loose scales have been removed.

2. Place fish in a baking pan, coat inside and out with a film of olive oil, and sprinkle with salt and pepper.

3. Rub the garlic, sparingly, inside the fish and also put the parsley inside. Cover the outside of the fish with lemon slices. Add the wine to the pan.

4. Put a lid on the baking pan or cover with aluminum foil and bake in a preheated oven at 375° F. for 25 to 35 minutes or until the fish is cooked through. It will flake easily when tested with a fork. Uncover the baking pan during the last 10 minutes of cooking.

5. Serve with lemon wedges to 4 or more depending on the size of the sea bass.

This is a Florentine fishmonger's recipe for baked whole fish.
Sea bass, lake bass, trout, salmon trout, or red snapper may be used.

PESCE AL FORNO
Florentine Baked Fish

3 tablespoons extra virgin olive oil
2 or 3 sprigs of fresh rosemary
2 cloves garlic, peeled and halved lengthwise
1 whole fish, cleaned and scaled
salt and pepper
lemon slices
wine vinegar

1. Pour the olive oil into a baking pan. Add the sprigs of rosemary and garlic pieces and lightly brown in a preheated, 375° F. oven. Remove from the oven.

2. Season fish inside and out and place 1 or 2 lemon slices inside.

3. Place the fish on the rosemary and garlic in the baking pan. Return the baking pan to the oven and bake fish 25 to 35 minutes or until cooked through. Fish is done if it flakes easily when tested with a fork.

4. Carefully turn fish with a spatula half way through cooking. Serve immediately to 4 or more depending on quantity of fish.

My mother liked to prepare this tasty baked fish and potatoes in tomato sauce, on Fridays, as she did most of her fish dishes, because we all enjoyed it, and it did not take long to prepare.

PESCE E PATATE ALLA MARINARA
Baked Fish and Potatoes in Tomato Sauce

1 onion, finely chopped
2 cups peeled and chopped tomatoes, fresh or canned
4 potatoes, peeled and diced
salt and pepper
2 rounded tablespoons chopped parsley
1 rounded tablespoon chopped basil
1 1/4 pounds white fish, skinned and boned and cut into 4 pieces
1 tablespoon extra virgin olive oil
additional chopped parsley, optional

1. Preheat oven to 350° F. Combine the onion and tomatoes in a large baking dish that goes directly from the oven to the table. Cover and put into the oven.

2. Bake about 20 minutes or until onion is soft. Stir in potatoes, salt, and pepper. Cover and bake until potatoes are nearly done. Remove from oven. If sauce becomes dry, add a little hot water.

3. Stir in parsley and basil and add fish. Dribble olive oil over the top and sprinkle with salt and pepper. Cover and bake about 8 minutes or until fish is nearly done.

4. Uncover dish and continue to bake about 5 minutes or until fish and potatoes are cooked through. More parsley may be sprinkled over the completed dish. Serves 4.

In Naples, where this dish originated, cooks prefer to poach whole fish in the soup, remove it when it is done, skin and bone it, and serve the fillets to the diners with a ladle of soup over the fillets. I find it easier to serve if I poach fillets of fish, already skinned and boned, in the soup. Italians, of course, have the wonderful fish of the Mediterranean sea such as *spigola, orata,* and *cernia.* Americans can use sea bass, salmon, cod, halibut, flounder, or any other fresh fish with good flavor.

PESCE IN ACQUA PAZZA
Fish Poached in Crazy Water

8 cups water
1 onion, finely chopped
1 tablespoon extra virgin olive oil
1 stalk celery, chopped
1 carrot, chopped
3 small Italian-type plum tomatoes, peeled, seeded and coarsely chopped
(Use fresh tomatoes if in season.)
salt and pepper
1 1/2 pounds whole fish, or 1 1/4 pounds fillets
1 rounded tablespoon of chopped parsley

1. Bring the water to a boil and add the onion and olive oil. When the onion softens, add the celery. Bring back to a slow boil and add the carrot, tomatoes, salt, and pepper.

2. Cook until all the vegetables are tender. Shortly before serving add the fish and parsley, check seasonings, and poach until fish flakes easily with a fork.

3. Serve fish to 4 on individual, warmed, shallow soup plates. Ladle a little of the hot soup over the fish.

The Calabrian fishermen catch huge swordfish in the Strait of Messina between the toe of the Italian peninsula and the Island of Sicily. It is not surprising that swordfish is so popular in this part of Italy.

PESCE SPADA AL LIMONE
Swordfish with Lemon

seasoned flour for dusting fish
3 tablespoons extra virgin olive oil
4 swordfish steaks, about 1/4 to 1/3 pound each
1 small onion, finely chopped
2 tablespoons chopped parsley
juice from 1/2 juicy lemon
salt and pepper

1. Dust swordfish steaks with the seasoned flour.

2. Heat oil in a large skillet. Sauté fish over moderately high heat until fish is browned on both sides, but not thoroughly cooked. Remove fish and keep it warm.

3. Add onion to the remaining oil in the pan and sauté over low heat until onion is golden and soft.

4. Return fish to the skillet, turn heat to medium, and lightly brown the onion.

5. Add remaining ingredients and let swordfish cook gently with the lemon juice for 2 minutes. Turn fish carefully, and add a tablespoon of water if pan becomes too dry. When fish is cooked through, place on a warmed platter, spoon contents of skillet over swordfish steaks, and serve immediately to 4.

In Messina, where the world's best swordfish are found, Italians like to top the sautéed swordfish with their famous *Agghiotta* sauce. The sauce consists of many tasty and colorful ingredients which complement the fish perfectly.

AGGHIOTTA DI PESCE SPADA
Swordfish with Tomatoes, Raisins, and Olives

4 slices swordfish, about 5 ounces each
flour for dredging fish
salt and pepper
4 tablespoons extra virgin olive oil
3 tablespoons raisins
1 onion, chopped
2 cloves garlic, mashed
1 stalk celery, chopped
1 cup tomatoes, peeled and chopped
3 tablespoons pine nuts
1/3 cup green olives, pitted and thickly sliced
1 tablespoon drained capers

1. Coat the fish steaks with the seasoned flour. Heat 3 tablespoons of the oil and fry the fish steaks until they are browned on both sides. Remove fish from the oil, place in a baking dish, and keep warm.

2. Meanwhile soak the raisins in warm water for 15 minutes.

3. Add the remaining tablespoon of olive oil to the oil left in the pan where the fish was frying. Heat the oil and sauté the onion, garlic, and celery until soft and golden.

4. Add the tomatoes and simmer 10 minutes. Then add the pine nuts, olives, and capers. Drain the raisins, chop them, and add them to the sauce. Simmer 5 minutes. If the sauce becomes dry, add a little water. Add salt and pepper to taste.

5. Spoon sauce over fish fillets and bake in the oven at a medium–high temperature 375° F. for 10 minutes or until fish is cooked through. Serves 4.

Looking down from the Campanile, Pisa

Raisins are frequently used in Italian cooking to sweeten a dish or a sauce. They are combined in this dish with vinegar to create a delightful sweet-and-sour sauce for the trout. The lakes and rivers in both northern and southern Italy have an abundance of fine trout.

TROTE ALLA PIEMONTESE
Trout with Sweet and Sour Sauce

2 trout each weighing about 10 ounces, cleaned and boned
2 tablespoons golden raisins
2 tablespoons extra virgin olive oil
1 small onion, finely chopped
1 clove garlic, mashed
1 stalk celery, finely chopped
4 or 5 sage leaves, finely chopped
1 sprig of rosemary, finely chopped
2 tablespoons wine vinegar
grated rind of 1 lemon
1 cup fish stock
salt and pepper
2 teaspoons flour
1 teaspoon butter

1. Wash trout under running cold water and dry.

2. Soak raisins in 3 tablespoons warm water for 15 minutes.

3. In a large skillet, heat the oil and sauté the onion, garlic, celery, sage, and rosemary until soft but not browned.

4. Add the trout to the pan, lightly brown, and then add vinegar, lemon rind, raisins with their liquid, stock, salt, and pepper.

5. Bring liquid to a boil, lower heat, cover and simmer for about 10 minutes or until trout is done. Remove trout and keep hot in a warm oven.

6. Scrape up any bits on the bottom of the skillet and strain the fish sauce into a small saucepan, pushing hard on the solids in the strainer.

7. Blend the flour and butter and add to the sauce. Cook while stirring until sauce is smooth. Test seasonings.

8. Take the trout from the oven. Remove skin and open trout so that there will be 4 fillets. Spoon sauce over trout and serve to 4 immediately.

When I first tried swordfish with mushrooms, in Italy, I thought it might be an incongruous combination. In fact, they go together beautifully.

PESCE SPADA AI FUNGHI
Swordfish with Mushrooms

4 swordfish steaks
salt and pepper
flour for dredging the swordfish
4 tablespoons extra virgin olive oil
1/2 onion, finely chopped
1/2 pound brown mushrooms, sliced
1/2 cup white wine
1 rounded tablespoon chopped parsley

1. Coat the swordfish steaks with seasoned flour. Heat oil in a large skillet and brown swordfish quickly on both sides. Remove from pan and set aside.

2. Sauté onion in the skillet until golden and add the mushrooms. Sauté over medium-high heat until mushrooms are lightly browned. Add more oil, if necessary. Season mushrooms.

3. Return swordfish to the skillet. Pour wine over everything and add parsley. Cook until most of the wine evaporates and fish is cooked through. Add a little water to the pan, if necessary, to have about 1/4 cup of sauce in the pan.

4. Serve to 4, one steak each, some mushrooms, and a spoon of sauce.

This popular fish preparation is a joy to eat and is simple to prepare. It must be fresh. The Italians leave the shell on the shrimp when cooking and serving them because the flavor is better, but I like mine shelled and deveined. Buying the fish is fun in the Italian coastal towns where in the open markets you can find a great variety caught that day. For this dish, you need to buy small fish like smelt, small shrimp, small *calamari,* and small sole.

FRITTURA DI PESCE MISTO
Mixed Fried Seafood

1 1/2 pounds small seafood, i.e., tiny fish like smelt, small shrimp, small scallops, small *calamari*, and sole fillets
extra virgin olive oil for frying fish
1/2 cup all-purpose flour for dredging seafood
salt and pepper

1. Clean the fish. Remove the outer membrane from the *calamari* if it is not already done, and cut the *calamari* in rings. Cut the sole fillets in bite-size pieces.

2. Heat 1/4 cup oil in a large skillet for frying the fish.

3. Put the flour, salt, and pepper in a bag. Drop in the fish and quickly shake the fish in the bag to coat them.

4. Put the fish into the hot oil, piece by piece, not crowding them, until all is in the pan. If all the fish does not fit into the pan at once, fry the rest in another batch.

5. Turn the fish as it cooks and when it is golden brown, remove it to paper towels. Serve immediately with wedges of lemon to 4.

This is one of the most appetizing preparations of sole. If it is fried properly, the sole is crisp on the outside and moist on the inside.

Whenever frying fish, see that the oil is hot but not smoking before adding the fish, and do not crowd the fish in the skillet or the skillet will cool down. The oil should sizzle when adding the fish so that the coating on the fish does not absorb too much oil and forms a nice, lightly browned crust.

FILETTI DI SOGLIOLE FRITTE
Fried Fillets of Sole

2 eggs, beaten
1/4 cup milk
salt and pepper
12 fillets of sole (2 per person), skinned and boned
2 cups fresh bread crumbs, seasoned
extra virgin olive oil for frying
several sprigs of parsley
2 lemons

1. Put the beaten eggs in a shallow bowl and add milk, salt, and pepper.

2. Soak the fillets in the egg mixture for 30 minutes, turning them from time to time.

3. Put the bread crumbs on a plate for coating the fish.

4. Heat 3 tablespoons of olive oil in a large skillet.

5. Remove each fillet from the egg mixture onto the bread crumbs. Coat both sides of the fillet with the crumbs and place in the hot oil in the skillet. Continue to coat the fillets with the crumbs and place in the skillet until the skillet is filled but not crowded.

6. Fry fillets on one side until nicely browned and turn over to fry the other side. Remove fried fillets to a warm platter and continue to fry in batches until all fillets are cooked, adding oil to the skillet, if necessary, between batches.

7. Quickly fry the sprigs of parsley and place decoratively on the platter. Serve to 6 with lemon wedges.

Greens, especially spinach, are greatly appreciated by the Florentines. This attractive dish employs a bed of spinach to hold the delicately flavored sole.

SOGLIOLE ALLA FIORENTINA
Sole with Spinach

1 pound spinach
3 tablespoons butter
1 1/2 tablespoons flour
1 cup milk, heated
salt and pepper
pinch of nutmeg
1/2 cup white wine
4 fillets of sole (Each one should weigh about 4 ounces.)
1/4 cup grated *Parmigiano Reggiano* cheese

1. Cook the spinach in a covered saucepan with just the water clinging to its leaves after washing. Cook for 3 or 4 minutes or until all the spinach leaves are wilted. Do not over cook.

2. Drain and coarsely chop spinach. Spread spinach evenly over the bottom of a buttered, shallow baking dish that can go from oven to table.

3. Prepare a *besciamella* sauce: cook together 2 tablespoons of the butter and the flour over moderate heat, while whisking, for 3 or 4 minutes. Add the hot milk all at once and stir vigorously with the whisk until mixture comes to a boil and thickens. Add salt, pepper, and nutmeg and set aside.

4. Bring to a boil over moderately high heat, in a large skillet, the wine and the remaining tablespoon of butter. Add the sole in 1 layer, salt, and pepper. Cook for about 5 minutes, turning once. Fish should not over cook.

5. Carefully lift fillets onto spinach bed. Strain the juices from the skillet into the *besciamella* sauce and spoon sauce evenly over fish and spinach. Sprinkle with cheese.

6. Bake in a preheated oven at 400° F. for about 10 minutes or until bubbly and beginning to color. Serve immediately to 4.

This makes a very light and pleasing summer luncheon. In Salerno it is usually offered as a second course after *pasta*. It is served at room temperature with bread and a salad. Other fillets of small fish may be used for this delightful dish. Only the very best extra virgin olive oil should be used to dress the fish.

SOGLIOLE LISCE CON LIMONE
Poached Sole with Lemon

4 or 8 fillets of sole depending on their size
salt
extra virgin olive oil
parsley, chopped
lemon wedges

1. Boil about an inch of water in a skillet. Add the fillets of sole and keep the water boiling until the fish fillets are tender, about 10 minutes.

2. Carefully remove from the water so that they do not fall apart and place them on a plate. Remove any bones that may be in the fish and with the tip of a knife, scrape off any brown bits that may remain on the fillets, so that they will be totally white.

3. Place a portion of whole fish fillets on each of four plates. Salt fillets and spoon olive oil over them. Sprinkle with parsley and serve with lemon wedges at room temperature.

When olive oil and garlic combine with the shrimp, a flavorful and aromatic dish is the result. Not only shrimp but *calamari* and other seafood are excellent prepared in this manner. Use cleaned *calamari,* with the membrane removed, and cut into rings.

GAMBERI AGLIO E OLIO
Shrimp with Garlic and Oil

4 tablespoons extra virgin olive oil
2 cloves garlic, peeled and halved lengthwise
1/8 teaspoon crushed, dried red pepper
1 1/3 pounds fresh shrimp, peeled and deveined
salt
1 tablespoon chopped parsley

1. Heat olive oil and lightly brown garlic on both sides. Add the red pepper, swirl around in the pan, and add shrimp.

2. Toss in the oil, about 2 minutes, and add salt and parsley. Cook until shrimp is cooked through but not overdone. Serve immediately to 4.

In Italy cooking over an open fire is one of the most popular methods of preparing seafood, meats, and vegetables. This method brings out the finest flavor from shrimp. Sometimes the shrimp are put on skewers before grilling. Seafood can also be cooked under a broiler.

GAMBERI ALLA GRIGLIA
Grilled Shrimp

1/3 cup extra virgin olive oil
2 lemons
1 large clove garlic, mashed
salt and pepper
16 jumbo shrimp, cut down the back lengthwise, vein removed, but shells and remainder of shrimp intact

1. Combine in a measuring cup, olive oil, juice of 1/2 of one of the lemons, garlic, salt, and pepper.

2. If doing this on an outside fire, have coals burning hot. Saturate the shrimp with the olive oil sauce and place them on a grill about 5 inches over the fire. Cook about 4 or 5 minutes, turning once, until shrimp are cooked through. Brush olive oil sauce over shrimp frequently as it cooks.

3. If doing this under the broiler, dip shrimp into the sauce and place on a baking dish in 1 layer. Broil the shrimp about 5 inches from the heat, turning once. Baste with the olive oil sauce and broil about 4 or 5 minutes, depending on the size of the shrimp, until cooked through, but not over done.

4. Place the shrimp on a warmed serving plate. Cut the remaining lemon in wedges and arrange around the shrimp. Pour the sauce in the baking dish

over the shrimp and serve immediately to 4. Let the diners remove their own shells as the Italians do.

Variation:

If grilling or broiling fish steaks or fillets, use the same sauce for basting and cooking.

Mussels prepared in this manner are popular along the seacoast in southern Italy, especially in Bari. The seasoned breadcrumbs and extra virgin olive oil provide a tasty topping for the mussels which are enhanced by the fresh lemon that accompanies them. In Italy mussels usually are served as a first course.

COZZE GRATINATE
Baked Mussels with Breadcrumb Topping

2 pounds or about 2 dozen large mussels
10 tablespoons fresh, fine breadcrumbs
1 clove garlic, peeled and mashed
2 tablespoons finely chopped fresh parsley
salt and freshly ground black pepper
1 cup water
about 1/4 cup extra virgin olive oil
1 lemon, cut into wedges

1. Scrub mussels with a stiff brush under cold running water and pull off beards. Place mussels in a bowl of cold, lightly salted water and add a tablespoon of cornmeal to help further clean the mussels. Discard those that do not close when put into the water or those that have broken shells.

2. Combine the breadcrumbs, garlic, parsley, salt, and pepper in a small bowl and mix well.

3. Pour the water and a little salt into a large skillet with a lid and bring to a boil over high heat.

4. Meanwhile rinse mussels again and when water boils, place them in the skillet in one layer, if possible. Cover skillet and steam them open. This should take 2 to 5 minutes.

5. Remove skillet from heat and uncover. Discard mussels that have not opened. Remove and discard half of each shell and leave the mussels on the remaining half shell. If some of the mussels are small, you can put 2 on 1 shell.

6. Place mussel shells, side by side, in 1 layer in a baking dish. Moisten mussels with about 1/2 teaspoon of broth from skillet. Put a heaping teaspoon of breadcrumb mixture to cover each mussel, and dribble with 1/2 teaspoon of olive oil.

7. Place baking dish in a preheated, 425° F oven for about 10 minutes or until the topping turns golden. Serve very hot from the oven to 4.

The sauce of this *calamari* dish is tasty, and I like to serve it with crusty Italian bread.

CALAMARI IMBOTTITI
Stuffed Squid

8 *calamari* (about 5 inches long, not including tentacles), cleaned tentacles
from 2 of the *calamari,* finely chopped
4 tablespoons extra virgin olive oil
2 cloves garlic, peeled and mashed
3/4 cup fine, dry, plain bread crumbs
2 fillets of anchovy, cut in 1/2-inch pieces (optional)
12 black *Gaeta* olives, pitted and quartered
1 rounded tablespoon of capers, drained
salt and pepper
1/4 cup chopped parsley
2 cloves garlic, peeled and halved
a pinch of dried, red crushed peppers
1/4 cup dry white wine
2 medium tomatoes, peeled and chopped or 1 14-ounce can peeled and
chopped tomatoes
1 tablespoon chopped basil

1. Rinse the *calamari* and pat dry. Set aside.

2. Sauté the tentacles in 2 tablespoons of the olive oil until tender. Add the
mashed garlic and the breadcrumbs. Mix well.

3. Stir in the anchovy pieces, olives, capers, salt, pepper, and half of the
parsley. Also add 2 tablespoons of water and mix well. Remove the
breadcrumb mixture to a bowl to cool.

4. Fill the *calamari* with the breadcrumb mixture. Do not fill them too full or
they may split while cooking. Close the ends with a toothpick or a metal
pin and set aside.

5. Heat the remaining olive oil in a large frying pan over medium-high heat and place the filled *calamari* side by side in the hot oil. Add the garlic halves and red pepper. Sauté the *calamari* and garlic on all sides.

6. Add the wine and when it has nearly evaporated add the tomatoes. Cover skillet, lower heat and cook the *calamari* slowly, about 30 minutes or until fork tender.

7. Add salt, pepper, and basil. If liquid has evaporated, add a little water. Cook another 2 or 3 minutes and remove *calamari* to a warmed platter. Spoon sauce over *calamari* and sprinkle with remaining parsley. Serves 4 to 8.

Cappone Magro is a misnomer. *Cappone* refers to a capon chicken and *Magro* means thin, lean, or a day of abstinence. There is no chicken in this tempting Genoese fish and vegetable salad, and even though it is not a rich dish, it is definitely party food. In fact, it is a lavish presentation for a buffet table or dinner party with its great variety of seafood and vegetables beautifully arranged and topped with the piquant sauce.

CAPPONE MAGRO
Seafood and Vegetable Salad

2 beets
extra virgin olive oil
wine vinegar
salt and pepper
1/2 pound red potatoes
fresh lemon juice
1/2 pound slim, young green beans, left whole, topped and tailed
1/2 head of cauliflower
1 large carrot
2 stalks celery
3 eggs, hard boiled
1 pound salmon steaks or fillets about 1/2 inch thick
1 pound of a white fish, steaks or fillets 1/2 inch thick
12 mussels, well scrubbed and put in a bowl of cold water
12 clams, well scrubbed and put in a bowl of cold water
1/2 pound shrimp, peeled and deveined
1/2 pound scallops
1 lobster
1 small clove garlic, finely chopped
1/4 cup chopped parsley
1 tablespoon drained capers
8 green olives, pitted
1 tablespoon pine nuts
4 fillets of anchovy

1/2 cup extra virgin olive oil
2 tablespoons wine vinegar
slices of Italian homemade-type bread
12 oysters, fresh and cold, optional
1 small jar marinated artichoke hearts
1 small jar marinated mushrooms
olives

1. Boil the beets until they are tender. Cool, peel, and slice them, dress them with a little olive oil, vinegar, salt, and pepper, and set aside.

2. Boil the potatoes. Peel as soon as they are cool enough to handle. Slice them, put a dressing of olive oil and lemon juice with salt and pepper over them, and set aside to cool.

3. Steam for about 10 minutes, or until tender crisp, the beans, cauliflower, carrot, and celery. Cut the cauliflower into flowerettes, the carrots into rounds, and slice the celery on the diagonal. Pour a little olive oil and lemon juice dressing over them with salt and pepper and set aside to cool.

4. Peel the eggs and reserve.

5. In a large skillet with a lid, poach the salmon and white fish in 1 cup of lightly salted, boiling water. The salmon should be done in 5 minutes. Remove fish with a slotted spatula. Remove and discard bones and skin and dress with olive oil, lemon juice, salt, and pepper.

6. Bring the fish broth to a boil again in the skillet and put in the mussels and clams. Cover the skillet and cook for 3 to 5 minutes. Discard shells that did not open. Remove mussels and clams from skillet, leaving the broth behind. Remove half the shell and let the mussels and clams sit on the other half shell. Moisten each mussel and clam with a teaspoon of fish broth from the skillet, olive oil, and lemon juice. Set aside.

7. Bring the water in the skillet back to a boil and add the shrimp and scallops. Cover the skillet and boil the shrimp and scallops for 1 to 2 minutes depending on their size. Remove them from the skillet and dress them with olive oil and lemon juice. Chill all seafood and vegetables in refrigerator.

8. Bring to a boil a large pot of lightly salted water. Drop in the lobster, head first, and boil for 15 to 20 minutes depending on its size.

9. Make the sauce: put into a food processor bowl one of the hard boiled eggs, coarsely chopped, and the garlic, parsley, capers, olives, pine nuts, fillets of anchovy, and 2 tablespoons of wine vinegar. Process while slowly adding 1/2 cup olive oil. This may also be done in a blender.

10. Put enough slices of bread to cover the center of a large platter into a slow oven to dry out but not brown. Lightly rub a clove of garlic over the bread. Moisten each slice with olive oil and a few drops of vinegar. Lay them in the center of the platter and spoon a little sauce over them.

11. Arrange the vegetables over the bread in attractive patterns and the seafood around them. Place the oysters around the salad but use them only if they are absolutely fresh and icy cold. Sprinkle them with lemon juice.

12. Take the meat from the lobster, cut it in pieces, and place them on the platter. For a striking effect, garnish the salad with the lobster shell. Other garnishes that may be used are marinated artichoke hearts, mushrooms, and olives.

13. Pour the sauce over the salad just before serving. Enough for 8 to 10.

Variation:

Eliminate the salmon and white fish instead poach a whole fish. Remove the skin and backbone, but keep it otherwise intact. Place it in the center of the platter, over the bread, with the vegetables and other seafood arranged around it. In this case do not use the lobster shell.

Souvenirs, Florence

Le Frittate e le Uova

Fritatte and Eggs

Eggs in Italy are eaten for a light meal such as Italians might have in the evening,
but they might also serve as a second course of the main meal.
Eggs are not a breakfast food.

The Italian *frittata* is compared often to an omelet. There are similarities, but the two dishes
are somewhat different. An omelet, which seems to be more French than Italian in origin, is
prepared by pouring a thin layer of beaten eggs into a heated omelet pan with butter in it.
If other ingredients are to be added, they are sprinkled over the eggs as the omelet cooks.
The omelet is rolled and served in an oblong shape.

The *frittata,* of which there are many variations, is an egg-and-vegetable pie.
It usually is thicker than an omelet. Vegetables and herbs are sautéed in olive oil and seasoned.
Other ingredients may be added. Eggs are lightly beaten, seasoned, and often grated cheese
is added. The eggs are poured over the vegetables and cooked until the underside is lightly
browned. The *frittata* is next inverted onto a plate and slipped back into the frying pan so that
the other side can cook. It is then turned out onto a serving dish and cut into wedges like a pie.

Facing page: Chianti country, Greve

There are many variations of the easy to prepare *frittata* (egg-and-vegetable pie). The asparagus *frittata* is a favorite in spring when the new and tender asparagus is in season. My aunt tells me that the best is the wild asparagus which they used to find in the hills surrounding the small mountain town of Oliveto Citra in the province of Salerno.

To cut down on the fat content, this recipe calls for 4 eggs and 4 egg whites. More of the yolks may be eliminated for those needing to reduce cholesterol.

FRITTATA AGLI ASPARAGI
Asparagus Frittata

3 tablespoons extra virgin olive oil
1 large clove garlic, peeled and halved lengthwise
1 1/4 pounds asparagus, fibrous ends cut off and stalks peeled 2-inches from the bottom
1/2 cup water
4 eggs and 4 egg whites
salt and pepper
1/4 cup *Parmigiano Reggiano* cheese

1. Heat the oil in a 10-inch, non-stick frying pan and add the garlic pieces.

2. Cut the asparagus stalks in 1-inch pieces and add them to the pan. Sauté asparagus about 5 minutes or until lightly browned and add water. Cook until asparagus is tender and remove garlic pieces.

3. Meanwhile break eggs in a bowl, add salt, pepper, and cheese. Whisk with a fork until blended.

4. Pour the eggs over the asparagus and cook over moderately low heat, without stirring, until the under side is cooked. Loosen *frittata,* if necessary, with a spatula.

5. In order to cook the top side, place a large flat plate or lid over frying pan. Hold it tightly in place while you quickly invert the frying pan so that the *frittata* is resting on the plate. Slide the *frittata* back into the frying pan and cook the other side. The *frittata* also may be put under a broiler to cook the top.

6. The *frittata* should be cooked through but not be dry. Turn out on a plate and cut into wedges. Serves 4 to 6.

You can make a *frittata* from many of the vegetables or herbs. It is a quick and easy lunch or supper. This one is especially for the gardener who grows lots of *zucchini* in the summer. The buds are picked before they open into flowers. You may also add a couple of small *zucchini* to the *frittata*.

FRITTATA DI FIORILLI
Zucchini Buds Frittata

2 tablespoons extra virgin olive oil
1 clove garlic, cut in half lengthwise
a few flakes of dried, crushed red pepper
1/2 pound *zucchini* buds (*zucchini* flowers before they open)
1 or 2 very small *zucchini,* sliced
4 eggs or 2 whole eggs and 4 whites of egg
salt
1 rounded tablespoon grated *pecorino Romano* cheese

1. Heat oil in an 8-inch, non-stick frying pan. Sauté garlic halves, red pepper, *zucchini* buds and sliced *zucchini* in the oil until they begin to turn color. Add 2 tablespoons of water, put a lid on the skillet, and cook until the *zucchini* buds are tender but not mushy. Raise heat and cook without a lid until most of the water evaporates. Add salt.

2. Meanwhile beat the eggs with 2 tablespoons of water, salt and grated cheese.

3. Pour the eggs gently over the *zucchini* mixture and cook slowly, without stirring, until the eggs set. Loosen the *frittata* with a teflon turner, and when the bottom is lightly browned, cook the top.

4. To cook the top, hold a large, flat lid or a plate securely on the frying pan. Invert the pan in one quick movement so that the *frittata* is resting on the lid or the plate. Slide the *frittata* back into the frying pan and cook slowly until the under side is done. To cook the top side of the *frittata* without flipping it over, you may put the skillet under the broiler until the top is done.

5. Remove to a warm plate and cut in wedges as you would a pie. Serves 4.

A *frittata* makes a nice light lunch served with good, crusty Italian bread. This one, made often by my mother, was a family favorite.

FRITTATA DI ZUCCHINI E POMODORI
Zucchini and Tomato Frittata

1/2 onion, thinly sliced
3 tablespoons extra virgin olive oil
1/8 teaspoon crushed, dried red pepper
2 8-inch *zucchini,* sliced
1 cup peeled and chopped, Italian-type, plum tomatoes
salt
2 tablespoons chopped parsley
1 tablespoon chopped basil
2 eggs and 4 egg whites, or 4 whole eggs
2 tablespoons water
2 tablespoons grated *pecorino Romano* cheese

1. Sauté the onion in the olive oil with the pepper, in a non-stick skillet, until onion is golden. Add the *zucchini* and continue to sauté the vegetables until they are lightly browned.

2. Add the tomatoes and continue to cook until vegetables are tender. Sprinkle with salt and stir in parsley and basil.

3. Meanwhile break the eggs into a bowl, add water, grated cheese, and salt. Beat the eggs thoroughly.

4. Pour the eggs over the vegetables in the skillet and let them cook, without stirring, until the eggs are set. Loosen the *frittata* around the edges carefully so that it keeps its shape, and make sure that it is not stuck on the bottom. When the bottom is lightly browned, cook the top side.

5. To do this, hold a large, flat pan lid or plate securely over the skillet. Invert the skillet in one quick movement so that the *frittata* is resting on the lid or plate. Slide the *frittata* back into the skillet and cook slowly until the under side is done. To cook the top of the *frittata* without flipping it over, you may put the skillet under the broiler.

6. Slide *frittata* onto a warmed serving dish and cut into wedges. Serve to 4.

Potatoes and onions combine very well with the eggs in this tasty *frittata*. Fried potatoes alone or fried onions alone also make an excellent *frittata*.

FRITTATA DI PATATE E CIPOLLE
Potato and Onion Frittata

3 tablespoons extra virgin olive oil
1 onion, thinly sliced
1/8 teaspoon crushed, dried red pepper
1 pound potatoes, peeled and sliced about 1/8-inch thick
salt and black pepper
2 eggs and 4 egg whites

1. Heat 2 tablespoons of the olive oil in a non-stick skillet and sauté until the onion and pepper is soft and lightly browned. Remove from the skillet with a slotted spoon and reserve.

2. Add remaining tablespoon of olive oil to the skillet and when it is hot, fry the potatoes until they are lightly browned on both sides.

3. Return onion to the skillet, salt, and let cook, over moderate heat, until the vegetables are tender.

4. Meanwhile beat the eggs with 1 tablespoon of water, salt, and pepper.

5. Pour the eggs into the skillet to cover the vegetables. Cook, without stirring, until the eggs are set. Loosen *frittata* around the edges and when the bottom is lightly browned, cook the top.

6. To do this, hold a plate or flat pan lid securely on the skillet. With one quick movement, invert the skillet onto the plate so that the *frittata* falls on the plate or lid. Slide the *frittata* back into the skillet in its upside down position.

7. Cook until the *frittata* is cooked through but not dry. The top of the *frittata* may also be cooked under the broiler. Slide out onto a warmed serving dish and cut into wedges. Serve, while hot, to 4.

Sunset on the Arno, Florence

I have grown up with this egg preparation as have our daughter and son. It remains one of our favorites.

UOVA AL POMODORO CON ERBE FRESCHE
Eggs with Tomatoes and Herbs

2 eggs and 4 egg whites
salt and black pepper
2 tablespoons extra virgin olive oil
1 cup peeled, seeded, and chopped fresh tomatoes (Canned Italian tomatoes are preferable when tomatoes are out of season.)
a pinch of crushed, red pepper
2 tablespoons chopped fresh parsley
1 tablespoon fresh basil, torn

1. Beat the eggs with salt and pepper and set aside.

2. Heat the olive oil over moderate heat, in a non-stick skillet, and add the tomatoes and red pepper. Simmer about 10 minutes or until tomatoes are cooked.

3. Add 1 tablespoon of water if tomatoes become dry. They should remain moist. Add salt, parsley, and basil. Cook another minute, stirring, to incorporate the herbs.

4. Add the eggs to the skillet. Do not stir for 1 minute. Then start to turn the eggs with a spatula, gently, until the eggs and tomatoes have blended and are cooked through. Serve immediately to 4.

In this recipe "Hell" refers to the tasty red tomato sauce in which the eggs are fried.

UOVA ALL'INFERNO
Eggs in Hell

1 small onion, chopped
2 tablespoons extra virgin olive oil
1 3/4 cup Italian-type plum tomatoes, peeled, seeded, and chopped
(Fresh tomatoes should be used when in season.)
salt
freshly ground black pepper
1 tablespoon chopped basil
1 tablespoon chopped parsley
4 fresh eggs

1. Sauté the onion in olive oil, in a large skillet, until the onion is golden. Add the tomatoes and let cook until onions are soft. Season.

2. Add the basil and parsley and add a little water if the tomatoes become too dry.

3. Make 4 wells, with a wooden spoon, where the eggs will be placed. Break an egg into each well without breaking the yolk. Season the eggs and let cook over medium heat, without stirring, until eggs are set, but the yolks have not become hard. You may put a lid on to cook the tops of the eggs.

4. Lift the eggs onto 4 warmed plates and spoon some of the tomato sauce around them. Serve with crusty Italian bread.

I Contorni

Side Dishes

La Verdura
Vegetables

Italian preparations of vegetables emphasize the natural flavor. Vegetables are prepared
in a variety of ways and are enjoyed every day. Italian shoppers are very particular and
discerning about the quality of the vegetables that they buy and will reject any that are not
perfectly fresh. They eat their vegetables when they are in season, and thus the
vegetables always are of excellent quality.

In Florence the tiny artichokes unique to the area are truly appreciated,
and during the harvesting season the Florentines have them frequently.
One of the favorite preparations is fried artichokes (*Carciofi Fritti*).

In the southern regions of Italy tomatoes, eggplant, peppers, and greens are very popular,
and the Italian ways of preparing these vegetables bring out their vibrant flavors.

One of the great treats of spring is to eat the fresh, tender asparagus, coated in egg and flour, and fried in olive oil.

ASPARAGI FRITTI
Fried Asparagus

1 pound asparagus
flour for coating asparagus
1 egg
1 tablespoon grated *Parmigiano Reggiano* cheese
1 tablespoon water
salt and pepper
4 tablespoons extra virgin olive oil

1. Break off the tough ends of the asparagus.

2. Put the flour in a shallow bowl or flat plate. Beat the egg, cheese and water together in a shallow bowl. Season the flour and the egg mixture.

3. Heat the olive oil in a large skillet. Coat the asparagus spears with the seasoned flour shaking off the excess. Dip each spear of asparagus into the egg mixture and then set it into the hot oil.

4. Turn the asparagus while frying, over medium heat, so that they will brown on all sides. When asparagus are tender, serve immediately to 3 or 4.

This old family recipe continues to be the favorite *broccoli* preparation of family and friends.

BROCCOLI AGLIO E OLIO
Broccoli with Garlic and Olive Oil

1 large bunch of *broccoli*
3 tablespoons extra virgin olive oil
1 large clove garlic, cut in half lengthwise
dash crushed red pepper or 1 tiny dried red pepper
3/4 cup water
salt

1. Cut tough ends off *broccoli* stems and peel stems from the butt end as far up as possible. Slice stems on the diagonal and cut tops into flowerettes, or you may use only flowerettes. Wash, drain, and set aside.

2. Heat olive oil and lightly brown garlic halves on both sides. Add crushed red pepper or whole pepper, and when it turns a darker shade, remove pan from heat. Do not allow pepper to burn.

3. Add *broccoli* to the pan and cook while turning so that the *broccoli* is well coated with the oil and lightly sautéed. Add water and salt, cover pan, and cook until *broccoli* is tender, about 10 minutes. Do not overcook.

4. Spoon into warmed vegetable dish and serve immediately to 3 or 4.

I have seen this well-known, tasty dish served as an *antipasto*. In Sicily where it originated, however, it would be considered a side dish, usually accompanying meat or fish. Some Italians add cocoa which gives an interesting flavor.

CAPONATA
Sweet and Sour Eggplant

1 1/2 pounds firm eggplants
salt
1/4 cup plus 1 tablespoon extra virgin olive oil
1 onion, chopped
2 large stalks celery, coarsely chopped
1 1/2 cups peeled and chopped tomatoes
1/2 cup green olives, pitted and thickly sliced
2 tablespoons capers
1 tablespoon chopped, fresh basil
1 tablespoon sugar
1/4 cup wine vinegar
1/2 tablespoon unsweetened cocoa (optional)

1. Cut off the stems from the eggplants and cut them in 3/4-inch cubes. Place them in a colander and sprinkle evenly with salt. Place a plate and a weight over them and allow to drain for an hour. Rinse and pat dry the eggplant cubes.

2. Heat the 1/4 cup of oil and sauté the eggplant until soft and browned. Remove with a slotted spoon and set aside.

3. Add the remaining tablespoon of oil to the pan and sauté the onion and celery, stirring frequently, until vegetables are nearly done. Add the tomatoes and cook until vegetables are tender. Add the reserved eggplant and cook for 10 minutes.

4. Add the remaining ingredients, including the cocoa if using it. Cook another few minutes or until everything is soft. Adjust the salt.
Serves 4 or more.

This recipe of my mother's has always been my favorite artichoke preparation.

CARCIOFI RIPIENI
Stuffed Artichokes

4 large artichokes
2 1/2 cups fresh bread crumbs from homemade-type bread
2 cloves garlic, mashed
1 teaspoon *oregano*
salt
freshly ground black pepper
6 tablespoons extra virgin olive oil

1. Cut about 1 inch off the top of each artichoke. With kitchen scissors cut the spiky tops off the outside leaves. Remove the small leaves around the bottom of the artichoke. Cut off all but 1/2 inch of the stem. Make sure the artichoke will stand upright.

2. Carefully ease the leaves a bit open. The choke may be removed, but it is simpler to leave the choke intact and let the diners remove that portion while they eat their way from outer leaves to center.

3. To prepare the stuffing, combine bread crumbs, garlic, *oregano,* salt, pepper, and olive oil. With a teaspoon, put some crumb mixture into each of the outer leaves of the artichokes. If chokes are removed, put remaining stuffing into centers. If not, pack it into the tops of the artichokes.

4. Place stuffed artichokes in a pan of lightly salted water so that the artichokes fit loosely together and the water reaches about 3/4 inch up the sides of the artichokes. Use 1 1/2 to 2 cups water.

5. Cover tightly, bring to a boil over high heat, reduce heat, and boil gently for 45 minutes to an hour. If water level goes down much, add more. Test for doneness by pulling off an outside leaf. If it pulls out easily it is done.

6. Remove artichokes to serving dishes. Reduce boiling liquid over high heat to half and spoon just a little over each artichoke.

7. To eat artichokes, remove one outer leaf at a time, and insert most of it in the mouth. Then pull it out slowly between the teeth to scrape off the meaty part and the stuffing. Save some stuffing as you go, to eat with the heart. When you reach the very small, spiky leaves you can easily remove them with the choke. Only the delicious heart remains. Serves 4.

Girl watching, Sorrento

This dish is best when made with the tiny, purple artichokes found in Tuscany. Try to find the smallest artichokes for this delicately flavored artichoke preparation. They make an excellent first course or side dish and should be eaten soon after they have been fried.

CARCIOFI FRITTI ALLA FIORENTINA
Florentine Fried Artichokes

6 small, very young, tender artichokes (Frozen artichoke hearts may be used.)
flour for dredging artichoke wedges
1 egg
1 tablespoon water
3 tablespoons extra virgin olive oil
salt
1 lemon

1. Pull back the outer leaves of the artichokes, letting them break at the tender end. Cut off the pointed tips and any part of the leaves that are not tender and pale-colored. Drop the trimmed artichokes in a bowl of water acidulated with a little lemon juice.

2. Quarter each artichoke and cut out any choke that may have begun to form. Slice the quarters into thin wedges.

3. Dip the artichoke wedges into the flour, shaking off the excess. Beat the egg with the tablespoon of water.

4. Heat the oil to a medium temperature in a skillet. Dip each wedge of artichoke into the egg mixture and place in the hot oil. When the artichokes are browned and cooked through, remove to paper towels to drain.

5. Place the artichokes on a warmed plate and salt them. Serve immediately with wedges of lemon. Serves 4.

In Italy you are more likely to find green or purple cauliflower than white. The green Italian cauliflower has a more pronounced taste than the white or purple. Any of the colors may be used in this flavorful recipe. It may also be made without the olives.

CAVOLFIORE STUFATO CON OLIVE
Cauliflower Stew with Olives

1 cauliflower
3 tablespoons extra virgin olive oil
2 cloves garlic, peeled and halved lengthwise
1/3 cup water
2 ounces black *Gaeta* olives or green olives, pitted and coarsely chopped
salt
freshly ground black pepper

1. Cut the cauliflower into flowerettes and set aside.

2. In a large saucepan, heat the oil and lightly brown the garlic pieces. Add the cauliflower and stir to coat the pieces with oil. Add water, cover pan, and let cook over medium heat until cauliflower is nearly done.

3. Add olives and a little more water if water has evaporated, and cook until cauliflower is tender. Add salt and pepper. Serves 4.

You may use the green, purple, or white cauliflower to make this tasty dish.

CAVOLFIORE AFFOGATO
Cauliflower with Pine Nuts and Raisins

1 cauliflower
1/4 cup extra virgin olive oil
2 cloves garlic, peeled and halved lengthwise
2 tablespoons pine nuts *(pignoli)*
2 tablespoons raisins
salt and pepper

1. Cut the cauliflower in flowerettes and set aside.

2. Heat olive oil in a large saucepan and add garlic pieces. When they begin to brown, add the cauliflower. Sauté in the oil and turn pieces until golden on all sides.

3. Add 2 tablespoons of water, cover the pan, and let cook slowly, but do not let the cauliflower brown. If it begins to brown, add another tablespoons of water and let cook until cauliflower is nearly done.

4. Remove lid from pan and let water evaporate. Add pine nuts, raisins, salt, and pepper. Let everything sauté slowly until cauliflower is tender, but not brown. Serve to 4 or more.

My mother made this cabbage dish frequently because it is tasty, colorful, and healthful.

CAVOLO AI POMODORI
Cabbage with Tomatoes

1 medium head of cabbage, cut in 8 wedges
4 tablespoons extra virgin olive oil
2 cups peeled and coarsely chopped tomatoes and juice
(Fresh are preferred.)
1 large clove garlic, peeled and mashed
3 tablespoons fresh basil, chopped
3 tablespoons fresh parsley, chopped
salt and pepper
3 tablespoons grated *pecorino Romano* cheese

1. Set cabbage wedges, cut sides up, in a 6-quart pan with a well-fitting lid.

2. Dribble olive oil evenly over cabbage.

3. Combine tomatoes, garlic, basil, parsley, salt and pepper. Spoon over cabbage. Sprinkle with grated cheese.

4. Put lid on pan and bring to a boil. Reduce heat and simmer until cabbage is tender, almost an hour. Occasionally, check to see that there is adequate liquid in pan. Add water if it gets too dry. There should be some sauce on the bottom of the pan.

5. When cabbage is done, lift wedges onto a warmed, shallow bowl or platter. Spoon sauce from pan on cabbage and serve to 8.

These flavorful cabbage rolls are a complete meal by themselves, but my mother served them with fresh bread, and followed them with a salad, cheese, and fresh fruit.

PANZAROTTI DI CAVOLO
Stuffed Cabbage Rolls

1/2 cup long-grain rice (2 cups cooked)
1 large head of green cabbage
2 cloves garlic
3 tablespoons extra virgin olive oil
a pinch of dried, crushed, hot red pepper
1 1/2 cups peeled and ground tomatoes in puree
1 cup water
salt
1 pound lean ground beef
1 large clove garlic, mashed
1/4 cup grated *pecorino Romano* cheese
2 eggs
2 tablespoons chopped parsley
salt and pepper

1. Cook the rice according to directions on the package. Cool and set aside.

2. Remove 16 leaves from the head of cabbage. Blanch them in boiling water until they soften. Drain and cool them.

3. Prepare the sauce: brown the 2 cloves of garlic in the olive oil. Add the red pepper and then add the tomatoes and water. Let the sauce simmer for several minutes and add the salt.

4. In a bowl, combine the ground beef, garlic, grated cheese, rice, eggs, parsley, salt, and pepper. Mix thoroughly.

5. Cut out the tough part of the cabbage leaves at the base. Place 1 heaping tablespoon of the rice mixture on a cabbage leaf. Roll the bottom of the leaf over the mixture, fold in the sides in envelope-style and roll up the cabbage from bottom to top. Continue to fill the remaining cabbage leaves.

6. Put a good amount of sauce to cover the bottom of a broad-bottomed saucepan. Place the filled rolls over the sauce, side by side. Spoon some sauce over the cabbage rolls and place remaining rolls in a second layer.

7. Spoon the remaining sauce over the cabbage rolls. Simmer over low heat for an hour or until cabbage is tender. If necessary, add a little water if sauce is reduced. Serve with a little sauce spooned over the rolls. Makes 16 cabbage rolls.

Ciambotta is a vegetable mixture similar to ratatouille, the famous dish of Provence. It can be made with eggplant or *zucchini* or a combination of both. I always prepare *ciambotta* when my garden is teeming with *zucchini,* peppers, tomatoes, and herbs. It can be served as a first course or as a vegetable dish with the main course.

CIAMBOTTA
Vegetable Stew

7 tablespoons extra virgin olive oil
2 large green, red or yellow peppers, seeded and cut in strips
1 pound potatoes, sliced 1/8-inch thick
2 pounds *zucchini,* eggplant, or a combination of the 2, sliced
2 onions, sliced
1 large clove garlic, peeled and mashed
1/8 teaspoon crushed, dried red pepper, or to taste
1 1/2 cups tomatoes, peeled and chopped
salt

1. Heat 2 tablespoons of the olive oil in a large skillet and sauté peppers until lightly browned. Remove peppers with a slotted spoon and reserve.

2. Heat 2 additional tablespoons of olive oil in a skillet and fry potatoes until lightly browned. Remove potatoes with a slotted spoon and reserve with the peppers.

3. Heat 2 tablespoons of olive oil and fry *zucchini* and eggplant until lightly browned. Remove from skillet and reserve.

4. Add 1 more tablespoon of olive oil and sauté onion, garlic, and red pepper until onion is lightly browned. Add tomatoes and cook until some of the moisture of the tomatoes evaporates, about 15 minutes.

5. Add the reserved vegetables and salt and let everything cook together, stirring occasionally, until all vegetables are tender and flavors are blended. Enough for 6.

Cipolline d'Ivrea are small, flat, button onions cooked in the style of *Ivrea* in Piemonte. Frozen, small whole onions can be substituted if necessary. The onions are a delightful accompaniment for meats or poultry, especially roasts and game.

CIPOLLINE D'IVREA IN AGRODOLCE
Small Onions in a Sweet and Sour Sauce

1 pound small, whole, flat onions
1 tablespoon sugar
1/2 tablespoon butter
1/2 tablespoon flour
1/4 cup warm water
salt
1 tablespoon white wine vinegar

1. If using fresh onions, peel and parboil for 3 or 4 minutes. Drain and dry.

2. Heat the sugar in a saucepan, stirring constantly until it begins to caramelize and turns a light tan color.

3. Add the butter and flour and keep stirring until mixture is blended. Stir in the onions and then the water. Cook slowly, stirring occasionally, until onions are done. Add additional water if necessary.

4. Add salt and vinegar and simmer a few more minutes. Serves 6.

If you can find wild mushrooms or Italian mushrooms, especially *porcini* or *ovoli,* this dish will be even better than with cultivated mushrooms. The mushrooms are sometimes served on slices of grilled or sautéed *polenta.*

FUNGHI TRIFOLATI
Sautéed Mushrooms

1 clove garlic, quartered lengthwise
3 tablespoons extra virgin olive oil
1/8 teaspoon dried, crushed red pepper
1 pound wild or brown mushrooms, cleaned and sliced
salt
1/2 tablespoon chopped parsley
1 ripe Italian plum tomato, peeled, seeded, and chopped (optional)

1. Brown garlic in the olive oil on all sides and add red pepper and mushrooms.

2. Brown the mushrooms quickly, over high heat, and add salt, parsley and tomato. Cook until moisture is reduced. You may remove garlic pieces if you wish and sprinkle additional parsley over top when serving. Serves 4.

Young and tender garden beans are special cooked in this manner.
They may be dipped singly and cooked in the oil, or they may also be done with
a few together dipped and fried. I prefer the latter.

FAGIOLINI FRITTI
Fried Green Beans

3/4 pound thin, tender green beans, top and tail them but keep whole
flour for dusting the beans
salt and pepper
2 eggs
1 rounded tablespoon grated *pecorino Romano* cheese
4 tablespoons extra virgin olive oil

1. Steam the beans for 7 or 8 minutes. Drain and set aside to cool.

2. Put flour in a flat plate and season with salt and pepper.

3. Beat the eggs and cheese and add salt and pepper.

4. Heat the oil in a skillet.

5. Take one bean at a time or else take 3 or 4 at a time and coat them with
the flour.

6. Hold a few beans together and dip them into the egg mixture. Let the egg
drip back into the bowl and then put the cluster of beans into the hot oil.
Or, dip one bean at a time.

7. Cook until egg is set and turn to cook the other side. Serve hot to 4.

We had this dish served at home frequently because it was one of my father's favorite vegetable dishes. Any type of green beans may be used, but I prefer the flat, Roman-type beans when they are young and tender.

FAGIOLINI E PATATE AL POMODORO
Beans and Potatoes in Tomato Sauce

1 pound potatoes
1 pound green beans
2 tablespoons extra virgin olive oil
1 onion, chopped
1 1/2 cups Italian tomatoes, peeled and chopped
1 rounded tablespoon chopped, fresh basil (If fresh basil is not available, use fresh parsley.)
salt and pepper

1. Put whole potatoes to boil in water just covering them.

2. Top and tail beans and break into 2-inch lengths. Cook beans in a tightly covered saucepan with 1/2 cup water until they are nearly done.

3. Heat olive oil and sauté onion until soft and slightly brown. Add tomatoes and cook 15 minutes.

4. When potatoes are tender but not overdone, peel and cut into bite size pieces and add to the onion and tomatoes.

5. Add also the green beans with their remaining cooking-water. Add basil, salt, and pepper. Cook until vegetables are tender. Serves 4.

Very young, fresh Italian flat beans or thin green beans are best for this flavorful preparation.
The beans are delicious with or without the tomatoes.
If using tomatoes, fresh are better when in season.

FAGIOLINI AI POMODORI
Green Beans in Tomato Sauce

1 pound green beans
2 tablespoons extra virgin olive oil
1 clove garlic, peeled and halved lengthwise
3/4 cup peeled and chopped tomatoes (optional)
1 tablespoon chopped fresh basil
salt and pepper

1. Top and tail beans. Leave whole if they are small or break in halves.

2. Heat olive oil in a saucepan and add garlic pieces. When garlic just begins
to turn color, add the beans. Stir to coat with the oil and add tomatoes.
If you are not using tomatoes, add 1/2 cup water instead.

3. Cover pan tightly and cook until beans are barely tender. Add basil if
using tomatoes. Add salt and pepper. Cook another minute or until beans
are done and serve to 4.

Variation: FAGIOLINI AGLIO E OLIO—*Green Beans Without the Tomato*

Omit the tomatoes and basil from the above recipe.

This ancient and famous Tuscan preparation required a fire to cook the beans in the embers. They are best cooked that way. However, they can be done successfully, in a very slow oven. They have a superb flavor, and the only problem that I find is getting them out of the bottle. It is necessary to buy a bottle of *Chianti* wine of 1.5 liters which has the straw around it. Drink the wine or decant it to drink with the beans. Remove the straw and the labels from the bottle, but save the straw to make a plug for the top of the bottle. Do not cook the beans too long or they will be too soft to remove from the bottle.

FAGIOLI IN FIASCO
Beans Cooked in a Flask

1/2 pound dried *cannellini* beans
5 or 6 fresh sage leaves
2 large cloves garlic, unpeeled
1/3 cup extra virgin Tuscan olive oil
2 1/2 cups water
salt
freshly ground black pepper

1. Rinse the beans and drop them into the wine bottle. Add the sage leaves, garlic, olive oil, and water. Stuff the straw into the neck of the bottle.

2. The flask of beans can then be set near the embers of a fire or placed in a preheated, 225° F. oven. Keep in the oven for 3 hours. Pour the beans out of the bottle slowly, with a gentle shake. If they are still firm, cook a little longer in a saucepan.

3. Add salt and pepper and serve to 4.

Perhaps the beans resemble little birds, or perhaps the name comes from the fact that sage is an herb frequently used for cooking birds. Whatever the explanation, this is a traditional and popular Florentine preparation of beans.

FAGIOLI ALL'UCCELLETTO
Beans as Little Birds

2 cups dried or 4 cups fresh *cannellini* beans
4 tablespoons extra virgin olive oil
2 large cloves garlic, unpeeled
1 sprig (6 to 8 leaves) fresh sage
1 cup fresh tomatoes, peeled, some seeds removed, and chopped
(Canned Italian plum tomatoes may be used.)
salt and pepper

1. Sort through the beans, rinse them and add water 2 inches above the top of the beans. Bring to a rolling boil and cook for 1 or 2 minutes. Cover pan, remove from heat, and let beans rest for 2 hours. Cook beans slowly until nearly tender.

2. Meanwhile, in another large saucepan, heat olive oil and sauté garlic and sage until garlic turns golden. Add the tomatoes and let cook for 20 minutes.

3. Drain the beans and add them to the tomato sauce. Add salt and pepper and cook slowly until beans are soft. Serves 4 to 6.

My mother's beans were prepared according to the tradition of my father's family.
They were never over- or under-cooked, and they were seasoned to perfection.
She usually served them with greens (recipe follows) that were prepared in the family tradition
and always accompanied by homemade bread. The beans are healthful and delicious
and remain one of our family's favorite meals.

FAGIOLI DELLA NONNA
Grandma's Beans

1 pound dried great northern or *cannellini* white beans
1/3 cup extra virgin olive oil
2 large cloves garlic, peeled and quartered lengthwise
1/8 to 1/4 teaspoon dried, crushed red pepper
1 teaspoon *oregano*
salt

1. In a large saucepan, rinse and drain the beans which have been picked over to remove any bits of dirt, stones, or imperfect beans.

2. Add triple their volume of cold water (about 7 cups). Bring the water to a full rolling boil and cook about 1 minute, skimming the foam from the top of the water. Cover the pan, remove from heat, and let stand for 2 hours.

3. After the beans have rested, bring to a gentle boil and let simmer until tender, about 40 minutes. The older the beans the longer they take to cook.

4. Heat olive oil in a saucepan. Add garlic pieces and brown them lightly on all sides. Add red pepper, and when it becomes a shade darker, remove pan from heat so that pepper does not burn.

5. Pour olive oil, garlic, and pepper from the saucepan to the pot of cooked beans. Add *oregano* and salt and let beans simmer about 10 minutes to blend flavors. My mother would add a little more oil just before serving the 6 of us beans, greens, and homemade bread.

This is my grandmother's recipe from Oliveto Citra in Campania. She would use chicory or dandelion, mustard, turnip, beet leaves, swiss chard, or *broccoli di rape,* also called *rapini* greens. Our favorite was dandelion greens. They accompanied beans from the above recipe.

CICORIA AGLIO E OLIO
Greens with Garlic and Olive Oil

2 large bunches of dandelion or other greens
1/3 cup extra virgin olive oil
2 large cloves garlic, peeled and quartered lengthwise
1/8 teaspoon crushed, hot red pepper
1/2 cup tomatoes, fresh or canned, peeled and chopped (optional)
salt

1. Pick through the greens, wash thoroughly, and cut into about 3-inch lengths. Blanch the greens in a pot of boiling, lightly salted water. When water returns to the boil, drain greens and set aside. There should be about 3 cups of blanched greens.

2. Heat olive oil in a saucepan and brown the garlic pieces on both sides. Add red pepper, and when it turns a shade darker, remove from heat so that pepper does not burn.

3. If using tomatoes, add them and cook about 3 minutes. Stir in greens and salt and cook until greens are tender, stirring occasionally. Serve to 6 with the cooked beans and good Italian bread.

Bread is truly the staff of life in Italy. Italians insist on having excellent bread. They also want it fresh but do not want to waste good bread, so they have devised dishes whereby they can turn their dry bread into a tasty side dish or soup. When my mother served beans and greens for dinner, she would save some of them to make *pappone,* a favorite of ours, in which she used her stale homemade bread.

PAPPONE

Beans, Greens, and Bread

5 tablespoons extra virgin olive oil
4 cloves garlic, peeled and halved lengthwise
1/4 teaspoon dried, crushed red pepper (or to taste)
1 or more cups left-over beans from Grandma's Beans recipe (page 302)
1/2 cup or more left-over greens from Greens with Garlic and
Olive Oil recipe (page 303)
3 cups water
1/2 pound dried Italian bread, diced
salt

1. Heat oil and fry garlic pieces until they are browned on both sides.
Add red pepper and swirl in the oil to let it become a shade darker, but then
remove pan from heat so that pepper does not burn.

2. Stir in beans, greens, and water. Bring to a slow boil, cook about
5 minutes, and add diced bread. Add salt and stir and turn with a spatula
while bread absorbs the liquid.

3. The bread should become soft throughout. The *pappone* should be moist
but not soupy. If it becomes too dry, stir in a little more water. If soupy, cook
it longer, stirring and turning often. Check seasonings and serve to 4.
A dribble of olive oil may be added when serving.

Pane cotto is another tasty way to use stale bread even when you have no left-over beans and greens. This recipe makes an appetizing side dish for fish.

PANE COTTO
Cooked Bread

4 tablespoons extra virgin olive oil
4 cloves garlic, peeled and quartered lengthwise
1/4 to 1/2 teaspoon dried, crushed red pepper
salt
3 cups water
1/2 pound Italian bread, diced

1. Heat olive oil in a large skillet and brown garlic pieces on both sides. Add red pepper and salt, and when pepper becomes a shade darker, remove pan from heat so that pepper will not burn.

2. Add water, bring to a simmer, and let cook for 20 minutes.

3. Stir in bread and cook while turning with a spatula until bread absorbs the liquid and is soft throughout. If bread becomes too dry, add water. *Pane cotto* should be moist. If soupy, cook and stir longer. Check seasonings and serve to 4. A dribble of olive oil may be added when serving.

My neighbor Raffaelina Lambiase in Salerno had the most enticing aromas coming from her home each day when she prepared wonderful meals for her family. She has shared many samples and recipes from her kitchen including the following.

MELANZANE RIPIENE
Stuffed Eggplant

2 pounds small eggplant (oriental type), size of large eggs
salt
4 tablespoons extra virgin olive oil
1 heaping tablespoon of finely chopped onion
1 cup of crushed tomatoes
black pepper
1/2 pound *mozzarella,* grated
1 thin slice of *prosciutto,* chopped (optional)
2 rounded tablespoons of grated *Parmigiano Reggiano* cheese
1 rounded tablespoon of dried bread crumbs
1 egg
6 basil leaves, chopped

1. Remove stems from eggplants and cut in halves. Salt and let sit for 30 minutes. Quickly rinse, squeeze out water, and pat dry. Scoop out some of the pulp from the center to leave a space for the filling.

2. Prepare a tomato sauce: heat 1 tablespoon of olive oil and sauté onion until golden and soft. Add crushed tomatoes, salt, and pepper. Cook for 20 minutes. Add water if tomato sauce becomes too thick.

3. Fry the eggplant halves in olive oil, using 1 tablespoon of oil at a time. Remove the eggplants and fry the pulp.

4. Coarsely chop cooked pulp and put into a bowl. Add *mozzarella, prosciutto, Parmigiano* cheese, bread crumbs, egg, basil, salt, and pepper. Mix well.

5. Oil the bottom of a baking dish. Fill each eggplant half with the stuffing and set in the baking dish. Top each half with a spoon of tomato sauce and some grated cheese.

6. Bake in a preheated, 375° F. oven for about 30 minutes. Serves 4 to 6.

Triton Fountain (detail), Rome

In this preparation a light tomato sauce allows the distinctive, individual flavor of each ingredient to come through. The eggplant slices are broiled instead of fried so that less oil is absorbed and the procedure is quicker. The result is a well-flavored eggplant dish.

MELANZANE ALLA PARMIGIANA
Eggplant Casserole

3 medium-large eggplants (about 1 1/2 pounds each)
salt
1 heaping tablespoon finely chopped onion
about 1/4 cup extra virgin olive oil
2 cups peeled and chopped Italian plum tomatoes, fresh or canned
1 heaping tablespoon chopped basil
black pepper
1 pound *mozzarella* cheese, thinly sliced
1 cup grated *Parmigiano Reggiano* cheese

1. Top and tail eggplant and slice 1/2-inch thick.

2. Salt eggplant slices and stack in colander. Place an inverted plate over slices, put a weight on top, and let drain at least 30 minutes.

3. Make a tomato sauce: sauté onion in 1 tablespoon of the olive oil until golden. Add tomato and simmer about 20 minutes or until onion is soft. Add basil, salt, and pepper and cook another 5 minutes. Add a little water if sauce becomes dry.

4. Dry eggplant slices and line them closely on an oiled broiling pan without overlapping. Dab olive oil on both sides of each slice.

5. Set broiling pan about 5 inches from heat and broil eggplant at 500° F. about 5 minutes or until lightly browned. Turn slices over, and broil for 2 or 3 minutes until lightly browned. Remove slices from broiler pan and reserve. Broil remaining slices of eggplant. Makes about 45 slices.

6. Spoon a little sauce in a baking dish about 8 x 12 x 2 inches to barely cover the bottom. Line eggplant slices in dish. Place *mozzarella* slices and spoon just a little sauce over the eggplant. Top the layer with a sprinkling of *Parmigiano* cheese. Repeat layers of eggplant, *mozzarella,* sauce, and *Parmigiano* until all eggplant slices are layered in the dish.

7. Cover dish and bake in preheated oven at 350° F. for 20 minutes or until bubbling. Uncover dish and bake another 10 minutes. Serves 6.

This Tuscan specialty should be prepared in early summer when the fresh peas are still small and sweet.

PISELLI AL PROSCIUTTO
Peas with Prosciutto

3 pounds peas in their shells (12 ounces or 3 cups shelled)
3 tablespoons extra virgin olive oil
1 small onion, chopped
salt and freshly ground black pepper
1/2 cup water
2 ounces *prosciutto,* cut into 2-inch strips
1 rounded tablespoon chopped parsley

1. Shell the peas and set aside.

2. Heat olive oil and sauté onion until soft but not brown. Stir in peas, salt, and pepper. Add water and let cook uncovered until peas are nearly tender and water has reduced by half.

3. Add *prosciutto* and parsley. Check seasonings and when peas are tender, put into a warmed bowl. Serves 4 or 5.

This tasty preparation of peas goes well with a simply flavored main dish such as baked fish. It should not compete with a heavily flavored dish or sauce.

PISELLI E SCAGLIONI
Peas and Scallions

2 tablespoons extra virgin olive oil
2 1/2 tablespoons sliced scallions
1/4 teaspoon black pepper
10 ounces fresh or frozen shelled peas
salt
1/4 cup water

1. Heat olive oil and sauté scallions with black pepper until scallions are golden but not brown.

2. Add peas, salt, and water. Cook until peas are done. If using fresh peas, cover and check to see that there is sufficient water in the pan while peas are cooking. Frozen peas take only 2 or 3 minutes to cook. Serves 3 or 4.

The assortment of large, colorful peppers combined with tomatoes provides an attractive and tasty dish.

PEPERONI AI POMODORI
Peppers with Tomatoes

3 tablespoons extra virgin olive oil
1 clove garlic, peeled and halved lengthwise
1/8 teaspoon dried, crushed, hot red pepper
3 large peppers, 1 red, 1 yellow, and 1 green, seeded and cut into strips
1 cup peeled and chopped Italian tomatoes, fresh or canned
salt

1. Heat the olive oil in a large skillet and add the garlic pieces. When the garlic begins to color, add the dried red pepper.

2. When the dried pepper turns a shade darker, add the fresh pepper strips. Sauté the peppers, stirring occasionally, until they begin to brown and are about half done. Add the tomatoes and salt.

3. When the mixture comes to a boil, reduce heat and let simmer until peppers are cooked through. Add a little water if the sauce becomes too dry. Serves 4.

These versatile filled peppers can be used as a first course or side dish, and can be eaten hot, at room temperature, or cold. It is important to use small, sweet frying peppers. Our favorites in the United States are the Melrose peppers grown in the vicinity of Chicago. Traditionally, in Naples, the peppers are served with the Christmas Eve dinner.

PEPERONI PICCOLI IMBOTTITI
Filled Small Peppers

16 to 18 small frying peppers
2 cups fresh Italian bread crumbs
1 large clove garlic, mashed
1 teaspoon *oregano*
1 can anchovy fillets packed in olive oil, coarsely chopped, plus the oil from the can
5 tablespoons extra virgin olive oil
1 1/2 tablespoons red wine
vinegar
salt and pepper

1. Prepare peppers by cutting out stem ends, seeds, and membranes without breaking peppers.

2. Combine bread crumbs, garlic, *oregano,* anchovies with the olive oil from the can, 2 tablespoons of additional olive oil, vinegar, salt, and pepper. Fill peppers with the bread-crumb mixture.

3. Heat the remaining 3 tablespoons of olive oil in a large skillet and fry the peppers on all sides until lightly browned and cooked through. Serves 6 to 8.

Italians have found many ways to incorporate greens into their diet because of their healthful and flavorful elements. This dish is exceptionally tasty using the *broccoli di rape* or *rapini* greens.

PURE DI PATATE AL BROCCOLI DI RAPE
Mashed Potatoes with Broccoli di Rape

1 pound *broccoli di rape* or *rapini* greens
2 pounds potatoes, peeled and cubed
3 cloves garlic, peeled and cut in quarters lengthwise
1/3 cup extra virgin olive oil
a pinch of dried, crushed red pepper
3 tablespoons potato water
salt

1. Clean *broccoli di rape* and cut off the tough ends of the stems. Wash well, drain, and cut in 2-inch lengths. Put a pan of salted water to boil. When it boils, drop in the greens and just blanch them for 2 or 3 minutes. Drain and set aside.

2. Boil the potatoes in lightly salted water until tender. Drain, saving some of the water. Mash potatoes, but do not add anything to them. Set aside.

3. In a large skillet, lightly brown garlic pieces in the olive oil. Add the red pepper and let it darken slightly. Add the greens to the skillet and sauté them until they are tender. Add salt.

4. Add the mashed potatoes to the skillet and continue to mix and mash and turn until everything is well combined. Add a little potato water to keep mixture moist. Check salt. Serves 4 to 6.

This extraordinary treatment of mashed potatoes is prepared especially well by my sister Rosemary. It is attractive, full of flavor, and takes little time to prepare.

PURE DI PATATE AL CRESCIONE
Mashed Potatoes with Watercress

1 pound potatoes (about 4 medium)
1/3 cup extra virgin olive oil
1 chopped onion
salt and pepper
1 bunch watercress, thick stems removed and coarsely chopped

1. Peel potatoes, cube them, and boil in lightly salted water until tender. Drain.

2. Meanwhile heat oil in a skillet, add onion, and sauté until golden and soft, but do not brown. Add salt and pepper.

3. Add potatoes to onion and over low heat, mash and stir until well incorporated. Add watercress. Continue to turn and stir until watercress is limp but still retains its bright color. Check seasonings and serve immediately to 4.

Peppers preserved in vinegar and added to mashed potatoes with garlic and olive oil make a very tasty side dish and go especially well with pork or rabbit cooked with pickled peppers.

The recipes for pork and rabbit and pickled peppers are included in this book. See the index. Also, the mashed potatoes are very good with only the olive oil and garlic.

If you do not wish to preserve the peppers, you can buy Progresso brand peppers in vinegar, or another brand that does not add sugar. Add some *oregano* and a clove of garlic to the jar, and let it stand for a couple of weeks.

PURE DI PATATE ALL'AGLIO E PEPERONI SOTT'ACETO
Mashed Potatoes with Garlic and Pickled Peppers

6 large Idaho-type potatoes, peeled and cubed
1/3 cup extra virgin olive oil
3 cloves garlic, peeled and quartered lengthwise
a few small pieces of peppers preserved in vinegar, i.e., about 1/2 bell pepper
or 2 cherry peppers (optional)
salt

1. Cover potatoes in lightly salted, boiling water and cook until done. Drain and mash the potatoes without adding anything.

2. In a large skillet, heat olive oil and brown the garlic. Add pepper pieces, and fry them for a few minutes. Add the mashed potatoes and salt. Mix well and continue to mash and turn potatoes, with a spatula, until mixture is blended and well-flavored. Serve hot to 4.

In the northeast region of Trentino-Alto Adige, high in the Alps, the cooking is largely Austro-German. Potatoes, sauerkraut, *polenta,* and dairy products are staples.

PATATE ALLA TRENTINA
Potatoes with Fontina Cheese

1 onion, chopped
2 tablespoons extra virgin olive oil
1 tablespoon butter
2 large potatoes (1 pound), peeled and cut in 1/4-inch slices
salt and pepper
1 cup skim milk
2 ounces *Fontina* cheese, thinly sliced

1. In a skillet, sauté onion in olive oil and butter until golden and limp. Add potatoes and continue to fry until vegetables begin to brown.

2. Season the potatoes well and add the milk. Bring to a boil, reduce heat to low, cover skillet, and cook about 20 minutes or until potatoes are tender, milk has evaporated, and potatoes form a cake. If milk has not evaporated, turn up the heat and cook potatoes without a cover for a few minutes.

3. Distribute the cheese evenly over the potatoes, reduce heat, cover pan again, and cook about 2 minutes until cheese melts. Serves 3 or 4.

Well-flavored mashed potatoes blend with the cheeses and Italian sausage in a tempting potato cake which can be served as a main dish or as a side dish. It is important to buy a good quality, fresh, lean sausage.

TORTINO DI PATATE
Potato Cake

2 pounds potatoes
6 ounces fresh Italian sausage
2 ounces *prosciutto,* cut into small pieces
2 eggs, beaten
1/4 cup milk
1 cup grated *Parmigiano Reggiano* cheese
8 ounces *mozzarella* cheese, diced
2 ounces sharp *provolone* cheese, cut into small pieces
salt and pepper
2 tablespoons extra virgin olive oil

1. Boil potatoes with their skins until they are tender. Peel the potatoes, mash them well, and put them into a large bowl.

2. Remove the casing from the sausage and sauté gently while breaking the sausage meat into small pieces. Drain and cool.

3. Add eggs and milk to the potatoes and beat them until light and fluffy. Stir in the sausage, *prosciutto,* 3/4 cup of the *Parmigiano, mozzarella, provolone,* salt, and pepper. Mix well and put mixture into an oiled, round baking dish.

4. Smooth the surface and cover with olive oil. Sprinkle the remaining 1/4 cup of grated cheese evenly over the top and bake in a preheated, 350° F. oven for 40 to 50 minutes until the top is golden brown. Cut into wedges and serve to 6 as a main dish and 8 as a side dish.

In Italy vegetables are enjoyed not only roasted, but also cooked on a grill over hot coals. Italian roasted vegetables are now the rage in Britain.

VEGETALI ARROSTITI
Roasted Vegetables

1/2 cup extra virgin olive oil
2 cloves garlic, peeled and mashed
1/4 teaspoon *oregano*
1 teaspoon chopped fresh rosemary
1 teaspoon chopped fresh sage leaves
1 large onion, peeled and cut in wedges
1 pound new potatoes, scrubbed and cut in halves
2 peppers, 1 red and 1 yellow, cored, seeded and ribs removed, quartered lengthwise
1 long, thin eggplant, trimmed at the ends, halved crosswise and cut into wedges
2 *zucchini,* 5 or 6 inches long, trimmed at the ends and halved lengthwise
salt and pepper

1. Preheat oven to 400° F.

2. Combine olive oil, garlic, *oregano,* rosemary, and sage in a shallow bowl. Pass the vegetable pieces through the mixture and arrange, if possible, in a single layer on a large baking dish.

3. Dribble the remaining oil and herbs over the vegetables and sprinkle with salt and pepper. Put into the hot oven.

4. Bake 20 minutes and turn vegetables. Bake another 20 minutes or until vegetables are tender. If grilling them, place vegetables between a hinged grate and cook over hot coals or under the broiler. Serves 4 to 6.

Among the many benefits of growing *zucchini* and other summer squash in the garden are the beautiful and delicious, golden flowers that these plants produce. The male flowers grow alone on a stem, and the female flowers have tiny *zucchini* attached. Both are excellent for this recipe. A filling may be inserted in the flowers.

FIORI DI ZUCCHINI FRITTI
Fried Zucchini Flowers

1/2 cup flour
salt and pepper
2 eggs
3 tablespoons water
1/4 cup extra virgin olive oil
16 *zucchini* flowers

1. Season the flour on a flat dish.

2. Season the eggs, add the water, and beat until frothy in a shallow bowl.

3. Heat the olive oil in a large skillet over moderately high heat.

4. Rinse the *zucchini* flowers inside and out and dry on paper towels. Dust the flowers and stems and baby *zucchini,* if attached, with the seasoned flour. Shake off excess flour and pass through the egg mixture.

5. Fry in the hot oil until golden on one side. Turn and fry the other side. When golden brown on both sides, remove to paper towels to drain.

6. Serve while hot to 4 to 6.

Variation: FIORI DI ZUCCHINI RIPIENI—*Filled Zucchini Flowers*

Prepare a mixture of grated *mozzarella* cheese, a little chopped *prosciutto,* and a little of the beaten eggs to moisten filling. Stuff some of the mixture into the flowers before dipping them into the flour and egg. Fry and serve hot.

Santo Spirito, Florence

This vegetarian family recipe is attractive, has a tempting aroma, and always causes the partakers to exclaim on its good flavor. My sister Nancy prepares it frequently with eggplant as well as *zucchini* for her husband, Mort, and their three children. It can be a main dish or a side dish.

ZUCCHINI AL FORNO IMBOTTITI
Baked Zucchini Sandwiches

3 *zucchini* (1 3/4 to 2 pounds each)
2 cups dried bread crumbs
4 eggs, lightly beaten
1/2 cup or more grated, *pecorino Romano* cheese
salt
dash black pepper
4 heaping tablespoons finely chopped parsley
1 large clove garlic, peeled and halved lengthwise
4 tablespoons extra virgin olive oil
1/8 teaspoon dried, crushed red pepper
2 cups Italian plum tomatoes, finely chopped, fresh or canned

1. Slice *zucchini* about 3/8-inch thick, salt, and stack on a plate.

2. Prepare filling by combining breadcrumbs, eggs, 1/4 cup of the cheese, salt, pepper, and 3 heaping tablespoons of the parsley.

3. Prepare tomato sauce: sauté garlic in 2 tablespoons of the olive oil until lightly browned. Add red pepper, swirl around in the oil, and then add tomatoes. Let sauce cook 30 minutes. Sauce should not be too fluid. Add the remaining tablespoon of parsley and salt and cook sauce 5 minutes longer.

4. Dry the *zucchini* slices and spoon about a tablespoon of filling on a slice of *zucchini,* top with another slice, and press together to form a *zucchini* sandwich. Continue to make sandwiches with remaining *zucchini* slices and filling.

5. Heat remaining olive oil in a large frying pan. Put sandwiches in pan without crowding them and fry on both sides until lightly browned. Remove from pan, add more sandwiches, and continue to fry until all sandwiches have been browned. Add oil as necessary to complete frying.

6. If using eggplant instead of *zucchini* for the sandwiches, brush the eggplant sandwiches with olive oil and broil until lightly browned. Eggplant absorbs too much oil when fried.

7. To assemble, spoon very little tomato sauce on the bottom of a large baking dish to barely cover. Place sandwiches in one layer, side-by-side, over tomato sauce. Spoon a scant tablespoon of tomato sauce over each sandwich and sprinkle with grated cheese.

8. Place another layer of sandwiches on the first, close together, and top with more sauce and cheese. If there are any sandwiches remaining, make one more layer.

9. Bake at 350° F., uncovered, about 30 minutes until tender. Test with fork for doneness. Serves 8 to 10. It is an appreciated left-over the next day.

Any kind of pepper, hot or sweet, may be pickled. Bell peppers, seeded and cut into strips, work well and are decorative if you mix the colored peppers. They make a delicious *antipasto* when made into a salad with or without olives.

PEPERONI SOTT'ACETO
Peppers Preserved in Vinegar

distilled vinegar
water
salt
bell peppers or cherry peppers
garlic, peeled
oregano

1. Boil a mixture of half vinegar and half water, lightly salted, for 5 minutes and cool.

2. To prepare bell peppers, wash and dry them, remove stems, seeds, and membranes, and cut into wide strips. Leave the washed and dried cherry peppers whole with stems intact.

3. Fill clean, quart-size jars almost to the neck with peppers. Place a whole clove of garlic in each jar. Add 1 teaspoon of *oregano* and 1 teaspoon salt.

4. Pour the vinegar solution over peppers to fill the jars. Put lids on jars and store in refrigerator. Turn jars over once a week, for a few minutes, to distribute flavors. Top with more vinegar solution, if necessary, to keep peppers immersed in vinegar.

5. They will be ready in about 4 weeks and will last a year or longer.

6. To use, remove the peppers from the vinegar solution and place in a shallow bowl. Dribble with olive oil and add salt, pepper, and a little *oregano*. Add Italian olives if desired.

Note:

Whole cherry peppers, red and green, not only look attractive, but are useful when preparing tasty dishes. Pork chops fried with peppers, and potatoes mashed with peppers and garlic in olive oil are two examples. Look in the index for these recipes.

For this dish use small, thin, very hot peppers, if available. If not, use any fresh hot peppers. They are excellent served with *spaghetti,* on sandwiches, or with any dish that would be enhanced with hot peppers.

PEPERONI PICCANTI SOTT'OLIO
Fresh Peppers Preserved in Olive Oil

2 cups small, green, fresh, hot peppers
1 stalk celery, chopped
2 large garlic cloves, peeled and sliced
1 teaspoon *oregano*
salt
extra virgin olive oil

1. Use rubber gloves and scissors to cut the peppers in 1/4-inch lengths.

2. Spread the cut peppers on a tea towel to absorb some of the moisture and leave overnight.

3. Put the peppers into a bowl and make a salad with the remaining ingredients.

4. Fill small, clean jars to 1/4 inch below the neck with the pepper mixture, making sure that each jar has a couple of pieces of garlic, and cover completely with olive oil. Put lids on jars and let sit on a counter for 2 weeks.

5. Refill jars to cover peppers by 1/8 inch with olive oil and place in refrigerator.

6. After using some peppers from a jar, top with fresh olive oil, if necessary, to be certain that the peppers are completely covered with the oil. This will prevent mold from forming. The peppers will last a year or longer if always covered with oil.

These very hot, colorful peppers are usually put on the side of a dish to be eaten with the food as a condiment. They add interest to *pasta* dishes, *pizza,* or any dish where hot pepper is desired. They do not need refrigeration and will last over a year if they always are covered with oil.

PEPERONI ROSSI E SECCHI SOTT'OLIO
Dried, Hot, Red Peppers in Olive Oil

extra virgin olive oil
dried, red, hot, crushed peppers

Mix olive oil into the crushed peppers and place in small jars. Cover with olive oil 1/4 inch or more over the top of the peppers.

Le Insalate
Salads

Green salad (*Insalata Verde*) heads the list of salads as the one most eaten in Italy. There are many salad greens available in the open air markets. One can buy a variety of leaf lettuces, baby *arugula,* baby dandelion greens, endives, and the favored elongated-leaf *radicchio* of Treviso. Other ingredients, such as tomatoes, cucumbers, and peppers, can be added to one or more of these greens to prepare a mixed salad (*Insalata Mista*). Tomatoes selected for salads are firmer and lighter red than the riper tomatoes used for a sauce.

More elaborate salads, such as a seafood salad (*Insalata di Mare*) or a chicken salad (*Insalata di Pollo*), are popular but usually are served as *antipasti*.

Dressing a salad is simple. Italians use their most fragrant extra virgin olive oil and one of their wine or balsamic vinegars, together with salt and freshly ground black pepper.

Facing page: Oranges, Cinque Terre

Asparagus salad is enjoyed especially in spring when the new, tender asparagus is available. It makes a delightful *antipasto* simply dressed with fresh lemon juice and olive oil, freshly ground black pepper, salt, and if desired, shavings of *Parmigiano Reggiano* cheese.

INSALATA DI ASPARAGI
Asparagus Salad

24 asparagus spears
2 tablespoons extra virgin olive oil
juice of 1/2 lemon
salt
freshly ground black pepper
1/4 cup slivers of *Parmigiano Reggiano* cheese, optional

1. Snap off the woody ends of the asparagus spears. Peel about 2 inches of the butt ends.

2. Steam asparagus spears 10 to 12 minutes or until they are tender but still bright green.

3. Arrange asparagus on a platter and dribble with olive oil and lemon juice. Add salt and pepper. If desired sprinkle with slivers of *Parmigiano* cheese. The salad may be served at room temperature or chilled to 4.

This bright green, tempting salad must have freshly squeezed lemon juice and a subtle, fresh garlic flavor to be at its best. In Italy, this salad is more likely to be prepared with *broccoli di rape* or *rapini* greens. However, my mother used the typical American *broccoli*. It is delicious with both.

INSALATA DI BROCCOLI
Broccoli Salad

1 large bunch *broccoli* (about 4 stalks), cut into flowerettes
1/4 cup extra virgin olive oil
2 tablespoons fresh lemon juice
salt and pepper
1/2 of a small clove of garlic, mashed

1. Steam *broccoli* until tender but still bright green, about 10 minutes and put into a salad bowl.

2. Combine olive oil, lemon juice, salt, pepper, and garlic. Stir well and pour evenly over *broccoli*.

3. Toss salad and refrigerate until chilled or serve at room temperature to 4. Check seasonings before serving.

A salad of crisp, colorful, and nutritious carrots is always inviting. It is easy to prepare.

INSALATA DI CAROTE
Carrot Salad

5 carrots
4 tablespoons extra virgin olive oil
1 1/2 tablespoons fresh lemon juice
salt and pepper
chopped parsley for garnish

1. Peel and grate the carrots thinly.

2. Add olive oil, lemon juice, salt, and pepper. Mix well.

3. Top with chopped parsley and serve to 4.

4. The carrots also are delicious peeled, steamed until tender and cut into pennies. Use the same dressing for the cooked or raw carrots.

This sprightly salad has a striking appearance with the white cauliflower, red pepper, and black olives. It was often part of our Christmas Eve feast.

CAVOLFIORE ALL'INSALATA
Cauliflower Salad

1 cauliflower, trimmed and cut into flowerettes
4 fillets of anchovies, cut in 1/2-inch pieces
15 black Italian olives, pitted and quartered lengthwise
2 tablespoons drained capers
1 or 2 red cherry peppers packed in vinegar, cored, seeded, and cut in small pieces
salt and pepper
4 tablespoons olive oil
2 tablespoons red wine vinegar

1. Steam cauliflower until tender but not falling apart. Cool and put into a salad bowl rubbed with a piece of garlic.

2. Add remaining ingredients and toss. May be served at room temperature or cold. Serves 4.

The fresh mint and vegetables combined with the extra virgin olive oil dressing makes this a delightful salad. It keeps well for three or four days in the refrigerator. It may be served as a first course or as a side dish and also may be carried to picnics.

INSALATA DI FAGIOLINI E PATATE
Green Bean and Potato Salad

 2 pounds fresh green beans, topped, tailed, and cut in 1-inch lengths or longer
1 pound new potatoes
1/4 cup, loosely packed, chopped, fresh mint leaves
4 tablespoons extra virgin olive oil
3 tablespoons red wine vinegar
1 large clove garlic, mashed
salt
freshly ground black pepper

1. Steam beans until cooked through but not overdone. Drain and put into a large salad bowl.

2. Meanwhile, boil potatoes. When done, cool, peel, and cut into bite-size cubes. Add to the salad bowl along with the chopped mint.

3. Combine olive oil, vinegar, garlic, salt, and pepper. Pour over salad and mix well. Cover bowl and place in refrigerator. After about 30 minutes check seasonings and mix again. Serve to 6 or more.

This versatile and healthful potato salad may be served warm, at room temperature, or chilled. Lemon juice or wine vinegar may be used for the dressing. It is an especially flavorful accompaniment to fish.

INSALATA DI PATATE
Potato Salad

1 1/2 pounds red or baking potatoes
2 tablespoons finely chopped sweet onion, e.g., Vadalia or Texas 1015, or scallions
15 *Gaeta* black olives, pitted and quartered
1 rounded tablespoon of chopped parsley
salt
freshly ground black pepper
3 tablespoons extra virgin olive oil
juice of 1/2 lemon or 1 tablespoon of wine vinegar

1. Boil potatoes whole until cooked through. Peel while hot, cube the potatoes, and put them into a salad bowl.

2. Add the onion, olives, and parsley. Sprinkle with salt and pepper.

3. Dribble the oil and lemon juice or vinegar over the potatoes and toss well. Serves 4 to 6.

In the Florentine restaurants this salad is frequently featured during the summer months. For an elegant *antipasto,* the salad may be topped with caviar.

INSALATA DI FAGIOLI AL TONNO
Bean and Tuna Salad

1 1/2 cups dry *cannellini* or great northern beans or 2 cans beans
1/4 cup purple onion or other type sweet onion, e.g., Vidalia or Texas 1015, thinly sliced
1 7-ounce can tuna fish, preferably Italian packed in olive oil
1/4 cup extra virgin olive oil
1 tablespoon fresh lemon juice
1 rounded tablespoon capers
2 rounded tablespoons fresh parsley, chopped
salt
freshly ground black pepper

1. Sort through dry beans, rinse and put into a saucepan with about 2 inches of water over the top of the beans. Bring to a rolling boil. Boil 1 or 2 minutes while skimming off the foam, remove from heat, cover, and let beans rest for 2 hours. Bring them to a slow boil and cook gently until tender, but not mushy, approximately 45 minutes.

2. Drain the cooked beans and put them in a bowl to cool. If using canned beans, rinse in cold water, drain, and put into a bowl. Add the onion.

3. Add the tuna with the oil from the can and break tuna into chunks.

4. Add olive oil, lemon juice, capers, parsley, salt, and pepper. Mix the salad gently but thoroughly. Serves 4 to 6 as an *antipasto* or a light lunch.

This salad should be prepared in summer when tomatoes and peppers are just out of the garden. Green frying peppers are my preference, but large green or yellow peppers also combine well with the tomatoes.

INSALATA DI POMODORI E PEPERONI
Tomato and Pepper Salad

3 ripe tomatoes, cut in wedges
2 small frying peppers or 1/2 large green or yellow pepper, stems, ribs, and seeds removed, cut in bite-size pieces
8 leaves of fresh basil, torn
salt and freshly ground black pepper
3 tablespoons olive oil

Combine in a salad bowl tomatoes, peppers, basil, salt, and pepper. Dribble olive oil over and gently toss salad. Serves 4.

A salad of greens is the most popular salad in Italy. It usually follows the main course but is sometimes served as a side dish with the meat or fish. In Italy there are many varieties of salad greens that produce a tasty and interesting salad. In the United States we also are finding a greater selection of greens such as *arugula, radicchio,* and mixed wild greens.

A red wine vinegar usually is used in the dressing, but Italians also enjoy balsamic vinegar combined with their extra virgin olive oil. Balsamic vinegar is made only in Modena and is aged for many years in wooden casks. It has a rich sweet-and-sour flavor.

INSALATA VERDE
Green Salad

6 cups of bite-size pieces of a salad green or an assortment of greens
3 tablespoons extra virgin olive oil
1 tablespoon wine vinegar, balsamic vinegar, or a blend of wine vinegar and balsamic vinegar
salt and freshly ground black pepper

1. Put the salad greens in a large bowl. Dribble the olive oil and vinegar over, sprinkle with salt and pepper, and toss well. There should be enough dressing to coat the greens but none left in the bottom of the salad bowl.

Variation 1: INSALATA MISTA—*Mixed Salad*

Use the recipe above, but instead of greens alone, put together 6 cups greens and other salad vegetables, sliced. You may use tomatoes, cucumbers, fennel bulb, radishes, yellow or red peppers, green onions, celery, or whatever you find in season.

Variation 2: INSALATA VERDE CON L'ARANCIA—*Green Salad with Orange*

Use the above recipe for *insalata verde* but add an orange which has been peeled, the pith removed, quartered lengthwise, and sliced.

The tasty *Rivano* extra virgin olive oil is the choice of oil in this fresh, combination salad of Liguria. If you cannot find it, however, you may substitute another extra virgin olive oil. This substantial salad may be served as a light luncheon or supper or as an *antipasto*.

CONDIGGION
Mixed Salad of Liguria

1/2 clove garlic, to rub over salad bowl
2 large, firm, ripe tomatoes, cut into wedges
1 stalk celery, sliced
1 small, thin cucumber, sliced thinly
1/2 yellow pepper, sliced
1 spring onion, sliced
8 black olives, pitted and halved
3 fillets of anchovy packed in olive oil, cut in pieces
3 ounce can of tuna packed in olive oil, flaked
1 hard boiled egg, peeled and cut in thin wedges
1 rounded tablespoon of flaked *Parmigiano Reggiano* cheese
1 teaspoonful fresh *oregano,* chopped
6 basil leaves, torn
salt
freshly ground black pepper
3 tablespoons *Rivano* extra virgin olive oil
1 tablespoon red wine vinegar

1. Rub the salad bowl well with the garlic and discard the garlic. Put into the bowl all the ingredients, except egg, oil, vinegar, and *Parmigiano* cheese.

2. Sprinkle salad with salt and pepper. Dribble the oil and vinegar over the salad. Toss lightly and garnish with egg wedges and *Parmigiano* cheese. Serve to 4.

Dandelion greens are in abundance. They are not difficult to find, but it takes time to go out in fields to collect them. The long-leafed chicory, in the dandelion family, are found in farmers' markets, and even in supermarkets in Syracuse, New York, where I live. I sometimes buy these and cook the outer leaves with beans and use only the tender center leaves for salad. More often, I go out in fields in springtime and pick only the new tender dandelion leaves. I find it worth the time and effort to collect these in order to prepare this delicious salad.

In the Florentine farmers' markets, the young, tender, wild dandelion greens are readily available, carefully picked, and ready for the salad bowl.

INSALATA DI CICORIA
Dandelion Salad

6 cups young, tender, wild dandelion leaves, lightly packed
2 large cloves garlic, peeled and quartered
5 fillets of anchovy, packed in olive oil, cut in 1/2 inch lengths
salt and freshly ground black pepper
3 tablespoons extra virgin olive oil
3 tablespoons red wine vinegar

1. Put the dandelion greens in a salad bowl. Scatter the garlic and anchovy pieces over the salad.

2. Add salt and pepper, olive oil, and vinegar. Toss well and chill for 1 hour or longer. Toss salad again and check seasonings. You may remove garlic pieces if desired. Serves 4 or 5. Italian bread always accompanies this salad.

Zucchini alla Scapece is a salad or *contorno* (side dish), made from fried *zucchini* slices. It can be flavored with fresh mint when available, but parsley or fresh *oregano* can also be used. It is a popular dish in Campania.

ZUCCHINI ALLA SCAPECE
Fried Zucchini Salad

1 1/2 pounds *zucchini,* cut in 1/4-inch slices
3 tablespoons extra virgin olive oil for frying
salt and pepper
1 tablespoon extra virgin olive oil for dressing
1 tablespoon red wine vinegar
1 small clove garlic, mashed
2 heaping tablespoons chopped, fresh mint leaves

1. Sauté the slices of *zucchini* in hot oil until lightly brown on both sides. Salt and pepper, and with a slotted spoon remove to a plate.

2. Prepare a dressing with the olive oil, vinegar, garlic, salt, and pepper.

3. Layer the *zucchini* slices in a shallow bowl, spooning a little dressing and some mint over each layer. Cover bowl and cool. Refrigerate and serve the following day. It may be served cold or at room temperature. Serves 4.

In every coastal town in Italy you will find a version of seafood salad. They all rate good to excellent. This is a favorite of mine, and the selected seafood can be found in most good fish markets. If you cannot find all the seafood from this selection or if you prefer other kinds, it does not matter. Just use what is available or what you like.

INSALATA DI MARE
Seafood Salad

12 clams
12 mussels
12 shrimp
2 small squid
1 red bell pepper (optional)
4 small new potatoes (optional)
about 15 black *Gaeta* olives, pitted and halved
6 scallops
1/2 pound swordfish, cod, orange roughy, or other firm, white fish
1 tablespoon capers, drained
salt
freshly ground pepper
1/4 cup extra virgin olive oil
2 tablespoons fresh lemon juice (1/2 lemon)
1 clove garlic, mashed
1 rounded tablespoon chopped parsley

1. To clean clams and mussels, scrub them with a brush under cold running water, put them in a large bowl of cold, salted water, and sprinkle with a little cornmeal.

2. Rinse the shrimp in their shells and set aside. Try to buy squid already cleaned but, if they are not, remove the head, clean out the insides, and run under cold water while removing the outer membrane. The squid should be white when clean. Cut the tentacles in small pieces and set aside.

3. Place the pepper about 3 inches under the broiler and turn frequently until all the pepper is charred. Place in a paper bag, close it, and let the pepper stay there until it is cool enough to handle. Remove skin from pepper. Cut out stem, ribs, and seeds, and cut pepper into squares. Put pepper squares in a bowl.

4. Boil the potatoes until tender. Peel, slice, and add to the bowl.

5. The *Gaeta* olives are easy to pit if you hit each one with the bottom of a cup or glass, or with a mallet. The pit slips out easily. Halve the olives and put into the bowl with the peppers.

6. Put 1 cup of water to boil in a large skillet. When boiling, add drained clams and mussels in a single layer. Cover and let cook about 5 minutes until shells open and clams are done. Remove clams and mussels from their shells and put into the bowl with the peppers and olives. Put the liquor from the shells back into the skillet. Discard any clams or mussels that do not open.

7. Put skillet back over element to boil liquid. When it is boiling, add shrimp, squid, and scallops. Cook 2 or 3 minutes or until shrimp and squid are just cooked through and shrimp are pink. Do not overcook. Remove shrimp and reserve. Remove squid and scallops with a slotted spoon, cool, and add to the bowl. Peel and devein shrimp and add to the bowl.

8. In remaining liquid cook fish. Add a little water to the skillet if necessary. Cook until fish is cooked through, but not overdone. Remove from skillet onto a cutting board to cool. Remove and discard skin, bones, and dark meat. Cut fish into bite-size pieces and add to the bowl.

9. Add capers, salt, and pepper. Combine olive oil, lemon juice, and mashed garlic in a measuring cup. Beat with a fork and pour evenly over seafood salad. Mix salad carefully and refrigerate for two hours or more.

10. Before serving, adjust seasonings, and turn out, attractively, on a serving plate. Sprinkle with parsley. Serve with homemade-type Italian bread. Serves 4 to 6.

Granseole are large spider crabs found only in the Adriatic and regarded as a great delicacy in Venice. When cooked, the shells turn bright red and are used as containers for the salad. When *granseole* are not available, the meat from other crabs or crab legs may be used. Lump crab is especially delicious. If the shells are not available, the crab meat may be piled on a bed of salad greens as in the following recipe.

INSALATA DI GRANSEOLA
Crab Meat Salad

1/2 cup extra virgin olive oil
juice of 1 lemon
6 ounces mixed salad greens
salt and freshly ground black pepper
8 ounces crab meat
2 tablespoons chopped parsley

1. Combine the olive oil and lemon juice and pour about a third of it over a bowl of mixed salad greens. Add salt and pepper and toss well. Divide the dressed salad greens among 4 salad plates.

2. Pour another 1/3 of the dressing over the crab meat. Add the parsley, salt, and pepper. Mix well and spoon the crab meat on each plate of salad greens. Dribble the remaining dressing over each serving. Top with salt and pepper. Serve to 4.

This healthful salad, with whole-wheat Italian bread, makes a delightful, light lunch. You may use leftover boiled chicken if you have some on hand.

INSALATA DI POLLO
Chicken Salad

1 whole chicken breast or 2 halves
3 cups water
1/2 onion
a few celery leaves
3 sprigs parsley
salt and pepper
2 tablespoons raisins
1 pale-green inner stalk of celery, sliced
2 tablespoons extra virgin olive oil
1 1/2 tablespoons fresh lemon juice
romaine lettuce or endive

1. Boil the chicken breast in the water with onion, celery leaves, parsley, salt, and pepper until chicken is just cooked through and tender. Do not overcook. Remove from heat and let chicken cool in the broth.

2. Remove and discard skin and bones from chicken and set chicken meat in the refrigerator until completely cooled. Cut chicken breast into cubes.

3. Soak raisins in a little lukewarm water for 5 minutes, then drain. Combine cubed chicken, raisins, and sliced celery.

4. Whisk the olive oil, lemon juice, salt, and pepper. Drizzle dressing over chicken and toss. Spoon chicken salad onto lettuce or endive and serve to 4.

Panzanella, also called *Pan Molle,* is the famous bread salad featured in many of the Florentine restaurants in summer. The recipe comes from the Renaissance period before tomatoes were introduced to Italy, so I can imagine that it was a salad made of bread and onions with perhaps other vegetables.

These days you sometimes see the addition of tuna or anchovies, which could turn the salad into a light meal. It is essential that you use a homemade-type Italian bread, which will not turn mushy when soaked in water.

PANZANELLA
Bread Salad

1/3 pound stale or dried in the oven, homemade-type Italian bread
3 large, tasty, ripe tomatoes, cut in thin wedges
1 small, thin cucumber, peeled, halved lengthwise, and sliced
2 heaping tablespoons finely chopped sweet onion
10 black olives, pitted and quartered
10 basil leaves, torn
salt
freshly ground black pepper
1/4 cup extra virgin olive oil
1 tablespoon wine vinegar

1. Slice the bread, place in a bowl, and cover with cold water. Let stand for 15 minutes. Squeeze as much water out of the bread as possible, shred the bread, and put it into a salad bowl.

2. Add to the salad bowl the tomatoes, cucumber, onion, olives, basil, salt, pepper, and olive oil. Toss well and chill until ready to serve.

3. Just before serving, add vinegar, check seasonings, and toss again. Serves 4.

Relaxing on the Ponte Vecchio, Florence

Il Pane e la Pizza

Bread and Pizza

Bread is truly the "staff of life" in Italy. It is always on the table during a meal, and it is the basis for the Italians' simple breakfast of *caffe latte* and bread.

The Italian homemakers usually do not bake bread or even prepare a *pizza*. There are bakeries everywhere, and even most other food shops offer excellent breads, freshly baked and available at a reasonable cost.

The many *pizzerias* have wood-fired ovens, and they produce a fresh and flavorful *pizza* to be eaten on the spot or carried home. There is no reason to bake *pizza* at home. The recipes in this book come from a time when bread and *pizza* were home-baked.

Facing page: Head of Constantine, Rome

Tuscan bread is unusual, even in Italy, because of its lack of salt. It has a hard crust and a soft, yet textured, hearty center.

PANE TOSCANO
Tuscan Bread

2 packages of dry yeast (1/4 ounce each)
1/2 cup unbleached natural bread flour
1/2 cup warm water
5 cups unbleached natural flour
1 cup whole-wheat flour
approximately 2 cups warm water
cornmeal for baking

1. Prepare a sponge, in a small bowl, by combining yeast, 1/2 cup of unbleached bread flour and 1/2 cup of warm water. Cover bowl with plastic wrap and let sit for 3 or 4 hours at room temperature.

2. Combine unbleached and whole-wheat flours in a large bowl. Make a hollow in the center and add the sponge and the warm water. Mix with a wooden spoon or hands until a soft, sticky dough is formed.

3. Scrape the dough onto a well-floured pastry board and knead vigorously with the palms of your hands in a folding and pushing motion. Continue to add flour to the board as needed until dough is smooth and no longer sticks to hands. Kneading process takes about 10 minutes.

4. Place dough in a large, oiled bowl, rub some olive oil over it, cover with plastic wrap and a towel, and put in a warm place away from drafts. Let it rest until dough doubles in bulk, about 1 hour.

5. Punch down dough and divide in half. Form each half into a long loaf or into rounds and place 4 or 5 inches apart on a baking sheet, sprinkled with cornmeal. Cover loaves with a tea towel and allow to rise until doubled in bulk.

6. Preheat oven to 450° F. When ready to put loaves into the oven, first make a few slashes across the top of the loaves, using a very sharp knife or razor blade. Bake for 35 minutes or until well browned. Yields two 2-pound loaves.

My mother always provided homemade bread for us. This is an old family recipe
which I learned from her, and which she learned from her mother. Minor changes
have been made over the years but it is basically the same as that brought from Italy.
My grandmother made her yeast at home and always kept a starter for the next batch.
My mother used fresh and sometimes dried commercial yeast, and she always found the best,
natural, unbleached flour obtainable for bread making.

My grandmother would take her risen loaves to the local baker who would permit her to put
them into his wood-fired ovens after he finished the day's baking. Her hot loaves would be
brought home to be enjoyed by my grandfather and their seven children.

The original recipe is double the amount given below. I usually prepare the
double amount and freeze the extra loaves.

PANE DELLA NONNA
Grandma's Bread

2 1/2 teaspoons active dry yeast or 1-ounce cake of fresh
1/8 teaspoon sugar
3 cups warm water (110° F.)
2 1/2 pounds or 8 cups unbleached all-purpose flour
1 1/2 tablespoons salt
1 1/2 tablespoons extra virgin olive oil

1.Dissolve yeast and sugar in 1/2 cup of the warm water in a 1-cup measuring cup and let stand about 5 minutes or until foamy.

2. Combine flour and salt in a large bowl and make a well in center of the
flour. Add yeast mixture, 1/2 tablespoon of the olive oil and remaining 2 1/2
cups warm water to the well.

3. With one hand mix ingredients, gradually bringing in small amounts of
flour at a time, until dough is formed. Drizzle 1/2 tablespoon of olive oil on
bottom of bowl and over top of dough. Knead dough in the bowl until
smooth and elastic and no longer sticky, about 10 minutes.

4. Form the dough into a ball and spread the remaining olive oil over the ball of dough on all sides. Cover dough with plastic wrap and a kitchen towel and let rise in a warm place, free from drafts, until doubled in bulk, 1 to 2 hours. Punch down dough with fists, turn out on a floured board, and knead briefly.

5. Grease 2 (9 x 5-inch) loaf pans. Divide dough into 2 equal parts. Shape dough into loaves and place in pans. Cover and let dough rise until it reaches tops of pans.

6. Preheat oven to 350° F. Bake bread 50 minutes to 1 hour or until crust is golden brown and bread sounds hollow when tapped on bottom. Remove from pans and cool loaves on a rack. Butter tops of loaves while still hot, if desired. The loaves freeze well if double wrapped with plastic wrap and a freezer bag. Yields two 2-pound loaves of bread or two 1 1/2-pound loaves of bread and one 12 to 14-inch *pizza*.

Variation:

Set aside about 1 pound of dough for *pizza* (page 356).

This is an adaptation of my mother's bread recipe. It is very much like hers but makes whole-wheat loaves. I usually double this recipe and freeze the extra loaves.

PANE INTEGRALE
Whole-Wheat Bread

2 1/2 teaspoons active dry yeast
1/8 teaspoon sugar
3 1/3 cups warm water (110° F.)
1 1/2 pounds stone ground, whole-wheat flour (about 5 cups)
1 pound unbleached bread flour (about 3 1/2 cups)
1 1/2 tablespoons salt
1 1/2 tablespoons extra-virgin olive oil

1. Dissolve yeast and sugar in 1 cup of the warm water in a 2-cup measuring cup and let stand about 5 minutes or until foamy.

2. Combine flours and salt in a large bowl. Make a well in center of flour and set aside. Add yeast mixture, 1/2 tablespoon of the olive oil, and remaining 2 1/3 cups lukewarm water to well.

3. With one hand mix ingredients, gradually bringing in small amounts of flour at a time, until dough is formed. Drizzle 1/2 tablespoon of olive oil on bottom of bowl and over top of dough and knead dough in the bowl until smooth and elastic and no longer sticky, about 10 minutes.

4. Form the dough into a ball and spread the remaining olive oil over the ball of dough on all sides. Cover dough with plastic wrap and a kitchen towel and let rise in a warm place, free from drafts, until doubled in bulk, 1 to 1 1/2 hours. Punch down dough with fists, turn out onto a floured board, and knead briefly.

5. Grease two 9 x 5-inch loaf pans. Divide dough into 2 equal parts. Shape dough into loaves and place in greased pans. Cover and let dough rise until it reaches tops of pans. Loaves may also be shaped into long or round loaves and placed on greased baking sheets.

6. Preheat oven to 350° F. Bake bread 1 hour or until crust is golden brown and bread sounds hollow when tapped on bottom. Remove from pans and cool loaves on a rack. The loaves freeze well if double wrapped with plastic wrap and a freezer bag. Yields two 2-pound loaves or two 1 1/2-pound loaves of bread and a 12 to 14-inch *pizza*.

Variation 1:

Set aside about 1 pound of dough for a *pizza* (page 356).

Variation 2:

Add raisins and/or dates and chopped walnuts to one of the loaves.

Whenever I make bread, I set aside some dough for a large recipe makes enough whole-wheat dough for two 12-inch *pizze,* or a flattened bread such as the Tuscan *Schiacciata al Rosmarino.* If you prefer dough using solely white flour, you can still follow this recipe using white flour in place of whole-wheat.

In the following *pizza* recipes I suggest using only one-half of the dough so that you can make two different varieties with this one batch of dough.

PASTA PER LA PIZZA
Pizza Dough

1/2 cup tepid water
1 package dry yeast (7 grams or 1/4 ounce)
1/8 teaspoon sugar
1 1/2 cups whole-wheat flour
2 cups unbleached bread flour
1 teaspoon salt
1/2 cup plus 3 tablespoons tepid water
1 tablespoon plus 1 teaspoon extra virgin olive oil

1. Put 1/2 cup tepid water into a 1-cup measuring cup and add the yeast and sugar to proof the yeast. Stir to dissolve yeast and let it sit a few minutes until it develops a heady froth.

2. In a bowl, combine the flours and salt and make a well. Pour the yeast mixture, tepid water, and 1 tablespoon of the olive oil into the well.

3. Mix with one hand, bringing the flour gradually into the liquid ingredients. Knead with both fists, bringing dough up from the bottom, punching it down, and bringing up more dough to be punched down again.

4. Knead for about 10 minutes or until dough is smooth and elastic. If dough is too sticky, you may add a little flour. If too dry, add a little water. Form dough into a ball.

5. The dough also may be made in a food processor by combining flours and salt in the bowl, and while motor is running, add the yeast mixture, water, and oil. It takes only about 20 seconds to process.

6. Rub the remaining 1 teaspoon of olive oil over the ball of dough and around the bowl. Cover with plastic wrap and let rise about 30 minutes. Punch down and let rise again until dough has doubled in bulk. Makes two 12-inch *pizze*.

We cannot really make the true *Pizza Napoletana,* as they do in the *pizzerie* of Naples, unless we have a wood-fired *pizza* oven. We can come close to it, however, with our electric or gas ovens. This recipe is the true *Pizza Napoletana,* and the others are variations on this theme.

PIZZA NAPOLETANA
Pizza of Naples

1/2 recipe of *pizza* dough, using white flour, for one 12-inch *pizza*
1 cup peeled, seeded, chopped, and drained tomatoes, fresh or canned
1 clove garlic, thinly sliced
1/2 teaspoon dried *oregano* (Italians rarely use the fresh.)
salt and pepper (I use the crushed, dried red pepper.)
3 tablespoons extra virgin olive oil

1. Preheat oven to 400° F.

2. Flatten the dough. You may do this with your hands and even throw it around your fist if you like, but do not drop it, or you may roll it out with a rolling pin to about 1/4-inch thickness. Line a 12-inch, well oiled, *pizza* pan with the dough and make an edge.

3. Combine the tomatoes and garlic and distribute evenly over the *pizza.* Sprinkle with *oregano,* salt, and pepper. Dribble olive oil over all and put *pizza* in the oven. Bake for 20 to 25 minutes or until crust is golden brown. Take a peek under the *pizza* to be sure that the under crust is coloring. Do not let under side or top become overly brown.

Pizza Margherita, named for Queen Margherita di Savoia who once reigned over the Kingdom of Naples, remains the most popular of the *pizze.* One rule in Naples, which invariably is followed, is that *oregano* and cheese are never combined on *pizza* or in any other dish.

PIZZA MARGHERITA
Pizza with Mozzarella

1/2 recipe of *pizza* dough
1/3 pound *mozzarella,* thinly sliced
1 cup peeled, seeded, and chopped tomatoes, drained, fresh or canned
1 clove garlic, finely chopped or mashed
2 teaspoons chopped fresh basil
salt and pepper
2 tablespoons grated *pecorino Romano* cheese
2 tablespoons olive oil

1. Preheat oven to 400° F.

2. Stretch out the *pizza* dough with hands or with a rolling pin to about 1/4-inch thickness. Fit it into an oiled 12-inch *pizza* pan and make an edge.

3. Distribute the *mozzarella* slices evenly on the dough.

4. Combine tomatoes with garlic and basil. Spoon evenly over the *mozzarella.* Sprinkle with salt, pepper, and grated cheese. Dribble olive oil over all and pop into the oven.

5. Bake for 20 to 25 minutes or until the crust is nicely browned. Peek under the crust to see that the bottom is lightly browned. Serve immediately. Makes one 12-inch *pizza.*

Variation: PIZZA MARGHERITA BIANCA—*White Pizza Margherita*

The recipe follows a similar procedure but eliminates the tomatoes.

This *pizza* is fun to make because you can use your imagination for interesting toppings. Two thin strips of dough are put over the *pizza* to form a cross and to make four separate areas for the varied toppings.

The four toppings for this recipe are: (1) topping for *Pizza Margherita;* (2) anchovy and olive; (3) fried peppers and sausage; and (4) mushroom. You also may use clams, mussels, *prosciutto, salami,* or marinated artichoke hearts. Any of these toppings may be expanded to cover a whole *pizza*. I prefer making two of these *pizze* at one time because it is too much trouble for only one.

PIZZA ALLE QUATTRO STAGIONI
Four Seasons Pizza

1/2 recipe of *pizza* dough (If making 2, use 1 recipe of dough.)
1 cup grated *mozzarella* cheese, divided into thirds
2/3 cup peeled and chopped tomatoes, drained
1 teaspoon chopped basil leaves
salt and pepper
1/2 tablespoon grated *pecorino Romano* cheese
9 teaspoons extra virgin olive oil
2 fillets of anchovy
1/4 clove garlic, peeled and thinly sliced
6 black olives, pitted and quartered lengthwise
oregano
1 green pepper, cored, seeded, and cut into thin strips
2 ounces lean Italian sausage, sliced
1 clove garlic, peeled and halved lengthwise
1/4 pound fresh mushrooms, sliced
1 tablespoon chopped parsley

1. Cut off a little dough to make two 12-inch strips. Roll them to pencil thickness. Spread out the remaining dough to fit a 12-inch round *pizza* pan. Place the strips of dough over the *pizza* to cross in the center, leaving 4 areas for toppings. If making 2 *pizze,* double recipe and use 2 12-inch *pizza* pans.

2. In one quarter of the *pizza,* scatter 1/3 cup of the grated *mozzarella* cheese. Put on top of that 1/3 cup of the tomatoes combined with basil leaves. Sprinkle with salt, pepper, and grated *pecorino Romano* cheese. Dribble a teaspoon of olive oil over the quarter of the *pizza.*

3. For the second quarter, cut the anchovy fillets in small pieces and place them evenly on the dough. Place also slices of the quarter clove of garlic and the olives. Add very little salt, pepper, and *oregano.* Dribble with 2 teaspoons of olive oil.

4. For the third quarter, fry the pepper, sausage, and half of the clove of garlic, in 2 teaspoons of olive oil until tender. Drain and cool. Put on the third section of the *pizza* 1/3 cup of the *mozzarella,* the fried peppers and sausage, 1/4 cup of the tomatoes, salt, pepper. Dribble with 1 teaspoon of olive oil.

5. For the fourth quarter, fry mushrooms in 2 teaspoons olive oil and the remaining 1/2 clove garlic, over high heat, until browned. Add parsley, remaining tomatoes, salt and pepper. Remove from heat and cool. Put 1/3 cup grated *mozzarella* in the 4th area. Add mushroom mixture and 1 teaspoon of olive oil.

6. Put *pizza* into preheated, 400° F. oven for 20 to 25 minutes. Lift the crust slightly to see if it is browning underneath. Serve hot. Makes one 12-inch *pizza.* You may repeat this procedure for a second *pizza.*

This is a rolled *pizza,* filled with peppers, tomatoes, and *mozzarella.* My mother made this one frequently, doubling this recipe, because it was a family favorite. She preferred the small Italian frying peppers but, when unavailable, used bell peppers.

PIZZA ROTOLO AI PEPERONI
Rolled Pizza with Peppers

about 12 to 15 small frying peppers or 3 large bell peppers
1 tablespoon extra virgin olive oil
1 clove garlic, peeled and halved lengthwise
3/4 cup peeled, seeded, and chopped Italian plum tomatoes, fresh,
if in season, or canned
salt
1/8 teaspoon dried, crushed red pepper
1/2 recipe *pizza* dough
1/4 pound *mozzarella,* thinly sliced

1. Core and seed bell peppers and cut into strips, lengthwise. With small peppers, if seeds are very small, halve peppers and leave the seeds intact.

2. Heat olive oil and fry peppers and garlic until lightly browned. Add tomatoes, salt, and red pepper. Cook until peppers are tender and tomatoes have cooked down. This should not be soupy or dry. Remove from heat, discard garlic, and cool.

3. Roll out *pizza* dough in a rectangle about 1/4-inch thick, with the long edges at the top and bottom of the rectangle.

4. Spoon pepper mixture over *pizza* dough leaving a border at the long edge at the top of the *pizza.* Cover peppers with *mozzarella* and roll from the long, bottom edge without the border, ending with the border edge at the top.

5. Pinch the top and the ends closed and place the *pizza* roll on a floured baking sheet making a crescent shape. Stab the *pizza* roll in a few places along the top with a pointed sharp knife to let steam escape. Cover with a tea towel and let rise for 45 minutes.

6. Bake in a preheated, 375° F. oven for 45 to 55 minutes until nicely browned. Slice and serve hot. Makes one 12-inch *pizza*.

Variation: PIZZA ROTOLO ALLE OLIVE CONDITE—*Olive Salad*

Another filling for a tasty rolled *pizza* is made with *salami,* ham, sliced cheeses, and pitted and quartered olives in a salad.

This *pizza* is simple but very aromatic and tasty.

PIZZA AGLIO E OLIO
Pizza with Garlic and Olive Oil

1/2 recipe of *pizza* dough
6 to 8 anchovy fillets packed in olive oil, optional
2 cloves garlic, peeled and sliced thinly
salt and pepper
1 teaspoon dried *oregano*
3 tablespoons extra virgin olive oil

1. Line a 12-inch *pizza* pan with the *pizza* dough. Make impressions with fingertips, evenly over the dough, about 1 inch apart.

2. Cut the anchovy fillets in 1/2-inch lengths and place them in some of the impressions. Place the garlic slices in other impressions.

3. Sprinkle *pizza* with salt, pepper, and *oregano*. Dribble with olive oil and spread evenly over the surface with fingers or brush.

4. Bake in a preheated, 400° F. oven for 20 to 25 minutes or until *pizza* is golden and under the crust is browning. Serve hot. Makes one 12-inch *pizza*.

The Tuscan *schiacciata,* flattened bread, is tasty but very simple. It usually has a rosemary topping with coarse salt, but sometimes it is plain. It is great for sandwiches, cut in squares, opened and fillings put between the two pieces of bread.

SCHIACCIATA AL ROSMARINO
Flattened Tuscan Bread with Rosemary

1 recipe of *pizza* dough
extra virgin olive oil
1 tablespoon of fresh rosemary
coarse salt

1. Spread the dough about 1/2 inch thick on an oiled rectangular baking sheet and make indentations over the top with fingertips.

2. Dribble olive oil generously over the top, sprinkle with rosemary and coarse salt. Let rise about 30 minutes and bake in a preheated 400° F. oven for approximately 25 minutes or until golden brown and the bottom of the crust is lightly browned. Makes the equivalent of two 12-inch *pizze.*

Calzone, made from folded-over *pizza* dough, contains a variety of fillings.
This version is the most typical.

CALZONE NAPOLETANA
Filled Pizza with Ricotta and Mozzarella Cheeses

1/2 recipe of *pizza* dough
1/4 pound *ricotta*
1 small egg
salt and pepper
1 rounded tablespoon grated *pecorino Romano* cheese
1/8 pound *mozzarella,* diced
1/8 pound Italian *salami* or *prosciutto,* cut into small pieces

1. Divide dough in half and roll out 2 rounds about 1/4-inch thick.
Place them on a lightly oiled baking sheet.

2. Combine *ricotta* and egg in a bowl and beat them until fluffy. Add salt,
pepper, and grated cheese. Stir in *mozzarella* and *salami* or *prosciutto.*

3. Spoon the filling on half of each round, leaving a 3/4-inch border.
Moisten the borders and bring over the other end of the dough, across the
filling, to form a half moon.

4. Press and pinch the edges together to seal each *calzone* completely.
Bake in a preheated, 425° F. oven for 18 to 25 minutes until golden brown.
Serve hot. Makes one 12-inch *pizza.*

Variation 1: CALZONE CON POMODORO—*with Tomato*

Fill with peeled and sliced tomatoes, *prosciutto, mozzarella,* pitted and sliced olives, grated *pecorino Romano,* salt, and pepper.

Variation 2: CALZONE CON SCAROLA—*with Escarole*

Fill with escarole or swiss chard that has been blanched in boiling water and then sautéed in olive oil and garlic with a few pine nuts, raisins, salt, pepper, and perhaps a fillet of anchovy. A little *ricotta* may be added.

The flattened breads have always been a favorite food in Italy. They may be the *focaccia* of Liguria, made with sage or cheese, the *schiacciata* of Tuscany, topped with rosemary and coarse salt, or the *pizza* of Naples. All make excellent sandwiches cut into squares, cut open with interesting fillings inside.

FOCACCIA ALLA SALVIA
Flattened Bread with Sage

1 pound (3 1/2 cups) unbleached bread flour
1 teaspoon salt
1 package (7 grams or 1/4 ounce) dried yeast
1/4 teaspoon sugar
1 cup warm water
1/4 cup dry white wine
4 tablespoons plus 1 teaspoon extra virgin olive oil
1 rounded tablespoon chopped, fresh sage leaves
coarse sea salt

1. Combine flour and salt in a bowl and make a well in the center.

2. Dissolve the yeast and sugar in 1/2 cup of the warm water. When it develops a thick froth, pour it into the well in the flour. Pour remaining warm water, wine, 3 tablespoons of the olive oil, and chopped sage leaves into the well.

3. Mix with one hand gradually working in the flour until you have a soft dough. Knead well with both fists, bringing up dough from the bottom, punching it down, and bringing up more to be punched down again. Knead for 10 minutes or until dough is soft, smooth, and elastic. Make into a ball.

4. Use 1 teaspoon of the olive oil to cover the ball of dough and rub around the bowl. Cover the dough with plastic wrap and a tea towel. Leave the dough to rise for 1 hour or until doubled in bulk.

5. Spread out the dough to cover an oiled, 14-inch round *pizza* pan, or a rectangle baking sheet.

6. Make indentations with the finger tips, about 1 inch apart, all over the dough.

7. Dribble remaining tablespoon of olive oil over surface and spread evenly with fingers or brush. Sprinkle with coarse sea salt. Let *focaccia* rise 30 minutes.

8. Bake in a preheated, 400° F. oven for about 25 minutes or until it is golden brown and the bottom of the crust is lightly browned. Serve hot or at room temperature. Yields about the equivalent of two 12-inch *pizze*.

Variation 1: FOCACCIA CON OLIVE—*with Olives*

Mix into dough 1/3 cup pitted and coarsely chopped, Italian black olives.

Variation 2: FOCACCIA CON POMODORI SECCHI—*with Dried Tomatoes*

Mix into dough 1/3 cup coarsely chopped, sun-dried tomatoes.

These rolls are often used for small sandwiches which are very popular in Italy. My sister Rosemary makes them frequently to have on hand for making sandwiches for breakfast or lunch or for supper as dinner rolls.

PANINI
Bread Rolls

1 recipe *pizza* dough using all white bread flour (food
processor may be used) or 1/2 recipe Grandma's Bread dough (page 352).

1. After dough has risen to double in bulk, roll out the dough on a
well-floured board to about 1/4-inch thick.

2. Cut out rounds of dough with a 3-inch cutter and place them with 1/2
inch of space in between them on greased baking sheets. Cover them with a
towel and let them rise, away from drafts, for approximately 45 minutes.

3. Bake in a preheated oven 350° F. for 20 to 25 minutes or until they are
a light golden color. Remove to racks to cool. The rolls freeze well if
double-wrapped with plastic.

Variation 1:

Prepare sandwiches with any variety of fillings. Rosemary especially likes to use a filling of sautéed mushrooms (page 296) with *asiago* or *mozzarella* cheese over the mushrooms, then broiled briefly, or even a sautéed *Portabello* mushroom with the cheese, broiled.

Variation 2:

Another tasty sandwich filling is to prepare peppers with tomatoes (page 312), then fry or broil Italian sausage, slice the sausage, and place in the *panini* with the peppers and tomatoes.

Other Variations:

Simple fillings, such as a slice of *prosciutto, provolone* cheese, or another tasty Italian cheese, can be delightful.

This *ricotta* and sausage filled *pizza* is prepared every Easter holiday in my family. It comes from my grandmother on my mother's side. It has a tasty filling encrusted in an egg bread dough. It stands 2 or 3 inches high and serves as our Easter breakfast.

PIZZA PER PASQUA DELLA NONNA TENORE
Grandma Tenore's Easter Pizza

2 teaspoons active dry yeast
1/4 teaspoon sugar
3 cups flour
1/2 tablespoon salt
3 eggs
1/4 cup water
1/2 tablespoon olive oil
1 1/2 pounds *ricotta* cheese
1/2 pound lean Italian sausage meat
1/4 pound lean ground sirloin beef
1/2 cup grated *Parmigiano Reggiano* cheese
1/4 cup raisins
salt and freshly ground pepper
1 egg yolk

Prepare bread dough:

1. Dissolve yeast and sugar in 1/2 cup of lukewarm water.

2. Place the flour and salt in the bowl of a food processor. With the motor running, add one of the eggs, water, olive oil, and yeast mixture. Process about 20 seconds or until a dough is formed.

3. Knead dough briefly on a well floured bread board. Cover dough with a light coating of olive oil. Put into a bowl covered with plastic wrap and a towel and let rise until doubled in bulk, about an hour. The method for forming dough may also be done according to directions for Grandma's Bread (page 352) or in a mixer with a dough hook.

PREPARE FILLING:

1. Drain *ricotta* cheese for a few hours or overnight to remove excess moisture. Put *ricotta* into a bowl.

2. Crumble sausage meat into a skillet and sauté until cooked through. Drain on paper towels to remove excess fat. When cool add to the bowl. Add also ground beef, remaining 2 eggs, grated cheese, raisins, salt and pepper.

ASSEMBLY:

1. Oil a 12-inch, round *pizza* pan or a baking sheet. Preheat oven to 350° F.

2. Cut off about 1/2 pound of the dough and set aside. Roll out remaining dough in a 12-inch disk as if for a *pizza* and set on oiled pan. Mound filling on center of dough leaving a 2-inch overhang around edge of filling.

3. Cut off about 1/3 of reserved dough and set aside. Roll out remaining dough into a 6-inch disk and set it on top of the filling.

4. Bring up the sides of the 12-inch disk to meet the edges of the 6-inch disk and pinch all around to enclose filling.

5. Roll, with the palms of your hands, the remaining dough until you have about a 2-foot long rope about the size of your small finger. Place a strip of rope all around the seam of the *pizza*. Form a bow, an initial, or any decoration with the remaining piece of rope.

6. Beat the egg yolk with a teaspoon of water and brush all over the top and sides of the *pizza*. Pierce the top of the *pizza* with a fork in several places so that the *pizza* will not puff.

7. Place *pizza* into the hot oven and bake about 1 hour or until it is golden brown. Serves 8 to 10.

Torta Pasqualina means Easter pie and was prepared at Easter time in Liguria. Now it is enjoyed the year round. The recipe calls for fresh *borage,* but *borage* can be omitted if not available. Several layers of pastry need to be rolled out very thinly. A good time-saver is to use the Greek filo pastry, already prepared. All that is required is to brush each layer of *filo* with olive oil and to keep the pastry from drying out. A puff pastry may also be used.

TORTA PASQUALINA
Easter Torte

8 eggs
1 pound tender beet leaves or swiss chard
1/4 pound fresh *borage* (optional)
1 large clove garlic, peeled and quartered
3 tablespoons extra virgin olive oil
1/2 pound *ricotta* cheese, well drained
3/4 cup grated *Parmigiano Reggiano* cheese
1 rounded tablespoon chopped fresh marjoram
salt and pepper
1 recipe of pastry or ready-prepared *filo* pastry or puff pastry

1. Place 6 of the eggs gently into boiling water to cover. When the water returns to a boil, put a lid on the pan and turn off the heat for 15 minutes. Remove eggs from pan, peel, and set aside.

2. Parboil the beet greens and *borage* just until they become limp. Drain and chop them coarsely.

3. Sauté the garlic in the olive oil until it golden. Add the boiled greens and continue to sauté until greens are cooked through. Season and set aside to let the greens cool.

4. Put into a large bowl the *ricotta* and *Parmigiano* cheeses, the remaining 2 uncooked eggs lightly beaten, marjoram, the reserved greens with the olive oil, salt, and pepper. Mix well and check seasonings.

5. Stack 9 layers of very thinly rolled-out pastry sheets, brushing each with olive oil, to fit into a 9 1/2- to 10-inch, straight-sided, round, cheesecake pan with removable sides.

6. Spoon onto the pastry lining the pan, the greens and *ricotta* mixture. Make 6 hollows in it, including one in the center. Place a cooked egg in each of the hollows and cover with the remaining 9 pastry sheets, brushing each with olive oil.

7. Brush the top of the pie with 1 egg yolk beaten with 1 tablespoon of water. Bake in a preheated, 350° F. oven for 1 hour and 10 minutes or until the top is nicely browned. Serves 8 to 10.

PASTRY:

3 cups flour
1/4 teaspoon salt
1/3 cup olive oil
3/4 cup water

1. Mix the ingredients thoroughly and knead until you make a smooth and soft dough.

2. Cover the dough with plastic wrap and let it sit for an hour or more. Divide the dough into 18 pieces and roll each one into a paper-thin round, large enough to line a 9 1/2- to 10-inch cheesecake pan.

Milan

I Dolci

Desserts

Italian desserts are usually reserved for special occasions. Fresh fruit is always present and, for Italians, takes the place of the formal dessert. At more formal meals fruit is often served as a dessert in the form of fruit salad (*Macedonia di Frutta*).

Sometimes on a Sunday or holiday when the meal is more elaborate and prolonged, a late afternoon dessert will precede a tiny cup of *espresso* coffee.

Italian homemakers occasionally prepare a fine dessert at home, but more often they buy cakes, pastries, and cookies at a local pastry shop (*pasticceria*). The desserts offered in the shops are always freshly baked, free from preservatives, and very flavorful. If invited to a home for dinner, the guest often brings an assortment of pastries and cookies.

Desserts in wide variety are common to all regions of Italy, and each region has its specialties. Sicily, for instance, is renowned for producing the finest pastries, the best known of which are the *ricotta*-filled *cannoli*. Though fine in texture and delicate in flavor, the desserts throughout Italy generally lack the sweetness of those prepared in some other countries. Italians prefer to take their sugar in their *espresso*.

Facing page: Settignano

Fresh fruit is Italy's favorite dessert, and *macedonia,* a mixture of prepared fresh fruits, is a popular way to present Italy's delicious fruits.

MACEDONIA DI FRUTTA
Fruit Salad

8 cups diced or sliced fresh fruit of any combination
1/4 cup sugar
1/4 cup lemon juice
1/4 cup *Marsala* wine

1. Layer fruit in bowl with sugar, lemon juice, and *Marsala.* Chill in refrigerator. Stir and serve to 8.

Variation: MACEDONIA CON ZABAIONE

Prepare *zabaione* according to the following recipe and serve over fruit salad. Top dessert with a few crushed *amaretti* cookies.

Zabaione, also spelled *zabaglione,* is world renowned, and one of northern Italy's special desserts. It can be eaten warm or cold and served as a topping over a variety of other desserts including *macedonia* or pastries.

ZABAIONE
Marsala Wine Sauce

6 egg yolks
1/3 cup sugar
3/4 cup *Marsala* wine

1. Put egg yolks and sugar in the top of a double boiler (not over heat). Beat until thick and pale colored. Stir in the *Marsala.*

2. Set the pan over barely simmering water, taking care that the water does not touch the bottom of the pan. Continue to beat until the *zabaione* warms, rises in the pan, and is thick and fluffy.

3. Pour into stemmed glasses and serve warm with dry *biscotti di savoiardi* (Italian ladyfingers) or it may be chilled. Serves 4 to 6 in the glassware, or 8 to 10 over fruit or pastries as suggested above.

Cream caramel has to be considered an international dessert now because it is found in so many parts of the world. It is delicious, not overly sweet, and easy to prepare.

CREMA AL CARAMELLO
Cream Caramel

4 cups milk
3 whole eggs
4 egg yolks
1 cup sugar, divided in half
1/2 teaspoon vanilla

1. Preheat the oven to 300° F. Place a pan of very hot water into the oven that will accommodate the mold in which the custard will be baked.

2. Bring the milk to a boil in a heavy-bottomed pan and boil very gently, stirring often, until milk has reduced to 3 cups. Strain milk and cool.

3. Beat together the whole eggs, the 4 yolks, 1/2 cup of the sugar, and the vanilla until mixture is smooth and foamy. Blend the cooled milk into this mixture.

4. Put the remaining sugar into a saucepan with 1 tablespoon of water and heat, while stirring, until sugar melts and begins to color. Remove from heat. The color will continue to deepen from the hot pan. It should be a medium brown. Do not allow the sugar to become dark brown. Pour the caramel into a 1- to 1 1/2-quart mold (a ring mold works well) or into individual molds, tipping the mold to coat the bottom evenly.

5. Carefully pour the milk and egg mixture into the mold over the hardened caramel. Set the mold into the pan of hot water in the oven so that the water comes about 1/2 way up the sides of the mold.

6. Bake for 1 hour or when knife inserted in the center emerges clean. Lift the mold out of the pan of water, allow to cool to room temperature, and then chill in the refrigerator.

7. To turn out, first run a sharp knife around the edges to loosen, then place a serving dish over the mold, and invert the mold onto the serving dish with a quick snap of the wrists. Remove the mold. The custard looks very attractive with the caramel on the top and trickling down the sides to the plate. Serves 6.

Basket maker, Siena

This delightful, molded dessert is served in small quantities plain, with various accompaniments or sauces, or flavored with coffee. Donatella Nicolais, from the Naples area, who shared her recipe, prefers it flavored with coffee.

PANNA COTTA
Cooked Cream Mold

1 teaspoon unflavored gelatin
2 teaspoons water
1 cup heavy cream
1/4 cup milk
2 tablespoons sugar

1. Sprinkle the gelatin over the 2 teaspoons water in a small cup or bowl to swell the gelatin.

2. Combine cream, milk, and sugar in a saucepan. Cook over medium heat, stirring with a wooden spoon, until mixture comes to a boil.

3. Remove pan from heat and add the swollen gelatin. (You may add also 1 or 2 teaspoons, or to taste, of *espresso* coffee powder if you would like it to be coffee flavored.) Stir the mixture to dissolve the gelatin and let mixture cool.

4. Butter four 3-ounce ramekins or a small ring mold. Pour the mixture into the ramekins or ring mold. Place them on a tray and cover with plastic wrap. Refrigerate until set, about 5 hours or longer.

5. To serve, briefly dip each mold in hot water, run a knife around the sides of the ramekins or ring mold, place a serving plate on top and invert the plate and mold. Shake the mold to release the *panna cotta* onto the plate.

6. I love this just plain, but it also is wonderful with a few fresh berries set around it. Some like to spoon chocolate sauce or fruit sauce around the plate. This dessert can be made the day before you plan to serve it. Serves 4.

Mascarpone, the Italian cream cheese, is the basis for many desserts.
This easy to do dessert, from Mantova, seems light and fresh at the end of a meal.

COPPETTE DI MASCARPONE AL LIMONE E LAMPONI
Lemon-Flavored Mascarpone with Raspberries

8 ounces *mascarpone*
5 tablespoons sugar
2 tablespoons fresh lemon juice (juice from 1 lemon)
2 tablespoons heavy cream
4 thin, plain, crisp vanilla or butter cookies
about 1 teaspoon brandy or cognac
1 cup fresh raspberries (4 ounces)
1 tablespoon sugar

1. Combine *mascarpone,* sugar, and lemon juice. Add cream and beat until light and fluffy.

2. Place a cookie on the bottom of each of 4 small dessert bowls. Sprinkle 1/4 teaspoon of brandy on each cookie. Spoon *mascarpone* mixture evenly over the cookies and refrigerate.

3. Rinse the raspberries quickly. Do not soak in water. Drain well and put into a small bowl. Stir 1 tablespoon of sugar into the raspberries and refrigerate.

4. Just before serving dessert, remove from the refrigerator and spoon raspberries over each portion. Serves 4.

The popularity of the sensational dessert *Tiramisu,* meaning "pick me up," has quickly spread through Europe and the United States. A newcomer to Italian desserts, it was invented by a chef in Treviso in the Veneto region of northern Italy about forty years ago. As a result, *mascarpone,* the Italian cream cheese, is available not only in Italian grocery stores but in supermarkets as well.

There are now many versions of this recipe. This one was given to me by Marissa, the cook for the Contessa Federica di Picalomini in Florence.

TIRAMISU
Mascarpone, Coffee, and Chocolate Dessert

2 extra-large eggs, separated
1/2 cup sugar
4 tablespoons rum or brandy
8 ounces *mascarpone*
1/2 teaspoon vanilla
1/3 cup espresso coffee
6 ounces *biscotti di savoiardi* (crisp Italian ladyfingers)
1/4 cup cocoa
1 cup heavy cream
3 ounces bittersweet chocolate, grated (optional)

1. Combine egg yolks and sugar in the top of a double boiler, not over heat, and beat until pale and thick. Stir in 2 tablespoons of the rum or brandy.

2. Set over hot water, not quite simmering, and whisk until thickened, about 5 minutes. Remove from heat and cool.

3. Beat the *mascarpone* and vanilla into the cooled mixture and reserve.

4. Beat egg whites until they hold stiff peaks and set aside.

5. Whip the cream until thick and set aside.

6. Combine remaining 2 tablespoons of rum or brandy with the coffee. Quickly dip each *biscotti* into the mixture and line a 6-cup glass serving dish with half of the moist *biscotti*. Reserve the other half of the dipped *biscotti*.

7. Stir any remaining coffee mixture into the *mascarpone* mixture. Fold in the beaten egg whites and the whipped cream.

8. Spoon half the *mascarpone* mixture into the *biscotti*-lined dish. Sprinkle with half of the cocoa. Place the remaining *biscotti* evenly over the cocoa and spoon the remaining *mascarpone* mixture over them, smoothing the top.

9. Sieve the remaining cocoa over the top. Cover bowl with plastic wrap and refrigerate 3 hours or longer. Before serving, you may sprinkle the top with grated chocolate. Serves 6.

The fresh strawberry flavor dominates in this beautiful dessert which combines the delicate *mascarpone* cheese and fresh strawberries over the plain *savoiardi* cookies. It can be assembled in a large glass bowl or in individual glass dessert bowls.

COPPA AL FRAGOLE E MASCARPONE
A Bowl of Strawberries and Mascarpone

1 pound strawberries plus 8 strawberries for garnish
1 cup sugar
1/2 pound *mascarpone* cheese
2 teaspoons fresh lemon juice
2 teaspoons *Marsala* wine
8 or more *savoiardi* cookies (Italian ladyfingers)

1. Wash the strawberries and remove green tops from all except the eight reserved for decoration. Put those with tops removed into food processor bowl. These also may be mashed by hand.

2. Add sugar to the strawberries in the food processor and process until well-chopped but not pureed. Let strawberry mixture sit for a few minutes, then strain from it about 1/4 cup of the juice, and pour into a shallow bowl. Add lemon juice and *Marsala* to the strained strawberry juice.

3. Quickly dip the *savoiardi* into the juice mixture and line the bottom of the bowl with them. Cut some in halves and place around the side of the bowl. If using individual bowls, place 1 of the *savoiardi*, broken in half or in pieces to fit on the bottom of the bowl. Spoon any remaining juice mixture over *savoiardi*.

4. Drain off and discard any liquid that may have accumulated from the *mascarpone*, and then add the *mascarpone* to the strawberry mixture in the food processor. Process until thoroughly blended. Pour mixture into a large bowl or individual bowls lined with *savoiardi*. Cover and refrigerate 5 hours or longer. Decorate with reserved strawberries and serve 6 to 8.

You must use totally bitter chocolate for this dessert to be at its best.
It is rich, so you should serve small quantities.

COPPETTE DI MASCARPONE AL CIOCCOLATA
Mascarpone with Chocolate

8 ounces *mascarpone*
6 tablespoons sugar
4 tablespoons light cream
1/2 teaspoon vanilla
6 plain, crisp vanilla or butter cookies
1 1/2 teaspoons brandy or cognac
2 ounces (squares) bitter baking chocolate
6 tablespoons light cream

1. Combine *mascarpone,* sugar, 4 tablespoons light cream, and vanilla. Beat until light.

2. Place a cookie on the bottom of 6 small dessert bowls or cups and sprinkle about 1/4 teaspoon of brandy over each cookie. Divide the *mascarpone* mixture among the 6 bowls and flatten the tops. Refrigerate for at least 1 hour.

3. Shortly before serving, melt the chocolate with the 6 tablespoons of cream. Stir over a low fire until mixture is smooth and thick like a chocolate frosting. Remove from the fire and cool for a few minutes.

4. Remove desserts from the refrigerator. Spread a teaspoon of chocolate over the center of each dessert, leaving a ring of *mascarpone* around the edge of the chocolate disk. Serve to 6.

I have always been fond of rice pudding, but this version is my favorite. Try to find the Italian *Arborio* rice when preparing this recipe. It makes a great difference.

BUDINO DI RISO
Rice Pudding

1 1/2 cups *Arborio* rice
6 cups water, lightly salted, boiling
4 cups milk (2 percent), lightly salted
1/2 cup sugar
2 eggs
1 teaspoon vanilla
zest of 1 lemon
3 tablespoons raisins

1. Stir the rice into the boiling water and let it cook 5 minutes. Drain and reserve. Preheat oven to 350° F.

2. Bring milk to the boil, stir in the rice, and cook, stirring often, until the liquid has been absorbed by the rice and there is a nice, creamy consistency.

3. Remove rice from the heat and add the sugar. Beat the eggs and vanilla and stir into the rice with the lemon zest and raisins.

4. Pour mixture into a buttered baking dish and set the dish into a pan of hot water (not boiling). Set on a rack in the oven and bake 1 hour.

5. Cool and serve to 6. Pass a pitcher of cold milk to pour over the pudding. You may also serve it with sliced and sugared strawberries or raspberries, or run the sugared berries through a food processor and make a berry sauce to pass at the table.

In the summer when peaches are in season, this flavorful, light dessert is frequently served in the Piemonte area of Italy. The peaches should be ripe, sweet, and juicy. The *amaretti* are crisp macaroons made with bitter almonds. They are found in Italian grocery stores and in many special foods stores. The most common are in the attractive, red tins under the trade name of *Lazzaroni di Saronno.*

PESCHE RIPIENE AGLI AMARETTI
Peaches Filled with Amaretti Macaroons

6 peaches
5 *amaretti* macaroons (about 2 ounces)
2 tablespoons blanched, slivered almonds
3 tablespoons sugar
1/2 teaspoon cocoa
2/3 cup white wine

1. Preheat the oven to 375° F. Peel the peaches. If you dip them briefly in boiling water first, they are easier to peel. Cut them in half and remove the pits. Butter a baking dish and put in the peach halves, cut side up, in a single layer.

2. Scoop out from the hollow of each peach half just a little of the pulp to enlarge the space in the center. Reserve the peach pulp. There should be about 1/4 cup of pulp.

3. Place the *amaretti,* almonds, 1 tablespoon of the sugar, and the cocoa in a food processor. Process with the steel blade until ingredients are finely chopped. Add the peach pulp to the processor and process until well blended.

4. Stuff the peach halves with the macaroon mixture. Pour the wine on and around the peaches. Sprinkle the peaches with the remaining sugar and bake them for about 30 to 35 minutes. Check them periodically, especially near the end of the baking time, to be sure that the liquid does not dry up and continues to cover the bottom of the dish. Serve hot or cold to 6.

The Easter dove usually is baked in a cake pan in the shape of a dove, but if you do not have one it may also be baked in a 9 1/2-inch springform pan. This is a specialty of Milan but now can be purchased elsewhere in Italy and abroad. I believe the homemade cake is superior.

LA COLOMBA
Dove Cake

3/4 ounces dry yeast (3 packages rapid rise)
4 cups flour
4 egg yolks
a pinch of salt
grated rind of one lemon
1/2 pound (2 sticks) butter at room temperature, cut into small pieces
3/4 cup sugar
1/4 cup warm milk
1/4 cup chopped citron
1/4 cup chopped candied orange peel
1/3 cup golden raisins
20 whole, blanched almonds
1 egg, beaten with 1 tablespoon water
powdered sugar for sprinkling over top of cake

1. Dissolve yeast in 6 tablespoons lukewarm water in a medium-size bowl. Stir in 1 cup of the flour to make a firm dough. Roll into a ball, make a cross on the top with the side of the hand, and drop into a large bowl of lukewarm water.

2. After a few minutes the ball will rise to the surface of the water. Turn it over and let it float for approximately 15 minutes, turning it from time to time. It will expand.

3. Meanwhile put remaining flour into a large mixing bowl. Make a well and add the 4 egg yolks, salt, lemon rind, half of the butter, sugar, milk, and the ball of dough which has been floating in water.

4. Mix very well by hand and knead thoroughly, until smooth and elastic and no longer sticky. Form into a ball, put into a large bowl, cover with plastic wrap and a towel, and set aside for it to rise.

5. When risen by 1/2, put dough on a floured board, flatten a little, and add 1/2 of the remaining butter. Knead thoroughly again, flouring the board as necessary. Place the dough back into the bowl, cover, and let rise again by 1/2.

6. Meanwhile use some of the remaining butter to grease the mold. Then dust mold with flour. You may use the traditional Easter dove mold or a 9 1/2-inch springform pan.

7. When dough has risen again, place on floured board and work in remaining butter, candied fruits, and raisins. Put the dough into the prepared pan and let the dough rise for 30 minutes.

8. Place the almonds evenly over the top, pushing them slightly into the dough. Brush the surface with the beaten egg. Let the dough rest for 5 minutes and then bake in a preheated, 375° F. oven for 10 minutes. Reduce heat to 350° F., cover the cake loosely with foil, and continue to bake an additional hour or hour and 5 minutes until a wooden pick inserted in the center of the cake emerges clean.

9. Cool on a wire rack. Just before serving, sprinkle top with powdered sugar pushed through a sieve. This cake will keep well for a few days. Makes a 9 1/2-inch cake.

Parrozzo is a delicately flavored almond cake with a chocolate icing. It is a specialty of Pescara in Abruzzi. A good quality chocolate should be used for the icing as it is in Italy. I use Dove Bar dark chocolate as a substitute when I cannot find dark Italian chocolate.

PARROZZO
Almond Cake with Chocolate Icing

5 ounces (scant 1 cup) blanched almonds
2 or 3 bitter almonds (optional)
3/4 cup sugar
1/2 cup unbleached flour
1/3 cup potato flour
4 ounces butter
5 eggs, separated
2 teaspoons vanilla extract

ICING PREPARATION:

5 ounces bittersweet chocolate
1 tablespoon butter
1 tablespoon water

1. Grease an 8 1/4-inch layer cake pan and dust with flour. Preheat oven to 350° F.

2. Place almonds with 3 tablespoons of the sugar into a blender jar and blend until reduced to a powder. Set aside.

3. Measure and set aside the unbleached and potato flours. Melt the butter and set aside. Beat the egg whites until stiff. Set aside.

4. In a large bowl beat the egg yolks and vanilla, gradually adding the remaining sugar, and continue beating while you slowly add the almond-sugar mixture. Beat until light and fluffy.

5. Gradually add the flour mixture. The batter will be stiff. Beat in the butter and, lastly, fold in the egg whites.

6. Pour the batter into the prepared cake pan and bake for 40 minutes. The cake will have risen and the top will be firm. Cool the cake for 10 minutes and turn it out on a rack to cool completely.

7. To make the icing, melt the chocolate and butter with the water in the top of a double boiler or place in a microwave oven for a few seconds. Do not overheat the mixture, or the chocolate will lose its gloss.

8. Stir the icing and spread on the top and sides of the cooled cake and decorate with additional whole almonds which have been lightly toasted, or else with chocolate strands. Serves 10.

Torta della Nonna, which means "Grandmother's cake," is one of the favorite pastries in Florence. It has a delicate top and bottom crust. It is filled with a tasty custard and topped with whole almonds.

TORTA DELLA NONNA
Grandmother's Cake

PASTA FROLLA *(Pastry)*:

3 cups flour
1 cup butter, softened a little and cut into small pieces
3/4 cup sugar
2 egg yolks

1. Place flour in a bowl and cut or rub in the pieces of butter until it has the consistency of breadcrumbs.

2. Add sugar and egg yolks. Knead gently until it forms a smooth dough. Cover and let rest in refrigerator 30 minutes.

CREMA PASTICCERIA *(Filling)*:

4 cups milk
2 cups sugar
1 cup flour
4 eggs

1. Bring milk to a boil, stirring occasionally, so that milk does not stick to bottom of the pan or boil over. Remove from heat.

2. Combine sugar and flour in another saucepan. Add eggs, one at a time, mixing well after each is added. Slowly add hot milk while stirring.

3. Put saucepan over heat. Cook, stirring constantly, until custard is thick and begins to bubble. Remove to a bowl to cool. Cover custard so that a crust does not form.

ASSEMBLY:

1 cup whole almonds (Hazelnuts or pine nuts are sometimes used.)

1. Preheat oven to 375° F. Butter and flour a baking sheet. Set aside 2/3 of the dough. With the remaining 1/3 roll out a 10-inch circle.

2. Prick with a fork and bake 10 minutes. Do not let it brown. Cool on the baking sheet placed on a rack.

3. Spoon pastry cream onto baked pastry, leaving a 1-inch border free of the cream.

4. Roll out remaining dough into a 12-inch circle. Cover the cream with the dough. Press dough around the edge to seal.

5. Gently press whole blanched almonds into crust. Bake at 350° F. until golden. Cool on a rack and sprinkle generously with powdered sugar sifted through a strainer. Remove to a serving dish. Makes 8 to 10 servings.

It must be thought that grandfathers are fond of chocolate because
Torta Del Nonno is the chocolate version of *Torta Della Nonna*.

TORTA DEL NONNO
Grandfather's Cake

1. *Pasta Frolla:* use same recipe as for *Torta della Nonna* (page 396).

2. *Crema Pasticceria:* add 3 ounces of melted, unsweetened baking chocolate to the pastry cream.

3. Assembly: when the *torta* is complete with the powdered sugar, sprinkle the top with sifted cocoa.

Italians enjoy fruit at the end of a meal. Pears, stewed in a wine sauce, are a favorite.

PERE SCIROPPATE
Pears in Wine Syrup

5 or 6 ripe Bosc or Comice pears
1 cup sugar
2 cups rose or white wine
1/4 cup water
1 teaspoon fresh lemon juice

1. Peel the pears with a peeler. From the blossom end, core the pears carefully with a paring knife. Leave the stems intact. Use a saucepan in which the pears just fit standing on end. If the pan is too large, add another pear, and if too small, remove one. Take pears out of the pan and set aside.

2. Put the sugar, wine, water, and lemon juice into the pan and stir to dissolve the sugar. Place over moderate heat and bring to a boil.

3. Set pears in the syrup and bring to a boil again. Reduce heat and simmer until pears are tender, about 20 minutes. Remove pan from heat and let pears cool in the syrup.

4. Serve at room temperature or chill, if desired. Serve 1 pear per person with the wine syrup spooned over each. Serves 5 or 6.

Fresh *ricotta* is used in many desserts in all parts of Italy. It is light and blends well with other ingredients. It is especially delightful in this Florentine specialty.

TORTA DI RICOTTA
Ricotta Torte

PASTA FROLLA *(Pastry)*:

3 cups flour
1/2 cup butter, softened a little and cut in pieces
1/2 cup sugar
2 egg yolks

1. Place flour in a bowl and make a well in the center. Add butter, sugar, and egg yolks.

2. Blend all ingredients with your hands, working quickly. Do not over mix.

3. Form dough in a ball, wrap, and place in the refrigerator to rest for 1 hour.

FILLING:

14 ounces fresh *ricotta,* well drained
2 eggs at room temperature, separated
1/4 cup sugar
2 tablespoons raisins, tossed with 1 tablespoon flour
1 tablespoon pine nuts
grated rind from 1 lemon
2 tablespoons orange flower water (optional)

1. Beat *ricotta* until smooth. Beat in egg yolks, one at a time, and then the sugar until well blended.

2. Add the raisins, pine nuts, lemon zest, and orange flower water.

3. Beat the egg whites until stiff and gently fold into the *ricotta* mixture.

ASSEMBLY:

1. Roll out about 3/4 of the dough and line a 9 or 10-inch buttered and floured cheesecake pan with removable bottom. Reserve extra dough for lattice top.

2. Fill with *ricotta* mixture and even out the top. Roll out remaining dough, cut out strips, carefully place them over the filling in an attractive lattice pattern, and trim the *torta*.

3. Brush top with a lightly beaten egg. Bake in a preheated oven at 350° F. for 1 hour. Let cool on a rack for 5 minutes and remove ring from pan. Let cool completely and put on a serving dish. *È squisita!*

The success of this *crostata* depends on finding an excellent quality of sour cherry jam. My favorite is made by Hero, but there are others for this wonderful Roman dessert.

CROSTATA DI VISCIOLA
Cherry Tart

2 1/2 cups unbleached flour
10 tablespoons butter
2/3 cup sugar
3 egg yolks
grated rind of 1 lemon
1 tablespoon fresh lemon juice
pinch salt
13 ounces sour cherry jam
1 egg, beaten

1. Place flour in a bowl and cut or rub in the butter until the mixture resembles breadcrumbs. Add sugar, egg yolks, lemon rind, lemon juice, and salt.

2. Stir in with a fork and quickly knead to a dough. Work the dough as little as possible. Roll the dough into a ball. Wrap in plastic wrap and refrigerate for 1 hour.

3. Roll out about 3/4 of the dough on a floured surface to fit an 11 x 1-inch round tart or flan pan with a removable bottom. Keep remaining dough in the refrigerator.

4. Butter and flour the tart or flan pan and line with the rolled out dough. Spread the jam evenly over the dough. Preheat oven to 375° F.

5. Roll out remaining dough and cut in even strips, about 1/2-inch wide and 10 to 11 inches long. Carefully place the strips in an attractive lattice pattern over the jam and trim the *crostata* neatly.

6. Brush top of *crostata* with the beaten egg. Bake about 40 minutes or until pastry is golden. Cool on a rack for 5 minutes and remove from pan to a serving dish. Cool thoroughly. Serves 8 to 12.

Rome

Antonio Scorza, a scholar from Palomonte, a small town in the mountains inland from Salerno, lives and works in Salerno and, as a hobby, specializes in Italian desserts.
He shares one of his favorites.

I add lemon juice to the recipe, which is not in the original, because American oranges are so sweet. It is not necessary to use the lemon juice if you can find tart oranges.

TORTA DI MANDORLE ALL'ARANCIA
Almond and Orange Torta

1 pound blanched almonds
1 1/2 cups sugar
9 eggs
grated rind and juice of 3 very large oranges
juice of 1/2 lemon
1/2 cup of *Aurum all'arancia* (orange liquor)

1. Preheat the oven to 350° F. Oil and flour a 12-inch, springform, round cake pan, about 4 fingers high.

2. Grind the almonds finely, in 2 batches, with 1/2 cup of the sugar per batch, in a food processor, and set aside.

3. Separate the eggs and beat the yolks until light and creamy. Gradually beat in the remaining 1/2 cup of sugar and then the almonds. The batter will be stiff, but mix it thoroughly.

4. Gradually add the grated rind and the juice of the oranges and lemon and pour in the *Aurum all'arancia*. Mix thoroughly.

5. Beat the egg whites until stiff and fold them into the batter. Pour the batter into the oiled cake pan and bake for 1 hour or until the cake is nicely browned.

6. Remove pan from the oven and cool on a rack. Turn it out onto a plate and decorate with powdered sugar, perhaps with a design, and place a few almonds on top for decoration.

7. You may also, just before serving, add 2 strawberries to the decoration. Slice a large strawberry with a green stem, not all the way through. Fan out the slices and place it in the center. Place the whole strawberry next to it. Serves 12.

Florence

This delicately flavored, moist *torta* is a favorite in Campania where almonds are grown. The almonds should be ground very fine. Grinding them in a blender, a handful at a time with some of the sugar, facilitates the operation.

TORTA DI MANDORLE
Almond Torte

1 pound blanched almonds
1 3/4 cup sugar
4 eggs
1 teaspoon vanilla
1/3 cup butter
3 tablespoons milk
1/4 teaspoon salt
powdered sugar

1. Boil some water and drop in the blanched almonds. Boil for 1/2 minute. Drain and dry in a towel. This facilitates the grinding of the almonds.

2. Grind the almonds with sugar. If using a blender, do a handful at a time with some sugar. If using a food processor, do half at a time, again with the sugar. Put almonds and sugar into a large bowl.

3. Separate the eggs. Put the whites in a bowl where they will be beaten. Add the yolks to the almonds and sugar, stirring it in well. Add the vanilla.

4. Put the butter and milk in a small pan over a low heat until the butter melts. Stir it into the almond mixture.

5. Add salt to the egg whites and beat until stiff. Gently fold them into the batter.

6. Butter and flour a 10 1/2-inch or 11-inch pan 1 1/2 inches high. Pour in the batter and bake in a 350° F. oven for 35 to 40 minutes or until *torta* is golden brown and begins to pull away from the sides of the pan.

7. Cool. Remove to a serving dish and sprinkle with powdered sugar. Serves 12. It keeps well for 3 or 4 days.

Evening, Rome

We always waited with great anticipation for the Christmas holiday treats, which always included the freshly cooked *zeppole* topped with honey and powdered sugar. This is my mother's recipe, which produces, I believe, the best of these wonderful donuts. They should be eaten shortly after they are made.

ZEPPOLE DELLA NONNA
Grandma's Zeppole

4 2/3 cups flour
1/4 ounce of dry rapid rise yeast or 1/2 cake of fresh yeast
1 3/4 cups of lukewarm milk
1 egg
1/2 teaspoon salt
1 1/2 tablespoon vegetable shortening
canola oil or olive oil for frying *zeppole*
honey
powdered sugar

1. Put flour into a large bowl and form a well.

2. Dissolve yeast in 1/2 cup of the warm milk. Let it sit until it foams.

3. Pour the yeast mixture, remaining milk, egg, salt, and 1 tablespoon of shortening into the well. Gradually mix ingredients in the well with the flour using one hand. When well mixed, beat the mixture with the hand. Dough should be soft, but just barely firm enough to handle. Add more flour if too soft, or more milk if too firm.

4. Oil the top of the dough and cover with plastic wrap, and then a tea towel. Let the dough rise about 2 hours.

5. When you are ready to fry the *zeppole,* heat oil in a deep fryer or saucepan to about 350° F. Keep a small dish of oil handy for dipping fingers into while forming donuts.

6. Take a large spoon of dough at a time, shape it into a donut with a hole in the middle, and drop into the hot oil. Fry 2 or 3 *zeppole* at a time, turning them, until lightly browned, and remove to paper towels to drain. Continue to make and fry *zeppole* until all the dough has been used.

7. Arrange *zeppole* on a platter and dribble honey over each one and sprinkle with strained powdered sugar.

These chestnut-filled pastries are enjoyed throughout the region of Campania only at *Natale* (Christmas time). This recipe comes from Oliveto Citra, my father's birthplace. My aunt, Loretta Coglianese, always made them for us at Christmas time. These are also called by the dialect name, *"Caozoncelli,"* and *"Panzarotti di Castagne,"* broken stomachs of chestnuts (broken because you eat too many). Actually, it is a healthful dessert.

PASTICELLI DI NATALE
Filled Christmas Pastries

FILLING:

3/4 pound chestnuts
6 ounces dried pears
1/4 pound shelled hazelnuts
8 ounces good quality bittersweet chocolate
4 tablespoons cocoa
3/4 to 1 cup honey or to taste
grated rind of 1 tangerine
1/3 cup strong espresso coffee
2 tablespoons of an Italian liqueur, such as *Sambuca* or *Strega*

1. Remove outer peeling from chestnuts. If very difficult, try boiling them for 5 minutes. Boil another 2 or 3 minutes to help remove the inner peeling. Boil peeled chestnuts in about 1 1/4 cups of lightly salted water until they are soft. To mash the cooked chestnuts, put them through a ricer, or run them in the food processor. Put them in a large bowl.

2. Cook the pears in a cup of water until they are soft. This may take an hour.

3. Toast the shelled hazelnuts in a preheated 325° F. oven for 10 minutes or until golden brown. Put them in a kitchen towel, rub them in the towel to remove some of the skins. Pulverize the nuts in the food processor or in a blender. If using a blender, add a tablespoon of sugar to facilitate the blending. Put them into the bowl with the chestnuts.

4. Grate the chocolate or finely chop. This is done easily in the food processor. Add to the bowl of nuts.

5. The food processor may also be used to mash the pears.

6. Add the processed pears to the bowl as well as the cocoa, honey, tangerine rind, coffee, and liqueur. Mix well until the filling has a thick, creamy consistency.

PASTRY:

4 cups flour
3/4 cup sugar
4 ounces (1 stick) butter, cut in small pieces
5 eggs (3 whole and 2 yolks only)
2 tablespoons of the same liqueur used in the filling

1. Combine flour and sugar in a large bowl. Work in butter with a pastry blender. Make a well, add eggs and liqueur, and mix them into the flour gradually, with the hands, until a dough is formed.

2. Pastry may also be made in a food processor. Put flour and sugar into the processor bowl. Pulse it a few times. Add the butter pieces and eggs. Run the motor until the dough has formed a ball, about a minute.

3. Knead the dough a few times on a floured pastry board. Cover and let it sit for a few minutes. Roll out the dough, very thinly (thinner than pie crust), with a rolling pin or through the rollers of a *pasta* machine on a medium-thin setting.

ASSEMBLY:

olive oil or canola oil for deep frying
honey
colored sprinkles or powdered sugar

1. Cut the pastry into disks 2 1/2 to 3 inches in diameter. A donut cutter without the center hole or a round cookie or biscuit cutter will work. Put a scant tablespoon of filling on a disk and cover with another disk. Or you may make them smaller by putting the filling in the center and folding one edge of the pastry over to the other to make a turnover.

2. Seal the edges well in a decorative manner. You may make slits around the edges, about 3/8-inch wide making flaps, turning one flap up and the next down all around the pastry, or you may press the tines of a fork around the edge. Put the pastries into the refrigerator. They are chilled before frying.

3. Heat the oil, 2 inches deep in a 2 quart saucepan. When oil is hot, carefully lower 3 *pasticelli* into the hot oil. Fry for 2 or 3 minutes, or until golden. Do not let them become too brown.

4. Lift out, with a slotted spoon, onto paper towels and continue to fry 3 at a time, removing them to the paper towels until all are fried. Cool. These may be frozen if you wish to make them ahead.

5. Just before serving, warm the honey and dribble over the *pasticelli*. Some decorate them with tiny colored sprinkles and some sprinkle with powdered sugar put through a strainer before serving. Makes more than 50.

Cannoli may be the most popular of the excellent pastries of Sicily. They are a tradition at Carnival time, but are enjoyed year-round in many parts of Italy and elsewhere. The shells can be purchased at Italian bakeries or specialty stores and filled at home, but they also can be prepared at home with some equipment. You need to have metal tubes, about 3/4 inch in diameter or 5-inch lengths of wooden dowels. My father has made them out of a well-sanded broomstick. A machine that rolls out *pasta* dough is very useful too.

CANNOLI
Ricotta-Filled Pastries

SHELLS:

2 cups flour
2 tablespoons sugar
pinch salt
1/2 teaspoon cinnamon
1 egg yolk
2 tablespoons shortening
1/2 teaspoon vanilla
1/2 cup white wine
1 egg white
olive oil or canola oil for deep frying

1. Mound the flour on a pastry board and make a well in the center. Put the remaining ingredients, except the egg white, in the well.

2. Incorporate the flour gradually, into the ingredients in the well, with one hand. Knead the dough thoroughly with both hands. The dough should be firm, similar to dough for pasta.

3. Cover the dough with plastic wrap and keep in the refrigerator for several hours.

4. Roll out the dough very thinly and cut into 3 1/2-inch squares. Cover the part of the dough that you are not working on so that it will not dry out.

5. Wrap the squares loosely around the oiled *cannoli* forms diagonally, and seal the 2 corners that overlap with a little of the egg white.

6. Deep-fry 2 or 3 shells at a time in 2 inches or more of hot oil until lightly browned. Turn them as they cook. They will take less than 1 minute to be done. Do not allow them to become too dark.

7. As the cylinders are removed from the oil, tip them to let the oil drain back into the pan. Drain the shells on paper towels and let them cool enough to handle. Carefully slide out the *cannoli* cylinders and continue to form and fry the remaining shells. Makes about 50 shells. These will last for months in an airtight container.

FILLING:

1 pound *ricotta* cheese, well drained
1/2 cup powdered sugar
1/2 teaspoon vanilla
1/4 cup finely chopped citron or mixed candied fruit
2 ounces bittersweet chocolate, chopped (about 1/3 cup). The dark Dove bar chocolate works well and tiny chocolate chips could also be used.

1. The *ricotta* should be fairly dry. Add the powdered sugar and vanilla and beat with an electric beater, at high speed, until light, fluffy, and smooth. If mixture remains too dry, add 1 tablespoon of cream.

2. Stir in citron or other candied fruit. Shake the chopped chocolate in a strainer to eliminate the powdery chocolate. Add the chocolate pieces to the *ricotta* mixture.

ASSEMBLY:

12 *cannoli* shells
1 recipe of *ricotta* filling
1 tablespoon powdered sugar
natural, chopped *pistachio* nuts

1. Fill the *cannoli* shells with the ricotta mixture. This can be done with a small spoon or from a pastry bag fitted with a wide tip. They should be filled shortly before eating so that they do not become soggy.

2. Put a tablespoonful of powdered sugar in a strainer and sprinkle *cannoli* with the sugar. Decorate each end of the *cannoli* with chopped *pistachio* nuts.

Prato, located just north of Florence, is said to be the place where these almond-filled *biscotti* originated. *Biscotti* means "twice baked." The loaves are baked and cut into slices. If the sliced *biscotti* are not sufficiently cooked, they are put back into the oven for a few minutes for a second baking. These *biscotti* are very popular in Florence, served with *Vin Santo* or *Morellino* sweet wine. To conclude a typical Tuscan meal, the hard *biscotti* are dipped into the wine as they are eaten.

BISCOTTI DI PRATO
Almond Cookies of Prato

2 1/4 cups shelled almonds, with skins
4 cups unbleached flour
2 1/4 cups sugar
1 teaspoon baking powder
1/2 teaspoon salt
4 eggs
1 egg yolk (Reserve egg white.)

1. Preheat oven to 350° F.

2. Spread almonds on a baking sheet in a single layer. Bake 5 or 6 minutes until they are slightly toasted. Remove from oven and cool.

3. Heap flour on a pastry board or work surface. Make a well in the center and put into it the sugar, baking powder, salt, eggs, and egg yolk.

4. Mix well with one hand and knead with both hands to a smooth consistency. Work almonds into dough until they all are incorporated.

5. Divide dough into 6 equal parts and form long loaves about 4 fingers wide and 1 finger high. Place loaves, far apart, on buttered and floured baking sheets. Slightly flatten the long edges to form an arched shape.

6. Beat reserved egg white slightly and brush over tops of loaves. Bake 40 minutes or until nicely browned.

7. Remove from oven and immediately slice loaves on the diagonal about 1 finger wide. Turn the slices on their sides and return them to the oven for a few minutes. Watch them carefully so that they do not brown. Turn them once again to toast the other side. They should be golden but not brown and should be dry and hard. Makes about 7 dozen.

Variation: BISCOTTI DI ANICE—*Anise-Flavored Biscotti*

Anise-flavored *biscotti* are very similar to the *biscotti* of Prato. To make them, add to the dough 2 to 3 teaspoons of anise extract or to taste.

For the Christmas holidays my family would prepare large quantities of these delightful treats, topped with honey and powdered sugar. These are made in all regions of Italy and are also called *bugie, frappe, cenci,* and *nodi d'amore.*

CHIACCHIERE
Chatter Cookies

1 pound unbleached flour (3 1/2 cups)
5 1/4 tablespoons sugar
2 tablespoons corn starch
1/2 teaspoon salt
5 tablespoons extra virgin olive oil
4 eggs
canola oil for deep frying

1. To mix the dough, combine dry ingredients and make into a mound. Make a well in the center and pour in the olive oil and eggs. Mix the dough with one hand, gradually bringing the dry ingredients into the mixture. Knead with both hands on a floured board. Cover dough and let rest a few minutes.

2. The dough can also be mixed in a food processor with the plastic blade. Put the dry ingredients into the processor bowl. Run the motor while you add the olive oil and eggs. Process until the dough forms a ball. Knead on a floured pastry board.

3. Roll out very thinly. A *pasta* machine that rolls out dough is helpful. The setting next to thinnest is about right. Cut dough into diamond shapes. Make a one-inch slit in the center of each diamond and slip a long point of the diamond through the slit, carefully.

4. Deep fry until golden but not brown. Drain on absorbent paper.

5. Before serving, arrange cookies on a platter. Drizzle with honey and sprinkle with strained powdered sugar.

Variation: STRUFFOLI—*Neopolitan Christmas Honey Pastry*

Struffoli can be made with the same dough as *Chiacchiere* if the cornstarch is omitted. When the dough is in a ball, cut off a piece at a time and roll it into a pencil-thin log with the palms of the hands. Make these thin logs until all the dough has been rolled. Cut the logs in 1/2 inch lengths and deep fry the little pieces of dough until they are golden. Drain them on paper towels.

Warm some honey in a pan large enough to hold the pastries. Drop the *struffoli* into the honey and stir until they all are coated. Stack the *struffoli* on a plate in a cone shape. When ready to serve, sprinkle with strained powdered sugar or decorate with colored sprinkles.

These attractive cookies were made only at Easter in our home.
I think that they deserve to be eaten more often. My mother would make
twice as many as in this recipe because they would go so fast.

TARALLI DOLCI
Easter Cookies

1 1/2 pounds flour (about 5 1/4 cups)
5 teaspoons baking powder
scant 1/2 cup sugar
1 teaspoon salt
6 ounces butter, softened
6 eggs, beaten
juice of 1 lemon
glaze
"hundreds and thousands" colored sprinkles

1. Combine the dry ingredients in a large bowl and work in the butter.

2. Add the eggs and lemon juice and mix thoroughly. It will be a stiff dough.
Knead a few times and form a ball. Cover with plastic wrap and let it sit for
a few minutes.

3. Take a fistful of dough at a time and roll it into a log, about the thickness
of the small finger, about 4 or 5 inches long. Attach the 2 ends, joining them
well, to form a small donut shape and place on a cookie sheet greased with
shortening. Continue to make *taralli* until dough is finished.

4. Bake in a preheated oven at 350° F. until cookies are barely golden but not
brown, about 15 minutes. Remove *taralli* from cookie sheets when done and
place on racks to cool.

5. Make a glaze for *taralli:* mix in a small bowl, 1 tablespoon butter, 2 cups powdered sugar, 1 1/2 teaspoons vanilla and enough milk to make a soft, but not liquid icing for dipping.

6. Dip the tops and sides of the *taralli* in the glaze and set on racks. Quickly, before glaze dries, sprinkle with a few decorative, colored sprinkles, e.g., "hundreds and thousands." Let *taralli* dry. Makes about 120.

Vinci

My aunt Rose called these delightful cookies *biscotti* which means "twice cooked," but in this recipe they are baked just once. They are easy to make, are light and fluffy, and are good for you too.

BISCOTTI DI RICOTTA
Ricotta Cookies

2 cups flour
1/2 teaspoon baking soda
1/4 pound butter
1 extra-large egg
1/2 pound *ricotta* cheese
1 cup sugar
1 teaspoon vanilla

1. Measure flour and baking soda and set them aside.

2. Put the remaining ingredients in a mixer bowl and cream them very well with an electric mixer or by hand.

3. Stir in flour and baking soda by hand until well combined. Drop onto a lightly greased cookie sheet by teaspoonfuls.

4. Bake in a preheated, 375° F. oven about 10 minutes. The cookies will be brown on the bottom and just beginning to turn brown on the tops.

Baking these cookies used to turn into a social event when my mother and my aunts would get together to make them. They did not make the mere 40 cookies produced by this recipe. They started with 8 cups of flour and made about 160. Eating the cookies as they came out of the oven, we children quickly reduced the number.

BISCOTTI DI CIOCCOLATA
Chocolate Cookies

2 cups flour
1/2 cup sugar
1/2 teaspoon baking powder
1/8 teaspoon baking soda
1/4 teaspoon cinnamon
1/8 teaspoon cloves
5 tablespoons cocoa
1/2 cup nuts
1/4 cup raisins
1/4 cup olive oil
1/2 cup milk
1/2 teaspoon vanilla

1. Combine dry ingredients in a mixing bowl and then stir in olive oil, milk, and vanilla. Mix well with hands. This is a stiff dough.

2. Divide dough into 4 parts. Roll each part into a log, about the size of a quarter. Break off 3/4-inch pieces from the logs and roll into balls.

3. Place balls on buttered cookie sheets and bake in a preheated oven at 350° F. for 6 minutes. Rotate pans and bake another 6 minutes. Do not overbake.

4. When *biscotti* have cooled completely, frost them with a chocolate glaze and let them dry on a rack.

5. To make chocolate glaze, combine in a bowl, 1 cup confectioners sugar, 3 tablespoons cocoa, 2 tablespoons plus 1 teaspoon milk, and 1 teaspoon vanilla. Makes 40.

In the heat of summer, there is nothing more refreshing and cooling than lemon ice or one of the other ices. The *Granita di Limone* is a delightful end of a meal with a little *spumante* or vodka over it.

GRANITA DI LIMONE
Lemon Ice

2 1/2 cups water
1 cup sugar
1 cup freshly squeezed lemon juice, well strained
vodka or *spumante,* optional

1. Combine water and sugar in a saucepan. Bring to a boil over medium-high heat. Stir until sugar dissolves. When mixture begins to boil, cook for 5 minutes, remove from heat and cool.

2. Add lemon juice and pour the mixture into a flat, shallow, container, preferably stainless steel. Ice cube trays without the dividers work well.

3. Freeze for 4 hours or longer, stirring after the first hour and then after every half hour.

4. If you prefer a more icy texture as most Italians seem to, just stir mixture with a fork. For a finer grain snow-like texture put mixture into a cold food processor bowl and process until smooth. You may also beat it with a mixer in a cold bowl.

5. Divide mixture into 6 dessert glasses and spoon a little vodka or *spumante* over, if desired.

Variation 1: GRANITA DI ARANCIA—*Orange Ice*

2 cups water
3/4 cup sugar
1 cup fresh orange juice
1/4 cup fresh lemon juice

Variation 2: GRANITA DI FRAGOLE—*Strawberry Ice*

1 cup water
1/2 cup sugar
2 cups fresh ripe strawberries, pureed
2 tablespoons fresh lemon juice

Variation 3: GRANITA DI CAFFE—*Coffee Ice*

1 cup water
1/2 cup sugar
2 cups strong *espresso* coffee

After dinner, when clingstone peaches were in season, my father used to enjoy slicing some of a cold peach into his red wine, letting it sit there for a few minutes and then savoring the macerated peach. I think that was his favorite after-dinner treat. Fresh fruits of the choicest seasonal varieties and superb cheeses usually end the Italian meal. However, as described below, there are sometimes other happy endings.

AFTER-DINNER TREATS

Cheese:

One of my favorite cheese endings is to have good Italian bread with the best extra virgin olive oil dribbled over and served with slices of *Parmigiano Reggiano* cheese.

Fruit Ices:

As mentioned above, Lemon Ice served with a little vodka or *spumante* is a refreshing after-dinner treat.

Liquor:

In Tuscany, *Biscotti di Prato* dipped into one of their two sweet wines, *Vin Santo* or *Morellino,* is a delightful after-meal treat.

Grappa, the distilled liquor, is a favorite to sip after dinner all through northern Italy and down into Tuscany. Like Scotch, *Grappa* can be cheap or very expensive.

A sweet or bitter liqueur can also conclude the meal. Among the more popular are *Amaro* (bitters, made of artichokes), *Sambuca,* and *Anisette* (both sweet and anise-flavored), *Strega* (the witch's brew), *Mandorla* and *Amaretto* (both almond based), and *Limoncello.*

Balcony, Carrara

Limoncello, my favorite liqueur which we make at home, is a delightful cordial to enjoy at the end of the meal. Italians say that it is a *digestivo,* an aid to good digestion. Also called *Limone Liquore,* it is a product of the *Amalfi* coast in Campania where beautiful, fragrant, and very large lemons grow. It is made in many of the homes but also produced commercially, put in attractive bottles, and sold in the shops. In Italy, pure grain alcohol, diluted to 50 percent, is used for these cordials. If such alcohol cannot be obtained, unflavored vodka can be substituted.

LIMONCELLO
Lemon Cordial

8 lemons
1 liter unflavored, 100 proof, Absolut vodka
1 3/4 cup sugar
3/4 cup water

1. Try to find organically grown lemons, if possible. Wash lemons well and wipe dry with a kitchen cloth.

2. Peel the lemons, carefully removing only the yellow part of the peel. Save the peeled lemons for another use.

3. Put the lemon peels and vodka into a covered jar and leave for 2 weeks.

4. In a saucepan, dissolve the sugar in water over medium-low heat. When completely dissolved, remove from heat and cool.

5. Strain the vodka from the peels into a large pitcher. Strain the sugar-water into the pitcher combining the mixtures. Pour into bottles with lids and leave at room temperature for 1 month before drinking.

6. It is popular now in Italy to store some of the *limoncello* in the freezer and serve it icy cold.

Variations:

The peelings of other fruits, such as limes, mandarin oranges, or even mixed fruits, may be used.

Beach umbrellas

RECIPES

LE FRITTATE E LE UOVA — FRITTATE AND EGGS

I CONTORNI — SIDE DISHES